SCOUNDRELS, DREAMERS & SECOND SONS

Scoundrels, Dreamers & Second Sons

British Remittance Men in the Canadian West

Second Edition, Revised and Expanded

Mark Zuehlke

THE DUNDURN GROUP
TORONTO › OXFORD

Design: Bruna Brunelli
Printer: Transcontinental

Canadian Cataloguing in Publication Data

Zuehlke, Mark
  Scoundrels, dreamers & second sons: British remittance men in the Canadian West

2nd ed., rev. and expanded
Includes bibliographical refernces and index.
ISBN 1-55002-369-1

1. Remittance men—Canada, Western. 2. British—Canada, Western—History. 3. Canada, Western—Emigration and immigration—History. 4. Great Britain—Emigration and immigration—History. 5. Immigrants—Canada, Western—History. 6. Gentry—Great Britain—History. I. Title

FC3230.B7Z83 2001   971.2'00421   C2001-901949-1
F1060.97.B7Z83 2001

1   2   3   4   5   05   04   03   02   01

THE CANADA COUNCIL | LE CONSEIL DES ARTS
FOR THE ARTS | DU CANADA
SINCE 1957 | DEPUIS 1957

Canadä

ONTARIO ARTS COUNCIL
CONSEIL DES ARTS DE L'ONTARIO

We acknowledge the support of the *Canada Council for the Arts* and the *Ontario Arts Council* for our publishing program. We also acknowledge the financial support of the *Government of Canada* through the *Book Publishing Industry Development Program*, *The Association for the Export of Canadian Books*, and the *Government of Ontario* through the *Ontario Book Publishers Tax Credit* program.

Care has been taken to trace the ownership of copyright material used in this book. The author and the publisher welcome any information enabling them to rectify any references or credit in subsequent editions.
                                            J. Kirk Howard, President

Abbreviations Used for Photo Credits: British Columbia Archives and Records Service — BCARS; Glenbow-Alberta Institute — GAI.

Printed and bound in Canada.⊛
Printed on recycled paper.

www.dundurn.com

        Dundurn Press   Dundurn Press   Dundurn Press
        8 Market Street   73 Lime Walk   2250 Military Road
        Suite 200   Headington, Oxford,   Tonawanda NY
        Toronto, Ontario, Canada   England   U.S.A. 14150
        M5E 1M6   OX3 7AD

Acknowledgements

Thanks go to staff at the British Columbia Archives and Records Service in Victoria; Glenbow-Alberta Institute Library and Archives in Calgary; the Alberta Provincial Archives in Edmonton; the Saskatchewan Archives Board and the Saskatchewan Parks Branch, both of Regina; and the Kelowna Centennial Museum. Thanks also to Archivist Linda Wills and volunteer John Shephard at the Greater Vernon Museum and Archives. For the revised edition special thanks go to the Cowichan Historical Society, and author Tom Henry for insights into the remittance era of Duncan and Cowichan Valley. Special thanks to Louise Donnelly for reading early portions of this book and providing much encouragement; to John Shinnick for relating a story so well that it nagged at me until I had to write this book; and to Rosemary Neering for many suggestions and much sound counsel.

Completion of this book was aided by a short-term grant from the Canada Council.

CONTENTS

Preface   9

Chapter One   13
    The Plight of Gentlemen

Chapter Two   29
    Travelling Like a Gentleman

Chapter Three   41
    Westward Ho

Chapter Four   53
    By Jove! This will be Wizard!

Chapter Five   64
    Oh I Say! How Deucedly Unsporting!

Chapter Six   76
    Civilizing Wilderness — The Beautiful Art

Chapter Seven   94
    Cannington Manor

Chapter Eight   114
    Walhachin

Chapter Nine   134
    Duncan — Canada's Most English Town

Chapter Ten   148
    Adventures on the Prairie

Chapter Eleven   167
    Roughing It With Style

Chapter Twelve   185
    The Hazardous Undertaking

Chapter Thirteen   197
    A Wasted Youth?

Notes   205

Bibliography   215

Index   221

Author Information   231

PREFACE

There is a legend about the British remittance men — perhaps true, perhaps apocryphal. The setting is British Columbia's Okanagan valley and the time is 1914. Across the valley's dry golden hillsides, overlooking the pristine blue lakes of the valley floor and the green orchards of the surrounding bench lands, hundreds of young Britons had settled in rough cabins. Most were well educated, of aristocratic or upper-middle-class background, cultured, and supported by regular allowances sent to them by family back in Britain. It was the allowance that earned them the nickname of remittance men. That and the way they behaved.

The remittance life was a carefree one. They worked seldom, usually only when the latest installment from home had been too quickly squandered. Leisure was their strong suit. They rode to the hounds, played polo and cricket, hunted, fished, lazed about in the taverns, danced at the town balls, charmed the community's women, and provided a colourful backdrop against which the valley's professedly more serious-minded, productive, and responsible residents went about their lives.

Remittance man was meant to be a disparaging term. It reflected the fact that these young men had been sent to the colonies to spare their families continuing embarrassment or shame. At home they had been scoundrels, dreamers, and second sons without future prospects. Perhaps in Australia, or South Africa, or the Canadian west they would make something of themselves. If they didn't, at least they would be far enough away that little disgrace would fall upon their families.

The time of the remittance men was short: most were sent out from Britain during the years between 1880 and the opening shots of World War I. Wherever they settled, however, they left an indelible mark perpetuated by the stories and legends that sprung up around them.

Growing up in the Okanagan, I heard many tales of the remittance men. Most stories were comic, laced with humorous anecdotes of young Britons with prim accents scheming to ensure continuation of a remittance, or pursuing some quixotic dream, or making fools of themselves by not listening to the wise counsel of a stolid Canadian.

One tale was different. It told how the age of the remittance men ended. In the fall of 1914, the story goes, a ham radio operator named George Dunn was the first in the Okanagan to hear that Britain and the Commonwealth had declared war on Imperial Germany. The news was soon relayed to the remittance men. Although they shunned work in favour of living a life of ease and adventure, none shirked their duty. Within days they were ready to leave for war.

There remained, however, their cabins and older animals, such as hunting dogs and horses, for which the valley residents had no practical use. Hundreds of the young men struck a pact. On the morning they rode to war, each left his cabin without looking back. Instead he rode to the cabin of his nearest neighbour, just as another remittance man rode toward his cabin. At his neighbour's cabin he dismounted, took his rifle, and shot the aged animals.

As the last shots echoed back from the surrounding hills he spilled kerosene across the cabin's cracked floorboards and then set the building ablaze. Throughout the valley this scene was repeated until all the remittance men's shacks were burned, all their animals killed.

The decision to destroy all trace of their lives in Canada, say the story-tellers, reveals that the remittance men knew they rode away from their youth, toward either heroic death or a surviving hero's reconciliation with family in Britain. Why else burn the shacks? Why else kill the animals?

The curious thing about this legend is no evidence of its truth is to be found, yet it persists. No one telling the story ever puts a name to any of these young men. No one points out the charred remains of a cabin on an Okanagan hillside.

Yet the story has a poignancy that lingers. I wondered who these men had been and how their lives were lived. I tired to attach faces to the shadowy images of young men burning cabins and killing treasured animals, then riding off into history's misty shroud.

Finally I decided to look past the legends and stories and seek out the truth of who these men were, where they came from, why they came to Canada, and what their lives here were really like. That search brought me no closer to confirming or dismissing the truth of the Okanagan legend. I'm glad of that. What matters is not whether it really happened but that it speaks many truths about remittance men; truths of these young men who came to western Canada seeking adventure and who left their mark on the tapestry of a young nation's history.

CHAPTER ONE

THE PLIGHT OF GENTLEMEN

Wars signalled both the dawn and sunset of the age of the remittance man in Canada. On September 11, 1855, the Crimean War sputtered to conclusion when the Russian Army blew up the forts of its besieged garrison at Sebastopol and withdrew from the contested Crimea Peninsula.

The British public were little concerned with the war's outcome. At best Crimea was interpreted as a marginal victory for Britain and the other European nations allied with the Ottoman Turkish regime to block westward expansion by the Russian Empire. That may have been the view of politicians and military strategists, but most Britons thought the Crimean campaign a disaster. The debacle was attributed to the upper class which insisted it alone had the ability and means to command Britain's armies.

Casualties in Crimea had been appalling. Of the 111,313 who saw service during the war, 21,097 perished. Although only 4,774 of these died in battle or from resultant wounds, such casualties shocked a nation that had since the end of the Napoleonic wars in 1815 known little but peace. Weapons since the Napoleonic wars had improved, and even the ill-equipped Russian army proved capable of shredding the carefully assembled, brilliantly attired, high-stepping lines of marching British soldiers. Yet ponderous, ill-executed tactics seemed all the lords turned generals could conceive. The Charge of the Light Brigade at Balaclava came to symbolize both the waste of lives and the stoic heroism of troops sent forth to die stupidly and pointlessly for the British Empire.[1]

For every man who perished in battle, four times that number succumbed to disease. Cholera, typhoid, and pneumonia were rampant in the military camps. Deplorable housing and sanitary conditions, inadequate food, lack of winter-weight uniforms, and the absence of a properly trained and sufficient medical corps made service in the Crimea a gruelling and futile experience.

The travails suffered by the troops in Crimea were similar, of course, to those endured in other historical campaigns. This war, however, was different from those of the past in terms of more than just weaponry. The introduction of the fast steamship enabled war correspondents to report events in Crimea to a concerned British public within days of their unfolding. William Russell's detailed articles carried on the front pages of London's *The Times* graphically depicted the suffering of the average soldier and the military ineptness of Britain's leaders. Following the war's end, more sordid tales of corruption and incompetence by the high command surfaced. Testimony before boards of inquiry by people like Florence Nightingale further eroded public faith in the military command, and, consequently, the overall social and political authority of the aristocracy.

As one inquiry after another unearthed a litany of scandals, ranging from incompetence to cases of blatant racketeering by army commanders and upper-class businessmen, demands for immediate and full reform of the military's officer selection and promotion system grew. The corruption and incompetence in the military was increasingly viewed as only the tip of an iceberg of corruption that extended throughout the British social and political system. Everywhere upper-class positions of sinecure were subjected to criticism and study. So strong did the movement for reform become that by 1855, when the last shots were fired on the Crimean battlefields, the Administrative Reform Association was already pledging to "destroy the aristocratic monopoly of power and place" in both the military and civil service. [2]

Against this tide of censure British aristocrats could do little but hunker down and scuttle to cover. It was the beginning of a slow end to aristocratic power on the island kingdom, an end that would take many years but would proceed relentlessly until the aristocracy was reduced to a remnant of its former glory and social prominence.

Into these changing times were born the remittance men to be. Most were children of the nobility or landed gentry, which together constituted the traditional ruling class. The parents of others were members of the burgeoning upper middle class forming a new industrial and urban-based aristocracy. Since the industrial revolution's beginnings in the 1760s, Britain's upper middle class, composed of wealthy entrepreneurs and professionals, rapidly outstripped the traditional aristocracy in economic and political terms. Despite its increasing power the upper middle class did not seek to replace the aristocracy as Britain's ruling elite. Instead it emulated the aristocracy's behaviour, adopted its social values, and aspired to be accepted as an equal. Members of the upper middle class especially hoped their children would be indistinguishable from their aristocratic peers.

It was, however, a time of change and the very lifestyle the upper middle class hoped to attain was rapidly being displaced by the tide of liberal reform. In the military several reports proposing measures to stop the wealthy from purchasing commissions for their sons were tabled before parliamentary committees. It was suggested that young men training for leadership at the military academy of Sandhurst would only earn promotion through professional excellence. Merit, not privilege, became the reformers' battle cry. Slowly they had their way in both the military and the civil service. By the early 1870s most civil-service openings were filled by open competition; in 1871 the practice of purchasing military commissions was formally abolished. Two traditional doorways through which the aristocracy had counted on passing their second sons were slammed firmly shut. The doors closed just as stoutly on the sons of the new aristocracy. Suddenly, social position no longer guaranteed comfortable security in a gentlemanly profession.

So what to do with the sons? The other acceptable career paths had been the church, law, and medicine. But law and medicine were plagued by the same problems hampering access to civil and military service: schools were being opened to anyone with ability and the financial wherewithal to pay tuition. Advances in the science of medicine made its practice complex, requiring an advanced education. As society became more complex, so too did its laws. The broad principles that formed English Common Law were increasingly refined and complicated. Never before had the academic world been so demanding. Within the public schools, where the privileged sons were educated, the need to compete for a position in the medical, legal, and military schools was referred to disdainfully as entering the "competition wallah."

Becoming a clergyman was increasingly a less desirable pursuit because of narrowing ecclesiastical opportunity. Most of the urban dioceses were well stocked with clergy. There might be positions open in the small, poorer, rural dioceses but these were not popular with upper-class clergy. They wanted a well-to-do parish where they could live comfortably and mix with those of their congregation who were of similar class stature.

The clergy was also losing favour as a career path because of changing social values. Religion just wasn't as important in the mid- and late 1800s as it had been earlier. British society was becoming increasingly secular and the privileged classes were not immune to these influences. Young men were reluctant to cloister themselves in a lifestyle that would dominate their social and cultural lives and dictate how they lived and behaved. They were gentlemen and that was enough of a social burden to carry.

So in disfavour did the clergical path become that by the late 1880s only 5 percent of Rugby graduates chose it for a career. At Harrow, once a bastion of ecclesiastical preparation, merely 3 percent entered the clergy, compared to 40 percent of graduates in the 1830s.

This narrowing of upper-class careers most profoundly affected second sons — loosely regarded as all those following the first-born male. Since Medieval times Britain had practiced primogeniture inheritance law. Under this system the eldest son inherited the whole real property of the estate. If it consisted, as most aristocratic estates did, of a large country property generating agricultural revenue, the oldest son would inherit the property in its entirety. In the case of the upper middle class — the new aristocracy — factories, businesses, and other capital generating opera- tions would go exclusively to the first-born son. Not until 1925, when the Administration of Estates Act became law, was primogeniture abolished.

In Victorian society a daughter was expected to marry into another family that would support her after her family provided a sufficiently large dowry to the groom-to-be. The second sons were traditionally found suitable careers in other fields reserved for their social class. This system ensured that the economic strength of large landed estates was- n't diffused by the property being broken up into smaller units as the estate passed from one generation to another.

Only the personal property of the deceased father was divided between the heirs. This included cash, insurance policies, and other fluid capital. It also entailed such things as paintings, furniture, and hunting guns. But there was nothing that could be inherited by the sec- ond sons that would guarantee a means to eke out a lifetime's living — especially considering the stylish standard expected of a gentleman.

By the 1870s, second sons faced some tough circumstances when their fathers died. The cash they would inherit was usually good for only a few years. What would happen when the money was gone? It was a question many a father, and many a second son, agonized over as the boy grew closer to manhood.

Why didn't upper-class parents and children come to terms with the changing realities, adapt, and accept the need to compete with the emerging middle class for careers? For one thing, Britain's ingrained class system didn't allow acceptance of the concept of class equality: the upper class was distinct from the rest of society and must remain so. This was a premise few Victorian aristocrats would even think to question. And the new aristocrats, firmly clutching the coattails of the old aristocracy, heartily agreed.

As each new generation came along, young men were taught from birth that they were superior beings. And the public school was a most effective way to inculcate this belief. From eight to young manhood, upper class boys spent most of their time under the influence of their school. Writing of public school boys in 1858 Henry Hayman said, "I will venture to say that there is little of that honourable love of truth, which distinguishes English public school boys, to be found in the homes of the lower classes."[3]

Their education had little to do with accumulation of knowledge or skills. Although they represented themselves as being the finest learning institutes in the world, the British public schools of the 1800s were amazingly backward. There was an obsession with teaching classics. Anywhere from 75 to 35 per cent of class time throughout the mid-1800s was devoted to studying classical languages and literature. This study mostly entailed learning the works of classical writers, such as Virgil and Cicero, by rote. Winston Churchill, for example, won a prize for learning twelve hundred lines of Macaulay's *Lays Of Ancient Rome*. He was also, due to his hopelessness at actually being able to read, write, and speak Latin and Greek, held back three times as long in the bottom form as anyone else in his school. Yet he won a much-lauded prize for memorization ability.

If the teachers at the public schools comprehended that the ability to memorize lines of a classical language didn't correspond with being competent in that language, they kept this knowledge to themselves and made little effort to teach language comprehension and usage. Lord Robert Cecil wrote of his school days in the 1880s: "When I went up to the university after twelve to fourteen years' tuition in the classical languages I was unable to read the easiest Latin authors for pleasure...we were taught no English literature....Nor do I remember learning any history."[4]

He also probably learned very little math or science. In 1875 the Devonshire Commission examined 128 public school and small endowed grammar-school curriculums. The commission reported that science was taught in only 63. Thirteen of this number actually had a laboratory, eighteen any apparatus for carrying out experiments. The public schools and the upper class seemed bent on conspiring to ensure their sons emerged from school with no ability to function in the modern industrial world.

But these boys would know how to play games. Beginning in the 1850s the playing of games in the public schools took on the nature of a mania. Throughout the 1860s, '70s, and '80s the pursuit of games seemed to eclipse academic study in importance both within the student body and faculty. Dr. Ridding, headmaster at Winchester, boasted: "Give me a boy who plays cricket and I can make something of him."[5]

The theory was that if you took a boy and immersed him in games he must become a gentleman. In the process of rigorous physical training, restricted diets, and need for team play and co-operation, the students learned traits of character that would serve them well in the real world. Team spirit was everything. House officers, often retired teachers of advanced years, were seen to break down in tears if their house team lost a competition. Your house, team, mates, school commanded the greatest loyalty.

The classics trained only a boy's mind; the games trained mind, character, and body. "A truly chivalrous football player," said an article in the *Marlburian*, "was never yet guilty of lying, or deceit, or meanness, whether of word or action."[6]

Boys in public schools didn't just play one game. They played cricket, tennis, rugby, football; they rowed and competed in gymnastics and track and field. Those who excelled at games and made it onto the school teams formed groups that often behaved like modern street gangs in terms of bullying others, adopting secret rituals, and exhibiting a fierce loyalty that excluded those outside the group. The lesser able, more bookish students were often bullied and pushed around by their more athletic counterparts. Yet, mostly this hoodlum behaviour was overlooked by the schoolmasters or dismissed as mere innocent rambunctiousness. To do otherwise would be to question the character-building value of games.

The importance of British games remained fervent for public schoolmen even after they immigrated to Canada. Duncan cricket team in 1912.
Cowichan Historical Society N987.1.6.1.

At graduation the young men emerged from the public schools as gentlemen. A graduate was now an old boy in the parlance of the system and as such he would uphold traditional values, respect authority, be well mannered and chivalrous, and have a keen sense of duty. Just as important, he would place a higher value on behaving respectably than on amassing material wealth. Indeed, he was expected to show an open disdain for soiling himself by pursuing too enthusiastically the accumulation of money. Money was a mere tool necessary only to maintain the lifestyle of a gentleman.

That lifestyle happily focused on the enjoyment of leisure and relaxed study. Hunting, riding to the hounds, playing games, trying after fourteen years of having little or no contact with the female sex to be witty, charming, and chivalrous at parties and balls, reading, listening to music, drinking, and visiting with your old school classmates were the pursuits of a gentleman. After all this came the trying task of doing something worthy and fitting to benefit society.

Once this was accomplished by serving in the military, joining the civil service, practicing law or medicine, entering the clergy, or going to university — all paths that graduating old boys could enter only after passing an entrance examination. Suddenly, the ability to memorize classical writings and win at cricket paled in importance. Some, like Winston Churchill, were turned over to a tutor and put through a crash course in the material needed to pass the entrance exams. In public school vernacular this was known as "doing the crammers."

But not everyone had the agile brightness of a Churchill, or the desire to go on to university. Young remittance-man-to-be Frederick Montague DelaFosse, for example, attended Wellington College in Berkshire and was supposed to be in training for entry to Sandhurst, as Wellington was specifically established to educate the sons of army officers. Young DelaFosse's last term was a disaster. He placed twenty-sixth out of twenty-seven in classics, divinity, and history; twentieth out of twenty in mathematics, and ninth out of eighteen in French. Furious at his failure, his uncle and guardian, H. G. DelaFosse, sent him off to Canada hoping he might come to some good in that foreign land.

Sending superfluous sons overseas was the solution increasingly adopted by many of the fathers and guardians of old boys graduating from public schools who had no obvious future awaiting them in Britain. It was an easy solution to look afield to the colonies and Dominion as a convenient spot for second sons to get a fresh start in life.

There was a logic in this approach. Life in Britain was expensive. Throughout much of the mid-to-late-1800s Britain was caught in a long, draining economic depression. Fathers were hard-pressed to provide their sons with enough money to maintain the quality of life that was their due as gentlemen. The boys themselves were usually unable to find work that was suitable.

Overseas, however, a small monthly remittance might support a youth comfortably until he was able to do something that was most acceptable — buy land and establish an agricultural estate of his own. In short, it was hoped that the young gentleman would build a country lifestyle and produce a new agricultural estate that would perpetuate the family name and sustain upper-class British traditions in a foreign land. To many a father this seemed a perfect solution to an increasingly vexing problem. Having reached the fateful decision, all that remained was to parcel up the second son and ship him overseas with the assurance that he would receive a small remittance on a regular basis, or to present him with a large grubstake as start-up capital.

To most it was not really an objectionable fate. In Britain they faced a life with little future. And after the excitement of a life filled with eternal games at the public schools, many an old boy thirsted for further adventures. They dreamed of being like Richard Burton, the famous explorer and scholar, who discovered Lake Tanganyika and penetrated forbidden Muslim cities after being expelled from Oxford. Dreaming of far-off lands where gold was waiting to be discovered, savage natives lurked, and untamed forests teemed with game to be hunted, many a young Briton was willingly coaxed into going abroad. Frederick DelaFosse thought the idea of going to Canada would prove vastly exciting. He wrote: "I discovered that Canada possessed boundless resources, and when I read of its wonderful prairies and magnificent forests, of its splendid lakes and rivers, of the fishing and the hunting, of its glorious summers and bright cheery winters, the sporting heart within me leapt, and I was almost reconciled to the abandoning of my summer's cricketing."[7]

Most Britons saw Canada, especially the west, as a wilderness idyll, a land yet untainted by the crasser aspects of the industrial revolution, a place where golden opportunity awaited. Popular men's magazines, such as *Field* and *Badminton Library*, and books by British adventurers were full of tales of gentlemen foraying into the wilderness of western North America. As early as 1841 British noblemen, such as Lord Caledon and Lord Mulgrave, were travelling to the outposts of Lachine and Fort Garry to hunt buffalo and explore the Rocky Mountains. The lords, believing their personal adventures and intellectual insights fascinating, wrote books about their experiences. The Earl of Southesk, for example, published an account of his hunting expeditions entitled *Saskatchewan and the Rocky Mountains*. Mixed in with the wilderness tale was forty-seven pages of reflection on Shakespeare's works, Bunsen's *Hippolytus*, and the general subject of *Patience and God's Providence*.

The peers came to Canada for sport and for that purpose they came well equipped. A Viscount Kilcoursie wrote in *Badminton Library* in 1898 of a trip to High River, Alberta. He and his friends, related Kilcoursie, each carried one thousand cartridges and several guns into the field. "We were mad keen to kill," he said, and kill they did. On one fine morning the small group brought down forty-seven brace of duck. One friend, identified only as Eustace, ran out of ammunition and flung his empty gun at some geese flying past.[8]

By the 1880s and 1890s accounts of British adventurers in western Canada were must reading among the British upper class. Edward Clive Oldnall Long Phillipps-Wolley's *A Sportsman's Eden*, published in 1888, extolled the sporting virtues of British Columbia. In a novel entitled *One of the Broken Brigade*, Phillipps-Wolley wrote of sport: "It is not the only thing worth living for, I grant you, but it is better than money-

"We were mad keen to kill." Hunting party near Calgary, circa 1900-1902. GAI NA-2831-6

grubbing. If there is no sport in America, there would have been mighty few Englishmen developing it to-day. It is the love of sport, or something uncommonly like it, which makes Englishmen colonize at all."[9]

Warburton Pike added to the sporting lore with *The Barren Ground of Northern Canada*, and *Through the Sub-Arctic Forest*. William Adolph Baillie-Grohman, often writing under the pseudonym "Stalker," added a host of books and magazine articles to the genre. Books, such as *Camps in the Rockies*, and *Fifteen Years' Sport and Life in the Hunting Grounds of Western America and British Columbia*, established Baillie-Grohman as a renowned sportsman. They also coincidentally made it easier for him to raise capital in Britain for many of his grandiose schemes to develop the wilds of British Columbia.

Baillie-Grohman was but one of a host of British gentlemen and financiers who saw in the Canadian west the opportunity to build Edenic British communities that would perpetuate the values and ideals of Britain's embattled agrarian-based upper class. In the valleys of British Columbia's interior, on the wide expanses of Saskatchewan prairie, in the Rocky Mountain foothills dreamers and schemers alike saw the possibility of both realizing personal profit and creating British utopian townships. These communities would be utopian in the sense that they would foster and sustain the traditional British aristocratic lifestyle. They would be agricultural townships, with fine British aristocratic homes; servants and workmen would labour and landowners would create a sophisticated culture that mirrored the best of British society.

Cannington Manor in Saskatchewan, Walhachin in central British Columbia, Windermere in the Kootenays, and many other such communities were touted as British Edens. Many a British family decided to send their sons overseas solely on the basis of promotional pamphlets and brochures. The Windermere advertising pamphlet, for example, shows a young, elegantly dressed mother alongside a sweetly dressed daughter of about seven. These two healthy, red-cheeked ladies are surrounded by the fruit-laden branches of an apple tree. The little girl has an apple in her lap and is in the act of raising another perfect fruit toward her lips. Inside the brochure are sketches of English-style cottages surrounded by flowers, of vehicles driving down well-maintained roads that wind through spectacularly scenic mountains. In reality Windermere was set in a narrow valley choked with virginal fir forest that would have to be cleared before even the most rudimentary agriculture could be undertaken. The harsh winters made fruit growing difficult at best and there was no way of transporting fruit to a viable market.

Amid all the material promoting western Canada, there were some that offered sensible advice and cautionary tales — but for the most part these were ignored. Harvey J. Philpot's *Guide Book to the Canadian Dominion Containing Full Information for the Emigrant, the Tourist, the Sportsman, and the Small Capitalist* warned that Canada was no place for "Old Country" farmers, professional men, or the sons of privileged families.

> Let me warn the disappointed parent against sending to Canada the son, who through his dissipation and extravagant habits has brought discredit upon his family...hoping thereby to give him a chance of "sowing his wild oats," and eventually becoming responsible. Never was a more cruel mistake made, nor one attended in most cases with more disastrous consequences. The poor youth('s)...hands, more accustomed to dealing cards and handling champagne glasses, are totally unfit to handle a plough, or cradle a field of wheat; his ideas do not harmonize in the least with the ruder ones of his practical neighbours; he soon becomes discouraged, and finally, thoroughly disgusted with the life he has been compelled to enter upon, his natural pride forsakes him; he sinks lower and lower in the human scale. We find him at last an outcast from society, living with a few more of his own stamp in some remote settlement, long ago lamented as dead by his friends in the old country, and where known at all, known as a "loafer" among his more fortunate neighbours.[10]

Illustrations such as this from the Windermere promotion brochure lured Jack and Daisy Phillips from Britain to Canada. BCARS collection.

The harsh reality Philpot depicted was too grim for most parents to consider; they chose instead to believe that things would work out. What were the alternatives? There was the certain knowledge that in Britain little opportunity existed for their sons; in Canada they might have a chance.

Even Philpot offered such hope with his advice to "the broken down gentleman possessed of small means in the shape of an annuity of 100 pounds or 200 pounds." Such men, he said, would find the money went further in Canada than at home, and "what is more gratifying still, he will not find himself elbowed out of the society, with which he means to mingle on fair and even terms, by reason of his poverty. Poverty in Canada, where every one begins by being poor, is not made a disgrace, except it be brought on by idleness and dissipation."[11]

For some of the young public schoolmen, flight to the colonies offered not only the chance of ultimately attaining a self-sufficient life but also a path of escape from the rigidity of Victorian society. In 1887, at the age of sixteen, Charles William Holliday was sent to sea aboard the four-masted windjammer *Eleanor Margaret*. He was a sickly young man, and his uncle, who operated a family-owned shipping company, secured Holliday an apprentice sailor's position in the hope that the experience would breathe some vigour into the frail boy. Holliday sailed around Cape Horn to San Francisco, thrived physically and mentally, and developed a taste for adventure and wide open spaces. Upon his return to Britain Holliday looked around the English countryside and felt "cramped; everything seemed so finished — set in an unchangeable pattern, each individual in his own little social orbit and content to stay there, confirming to his own silly social conventions; they were exasperatingly 'sot' in their ideas. You couldn't do this and you couldn't do that; there were so many things that just were 'not done.' 'Oh hell!' I said to myself; 'can I stick this?'"[12]

His family meanwhile was pondering what to do with this footloose lad.

> It was suggested that I might go into some business office in London; or be articled to a solicitor and go in for law. What a life! Going up town by the same train day after day, week after week, year after year with a deadly soul-killing monotony; going to church every Sunday, playing tennis or cricket every Saturday afternoon with the same correct uninteresting people. I would rather be in overalls, doing some healthy honest work out in the sunshine. But that was one of those things that were not done in my particular stratum of society — of course you could do that sort of thing in "the Colonies"; but if you did the same thing "at home" you would disgrace your family. Oh hell, again![13]

After flirting briefly with the idea of becoming a barrister, Holliday, confronted at every turn by the restrictions of British social convention, signed on as a crewman aboard the twelve-hundred-ton *Grasmere* and sailed for San Francisco. His uncle, who had taken an interest in the young man, again arranged Holliday's escape. His family was not impressed with Holliday's becoming yet again a merchant seaman. "It would be all right if he were in the navy," one aunt commented upon hearing of Holliday's plans.[14] Others in the family, however, suggested Holliday perhaps should stay at sea and away from Britain. No doubt they felt he would be less an embarrassment that way.

Certainly Holliday's earlier time at sea had undermined his sense of propriety and etiquette. Even his tolerant Uncle Willie, who fostered and abetted his growing wanderlust, was often scandalized by Holliday's behaviour. Once Uncle Willie invited Holliday to lunch in London. "It was a hot day, and I was clad in comfortable white flannels and a straw hat, and appeared at his office in this unconventional garb. 'Good Lord, Billy!' exclaimed my uncle, 'you don't think you can come to — 'his club, or whatever it was — ' in that getup, do you?' So we went to some more obscure place, which I daresay was more comfortable."[15]

On another occasion, walking with a younger uncle in the West End of London, Holliday filled his pipe and was about to light it when his uncle exclaimed in shock that he couldn't smoke. Holliday suddenly remembered that on these particular streets after a certain time of day "no gentleman smoked a pipe...Oh, my sainted grandmother! what a society; was it any wonder that so many of the young Englishmen fled to the Colonies?"[16]

And was it any wonder so many families were desperate to get rid of their young men? Scoundrels and the fallen abounded in the upper class. Gambling was rife and many a young man was drawn into the London casinos by old classmates. It was all good sport at first, but quickly it turned to drunkeness, indebtedness, and consorting with whores and other fallen women. Warburton Pike, after growing bored and dropping out of Oxford, spent a number of months slumming in the East End of London. He met many of his fellows in the whorehouses, taverns, and casinos. Finally, independently wealthy upon reaching his majority, he decamped for Canada to spend a lifetime hunting and making millions of pounds in a series of dubious business dealings in British Columbia.

Had he not been independently wealthy and opted to take his own leave of Britain it is likely his father would have shipped him out to the colonies in order to save the family name. Scandal was something every upper-class family feared. In the Victorian era a family name was easily compromised. A son's shameful behaviour was seen to reflect a lack of moral vigour in the whole family. If he turned to liquor, happened to get a young upper-class woman pregnant, consorted with prostitutes, gambled, or behaved in a manner unbefitting a gentleman in his way of dress, speech or table manners, it indicated that his family had been incapable of inculcating in him correct gentlemanly behaviour. There was about much of Victorian Britain a stifling atmosphere of conformity that resulted in many unintentional falls from grace, or the deliberate trashing of values by the likes of Warburton Pike. Both these categories of young men were likely to be shipped overseas.

Not all the sons, of course, were the perpetrators of scandal — some were themselves victims of the scandals of their elders. Such an event was just as damning, however, for a Victorian family. Jack Phillips came from a London family who had been grain and coal merchants in Knightsbridge for three generations. His father, Thomas Edward Phillips, frittered away a fortune, especially investing large sums to organize, outfit, and maintain a mounted company of the Volunteer Queen Victoria's Rifles. Phillips had three sons, Francis, Jack, and Kenneth. The boys spent much of their youth on the family estate where Phillips employed a dozen men and seven boys.

The depression plaguing Britain in the late 1880s caught up to the Phillips family in 1887 when the estate had to be given up. Two years later, when Jack was fourteen, his mother died. Phillips became a drunk and married his housekeeper, a mixing with the lower classes that led to his being ostracized by his brothers and sisters. Meanwhile, Jack struggled through a poor public school education that culminated in his failing the Sandhurst entrance exam. In 1895 Jack stunned the entire Phillips family by enlisting as an ordinary soldier in the Devonshire Regiment. First a father who married a housekeeper, now a son who became a common soldier; what was the world coming to? The fact that both father and son were to a large extent caught by the economic pressures of the time was lost on their family and friends. What they did simply was not done in this society and they were appropriately censured by being cut off from most of their former upper-class contacts.

One of the great weapons used to punish those who offended or violated upper- class values was the cutting off of family funds. This was the fate that befell Coutts Marjoribanks of Guisachan, Scotland when his father decided he had had enough of Coutts's scandalous behaviour. (The details of this scandal remain unknown, for, as was common at the time, they were neither spoken of in public or written down.) Most such young men, as was the case with Coutts, were not, however, allowed by all the extended family to fall into total disgrace and abject poverty while still in Britain; it would have been too shameful for their family, their parish, their community, and their class. When Coutts was cut off from any remittance by his father, Lord Sir Dudley Coutts Marjoribanks of Tweedmouth, his older sister, Ishbel, wife of Lord John Hamilton Gordon Aberdeen, Earl of Aberdeen,

Marquess of Aberdeen and Temair, and soon to be governor general of Canada, arranged a regular annual allowance averaging four hundred pounds to support "Couttsy." In late 1884, Ishbel, now Lady Aberdeen, financially backed and encouraged his immigration to the United States. Reportedly he was given start-up capital of six thousand pounds by his father, but there was speculation the money actually came from Ishbel's husband, who interceded somewhat grudgingly on Coutts's behalf at Ishbel's request. Coutts bought a large spread of land in the Dakotas and built a ranch which failed grandly in 1890. From there Ishbel brought Coutts to British Columbia where he proceeded to mismanage disastrously the Aberdeen's ranch estates of Guisachan and Coldstream in the Okanagan Valley.

With the promise of a remittance, and a chance to withdraw from scandal with all the grace a gentleman should display, most sons who fell into disrepute accepted their father's or family's offers and set forth for the adventure that awaited them in Australia, India, or Canada. Increasingly, in the late 1880s Canada grew in popularity as a destination for remittance men. From Liverpool the ships sailed for Quebec with the first-class and tourist-class berths sporting an odd assortment of young old boys setting off on a potentially grand adventure in a new land. Neither Canada nor the old boys were prepared for each other.

CHAPTER TWO

TRAVELLING LIKE A GENTLEMAN

Not many remittance men followed Charles Holliday's example. He sailed as a crewman on a windjammer that would brave the storms of the south Atlantic, round Cape Horn, and fight against Pacific winds to reach North America's sparsely settled west coast. Such an adventurous approach was not the way that a young man of good breeding was supposed to undertake a transoceanic journey. By the late 1870s upper-class Britons had managed to stylize, regiment, and instill an atmosphere of conformity upon the experience of travel abroad that would allow a Briton to remain British at all times and in all places. There was, even in travel then, correct and incorrect behaviour. Life was indeed happily ordered and dependable.

Most young remittance men sailed for the colonies from the port of Liverpool and, if going to North America, put ashore either at New York City or Quebec City. (So insular was much of British upper-crust society that some, such as Holliday's aunts, thought all North America was still part of the Empire.) Steamships had reduced what had historically been a dangerous, slow journey under sail to a fast seven- to eight-day crossing. The steamers of the Allan, Dominion, and, later, Canadian Pacific Railway lines were part of the passenger fleet. These were the glory days of steam travel. The era would reach its ascendancy with the launch of the *Titanic* and begin a slow decline only days later with that ship's tragic sinking on April 14, 1912, south of Newfoundland's Grand Banks.

The ships sailed between April 1 and November 1 of each year, departing weekly. Each passenger was allowed a maximum of 150 pounds of freight, but *The Englishman's Guide-Book to the United States and Canada*, published in 1884, advised prospective travellers that luggage was never weighed, so as long as it was not excessive the weight limit could be exceeded. A special type of luggage trunk, known as a steamer, was advised. Steamers were specially designed trunks that fit snugly in the fifteen-inch space between the berth and the floor of the luxury- and saloon-class cabins. The trunks were sturdily built, often with heavy brass corners, hasps, and locks. Upon disembarking in Canada, most gentlemen immigrants continued to transport their worldly possessions in their steamers. The presence of such a trunk was a telltale sign that a young man coming into a western Canadian community was probably a remittance man.

Much thought was invested in determining what should be packed into the steamer. Several guidebooks offered extensive itemized lists of the provisions, gear, and clothing that a British gentleman should carry when travelling abroad. Some specifically addressed the challenge of identifying the necessities for travel in western Canada. After consulting such lists many visited London's famous colonial outfitter store — S.W. Silver & Company — to assemble their kit.

Among the equipment guides published were a number written and compiled by young remittance men already living in western Canada. The Church brothers, Herbert Edmund and Richard A., came to Canada in 1886. They later sent a list of the outfit they thought indispensible to a Briton coming to Canada who was of respectable birth and modest means. The list was published in 1889 by their father, Rev. Alfred John Church in *Making a start in Canada, Letters from two young emigrants*.

Here's what the Church brothers deemed vital:

- Dress suit
- Best tweed suit
- Tennis suit
- One cloth suit of 'leather suiting'
- Extra trousers of ditto
- The three suits that they had in wear
- Two pair of corduroy trousers
- Ulster coat
- Pea jacket
- Mackintosh

- Dressing-gown (useful as an extra warm garment)
- Twelve flannel shirts
- Two white shirts
- Four pyjamas (of flannel)
- Four pairs of winter and summer drawers
- Four vests
- Twenty-four pairs of socks
- Six collars (the flannel shirts being furnished with collars)
- Cholera belt [A flannel or silk waistband worn to prevent stomach ailments.]
- Trunk (which should be of a manageable size)
- (An india rubber bath should have been added, and some coarse cotton shirts)
- Portmenteau for cabin
- White cravats and cuffs
- Cardigan
- Two jerseys
- Twelve pocket-handkerchiefs (some coarse coloured handkerchiefs might be obtained in Canada)
- Six Turkish towels
- Waterproof sheet (should be large, and of the best quality)
- Blankets (should be an undivided pair of large size, and thick)
- Rug
- Six pairs of dress gloves
- Three hedging and ditching ditto
- Two pairs of Canada mittens
- A housewife with buttons, needles, etc., of all kinds (saddlery needles included)
- One pair of high boots (others can be bought in Canada)
- Pair of boots
- Dress shoes
- Pair of shoes (not nailed)
- Pair of slippers
- Ambulance braces
- Helmet of Jaeger wool

"It should be easily remembered that pieces for repair of garments should be sent out: also all old clothes available should be included. And let everything be made large," they cautioned at the end of their list.[1] The Churches themselves had also taken along fishing rods, a gun each, a box of games, and a chest of medical supplies. The India rubber bath was their greatest regret it seemed, for they often lamented its exclusion.

Other items packed into travel kits were Norfolk jackets; straw boaters; riding boots; small arsenals of sporting rifles and shotguns complete with cartons of cartridges; double-edged axes; cricket bats; tennis rackets; books of verse; paint sets and easels; a variety of musical instruments ranging from penny whistles to violins, and, in at least one case, a tuba; croquet sets; numerous bottles of single malt Scotch; and full tea services of the finest china and silver.

An especially vital addition to the travelling kit were letters of credit that could be redeemed in all parts of the United States and Canada. The letters of credit were made available from leading banking houses in London; the most popular and recommended was Brown, Shipley & Company, which had offices in Liverpool, London, and New York. British gentlemen gave a lot of thought to money and the difficulties of currency management and exchange. After all the standard of living required in Britain soaked up money at a frightening rate. *The Englishman's Guide-Book to the United States and Canada* counselled that such letters were a fundamental requirement for those coming to North America, as neither Canada or the United States were countries in which a man's status as a gentleman automatically guaranteed that a bank manager would advance a loan.

The guidebook went on to recommend the British traveller carry a goodly sum of Bank of England notes because these were salable in large towns at full value. In the smaller outback towns of the west, however, it was advised to carry smaller denominations of either Canadian or American circular notes purchased in the larger cities. This, the guidebook counselled, would avoid problems with exchanging Bank of England currency. These smaller bills, the guidebook noted with some surprise, could be cashed on sight without the necessity of providing references or identification. It seemed in North America that no one really cared who you were as long as you had a pocket full of cash. This was a warning many a young gentleman failed to sufficiently note.

Singly or in groups, between 1880 and 1914, young men gathered at the Liverpool docks each week to sail for North America. In the late 1800s Liverpool was the second largest city in the United Kingdom. Its port was huge. A long line of docks was continually crowded with ships unloading raw materials to feed the vast British industrial engine. Freighters leaving the docks were loaded with manufactured goods for

A group of Cannington Manor residents, dressed as they were when they first arrived in Canada, pose with a Moosomin Indian Reserve friend. Saskatchewan Archives Board R-A4740.

export to markets around the world, especially the colonies and dominions. Standing on the docks, awaiting the arrival of steamboat tenders that would transport them to the passenger steamers standing offshore, it was hard for young well-to-do British men to not feel that they were the privileged citizens of the world's greatest nation boasting history's most successful culture and society. They were set to go forth into the world and bring to the wild lands of Canada their talent, knowledge, and cultural superiority.

Gathered with friends and family on the docks in 1878, eighteen-year-old Frederick DelaFosse reflected how his "addiction to sports" made him perfectly suited for "roughing it in the colonies." His relatives pitched in with departure gifts that were certain to prove worthwhile on this grand adventure. DelaFosse received an English saddle, an expensive pair of riding boots, and a large stock of Cockle's Antibilious Pills. So armed, he shepherded his steamer trunk onto a tender, which chugged out to a waiting Allan Line steamer, *Scandanavian*, and away he sailed for the Dominion of Canada.[2]

Perhaps DelaFosse took the advice of *The Englishman's Guide-Book* and secured a berth amidships, nearer the bow than the stern and the most stable part of the ship. If he did, the antibilious pills might have proven less essential during the voyage than feared. Another piece of advice offered by the guidebook was that the traveller, immediately upon boarding, register his name and the time desired for his morning "tub" with the barber or bathroom steward. Such prompt and decisive action would spare the traveller the need for a prolonged morning wait. This would allow more time to relax on the deck in the comfort of a steamer chair, which was another piece of luggage soundly counselled as vital to the British traveller. A steamer chair was a folding, wooden-framed chair with a canvas seat and back. As with so many of their travelling accoutrements, the chairs served as a signal that another remittance man had arrived in the Canadian west.

Despite the advice of the guidebook it was unlikely that many transoceanic travellers made much use of their chairs, for the trip across the Atlantic was usually a dreary, bleak voyage through rough seas. Many passengers were seasick and soon became bored and morose.

"Nothing can be drearier or more monotonous than a trip to Canada," groused J. Ewing Ritchie in his *To Canada with Emigrants*, published in 1885.

> After you leave Ireland, you see no ships — nothing but the sea, grey and dull as the heaven above. Now and then a whale comes up to blow hard, and that is all; and when the wind blows hard, you get nothing but big, lumpy waves, which set the ship rolling, and add only to the discomforts. And then you are on the Newfoundland banks, where you may spend dull days and duller nights — now going at half-speed, now stopping altogether, while the fog-horn blows, dismally every few minutes and when you can see scarcely the length of the ship ahead.
>
> Like Oscar Wilde, I own that I am very much disappointed with the Atlantic. The icebergs are monotonous — when you have seen one, that is enough. In the saloon, we are a sad, dull party; even in the smoking-room, one can scarcely get up a decent laugh. I pity the poor emigrants in the steerage.[3]

And well Ritchie should, for below the decks containing the luxury- and saloon- class cabins was the steerage class. Here the less fortunate lower-class Irish, Scottish, and British emigrants endured the trip in cramped quarters, while no doubt being able to hear and catch the odd glimpse of their betters experiencing the journey in relative comfort and amid notably posher surroundings. Ritchie's pity was, however, typically paternalistic and scornful in nature. "The steerage passengers," he commented, "are a difficult body to deal with; they seem so helpless and require much looking after."[4]

Ritchie made the passage in the steamship *Sarnia*, a ship of the Dominion Line. Her commander, Captain Gibson, was, Ritchie found,

> all that a captain should be — not a brilliant conversationalist, not one of those men who set the table in a roar; but cautious, skilful, fully alive to the responsibilities of his position and the dangers of his calling. As to the dangers, it is impossible to exaggerate them. There are more than a thousand of us on board, and were anything to happen, not more than three hundred of us could, I should think, be crowded into the boats, provided that the sea were quite calm, and that we had plenty of time to leave the ship; and in a panic and in bad weather it is clear that even such boats as the *Sarnia* is supplied with would be of little avail. Safety seems to me a mere matter of chance. You hit an iceberg, and down goes the ship with all on board, leaving no record behind.[5]

Twenty-seven years after Ritchie sailed on the *Sarnia*, his gloomy vision would be almost realized when the *Titanic* struck an iceberg and went down with 1,513 of its complement of 2,224 passengers and crew. It had life-boat space for 1,178 people, but in the confusion of the darkness many of the boats were less than full when launched.

Although impressed with Captain Gibson, Ritchie was less pleased with the facilities of the Quebec-bound Dominion Line ships. He lamented that the saloon accommodation and "the class of people you meet with on board" were not on a par with those of the ships sailing between Liverpool and New York. But perhaps, he ventured, this was for the best as "when the stormy winds do blow — when everyone is ill — when you are in that happy state of mind when man delights you not, or woman either — the gilded saloons, the velvet cushions, the plate glass and ornamented panels, seem quite out of place; to say nothing of the luxurious dinners, which not everyone is able to enjoy."[6]

Among those who found the transoceanic voyage less than enjoyable was newlywed Daisy Phillips, who made the journey with her husband, Jack Phillips, in 1912. Phillips was a rarity among remittance men com-

ing to Canada in that he was older than usual and married. Having
enlisted as a common soldier in 1895 after failing the Sandhurst
entrance examination, Phillips had been promoted to second lieutenant in the Lincolnshire Regiment in 1900. He fought as a mounted
infantryman in the Boer War, saw action at such battles as the Battle of
Spion Kop and the Relief of Ladysmith, and was wounded. After the
Boer War he served for three years in Uganda and the Sudan and was
garrisoned at Gibralter, before returning to Britain in 1912. Phillips
was, by this time, estranged from his father and the family's one
wealthy uncle, and faced the rancorous disapproval of a bevy of paternal and maternal aunts who had black-listed his father for marrying
his housekeeper and becoming a heavy drinker. They also remembered
all too well Phillips's own disgracing of the family by enlisting as a
common soldier.

Given this familial hectoring Phillips was understandably eager to
escape Britain for quieter surroundings. But at thirty-seven, Phillips
wanted to marry first. He proposed to family friend Daisy Oxley, then
thirty-five, and she readily accepted. To raise cash for his flight to
Canada Phillips sold some ivory he had gathered, raided his army pen-
sion funds, and was given some money by the Oxley family. From these
and other sources Phillips scraped together about one thousand
pounds and booked passage to Canada.

The Phillipses sailed saloon-class for Canada on April 5, 1912,
aboard the Canadian Pacific Railway Company's *Empress of Ireland*
(four days prior to *Titanic*'s departure from Liverpool) bound for St.
John, New Brunswick. The Phillipses' ultimate destination was the
newly created community, and ostensibly British-style Eden, of
Windermere in British Columbia's Kootenay region.

Jack and Daisy had tiered berths in their cabin. "I managed to sleep
fairly well to the noise of the rush of waves past the porthole," Daisy
wrote in a letter to her mother following her first night at sea. "There is
a vibration under the berths all the time as if at any moment you may
go 'up aloft.'"[7]

Daisy was swept up with a sense of adventure during that first day
at sea, when the coast of Ireland remained visible in the distance, and
the ocean was "a glorious blue green." Writing from a chair on deck,
she confided to her mother: "As I sit here, I can hardly believe it is 'me.'
In fact, I am sure 'me' is gone and it is a fresh somebody."[8] While Daisy
relaxed on deck, Jack spent hours striding around the ship satisfying
his "craze" for fresh air, as Daisy called it. Between on-deck outings, the
Phillipses enjoyed the grand meals served. "The meals are most won-

derful things," Daisy enthused, "and if you like you could eat enough to last you for twelve months, I am sure. Minced veal and poached eggs, sausages and mash, steak and onions for breakfast."[9]

By the next day, however, the ship was far from land and the swells were deeper. "How are the mighty fallen!" Daisy wrote with surprisingly good cheer.

After lunch yesterday the ship began to roll and I began to be very ill....This morning could not face breakfast, but Jack insisted on my getting up at 10:30 and coming into the fresh air and I am gradually reviving and have had two inches of cold chicken (on deck) for lunch and the boat is certainly steadier than it was.

The boards of the deck seem to jump up into ones face and bang your nose, but I am not the only one who is seedy. We do not get to Canada until Friday after all as we are using Canadian coal and only running at 16 1/2 knots an hour instead of 20....The twelve o'clock bell has just gone. We have a bugler for meals, but I am sorry to say I do not love the sound. My staple lunch is a little cold chicken! A thing I usually rather dislike. The sun is shining today and the water is deep blue and looks fairly smooth, but the boat keeps on slowly and deeply swinging through the rollers. I am no sailor bold! But it might be a great deal worse![10]

Indeed it might. Daisy, upon hearing of the *Titanic*'s fate, reflected that the *Titanic* might have been struck by the same ice her own ship had earlier passed. "In all probability," she wrote,

it was some of the same iceflow or field. We realized that our ship suddenly changed its course and went right south. We were then only 400 or 500 yards from the huge icefield in which were many huge bergs, and we were many hours passing it. The cold was intense, and I have never felt anything as icy as the wind. Our Captain was very worried and said he had never seen ice so far south before, luckily for us we passed it nearly all before night and we did not get into the fog which they usually get but of course they (the crew) were prepared and all on the look-out. The Captain told me that sailors 'smell' icebergs miles off.[11]

With stalwart hearts and usually squeamish stomachs the passengers at last caught sight of land. Soon most of the ships, other than those, like the *Empress of Ireland*, which docked at St. John, were steaming up the St. Lawrence toward Quebec City and everyone brightened considerably. "One hears much of the St. Lawrence, but it is hard to exaggerate its beauties," wrote Ritchie of his trip almost three decades earlier than Daisy's. "When you are fairly in it, after having escaped the fog of the Newfoundland Banks and the icebergs of the Gulf, on you sail all day and night amidst islands, and past mountains, their tops covered with snow, stretching far away into the interior, guarding lands yet waiting to be tilled, and primeval forests yet ignorant of the wood-cutter's axe."[12]

DelaFosse, settled no doubt in his steamer chair, eyed the woods with an uplifting of the heart. There in the thickets he imagined endless coveys of grouse, tender-fleshed deer browsing meadows, woods teeming with throngs of exotic wild animals awaiting the finely delivered shot of the marksman he imagined himself to be.

If this was eastern Canada, where the Empire had reigned supreme since winning the battle of the Plains of Abraham in 1759, what would the western wilderness be like? It made the heart quicken just to think of the possibilities.

The voyage had been thirsty, dangerous work, so there was pressing need to revitalize the constitution. Upon arriving in Quebec City, most saloon and first-class passengers set about relieving this thirst with a gusto that dismayed Ritchie even more than did Quebec City itself. There was little in Quebec to "attract the stranger," he wrote.[13] For those travelling in steerage this no doubt was doubly true as the passengers in steerage class were unceremoniously unloaded from the ship, passed into quarantine stations, and then required to wait sometimes for weeks for a special train that would carry them from Quebec to Montreal — assuming, of course, they weren't quarantined or deported back to wherever it was they came from.

Those with better-class berths were spared such discomforts, however, and a good many west-bound passengers spent the time it took disembarking those in steerage scouting out a good bar. Ritchie, spying this group, didn't hesitate to forsee their ultimate destiny symbolized in this one festive act.

> I am sorry to say, as regards some of the better class of emigrants, the long delay at Quebec gave them an opportunity of

getting drunk, of which they seemed gladly to have availed themselves. The future of some of these young fellows it is not difficult to predict. In a little while they will have exhausted their resources, and will return home disgusted with Canada, and swearing that it is impossible to get a living there. There was no need for them to go to the hotel at all. In the yard there was a capital shed fitted up for refreshments. I had there a plate of good ham, bread and butter and jam, and as much good tea as I wanted — all for a shilling.[14]

While Ritchie fretted and grumped during his voyage of little better than a week across the Atlantic, the adventurous Charles Holliday sailed from Britain in November aboard *Grasmere*, a barque of twelve-hundred tons. "As we sailed south we followed the summer all the way round, passing the Horn in midsummer. And there was nothing bleak or threatening this time; the air was fresh and exhilarating and alive with sea birds; and the night watch a pure delight, watching the sunset merge into the sunrise; it did not get dark at all and you almost hated to turn in when your watch was over. We had a fine run up the Pacific."[15]

Upon landing at San Francisco Holliday signed off *Grasmere* and set off in search of a family — the Spreckles — to which Uncle Willie had given him a letter of introduction. The Spreckles owned, among other things, a Pacific steamship line, a fleet of sailing ships in the South Sea Islands, and large sugar plantations in Hawaii. After months at sea, and in clothes that were somewhat threadbare from salt rot, Holliday found the Spreckles' offices awe-inspiring and imposing. Apprehensive about being rebuffed, Holliday gave his letter of introduction to a sceptical secretary, who returned moments later to usher Holliday into the private office of Adolph Spreckles. There, amid heavy mahogany furniture and deep-piled oriental carpet, Holliday was offered the chance of a job in pretty well any division of the company he wished. Spreckles said they should get together in three weeks, at which time Holliday could make a decision.

Holliday never made it back to the appointment. Several days after his visit to the Spreckles' office, Holliday saw two small steamers, the *Walla Walla* and the *Umatilla*, which made weekly trips up the coast. The ships made him feel restless. Acting purely on whim, he left a note apologizing to Adolph Spreckles for missing the appointment and booked passage on Walla Walla for Victoria, declared the capital of the province of British Columbia eighteen years earlier.

The nineteen-year-old travelled second class, which saved him ten dollars, but soon Holliday wished he had upgraded to first class when they took on board four to five hundred men bound for Seattle that he thought were "the sort of men who are aptly described as the 'scum of Europe.'"[16] To accommodate these men, who were destined for work on the railroad, the second-class berths were refitted with rough lumber bunks and bedding made of straw. The meals were served on boards laid across trestles.

Within hours of sailing the ship began to roll badly — one officer told Holliday this was why it was called *Walla Walla* — and soon the rails on both sides were thickly lined with heaving men. "The scene in the hold was indescribable; I had thought I could stick anything, but I couldn't go that," Holliday remembered.[17] The first officer, discovering that Holliday was himself a sailor, allowed him to take some old blankets and sleep on the deck for the rest of the voyage.

Like remittance men arriving on the east coast, Holliday was awestruck by the landscape he saw from the ship's decks.

I never could have imagined so many trees in the world; for all the way up, from the shore line up over the mountains as far as one could see, a dense, unbroken blanket of timber, eight hundred miles of it. Then, in the early morning of the fourth day, I walked down the gangplank on to the wharf at Victoria; my trunk following me on a truck. The boat pulled out; and there was I and all my worldly goods, sitting on that wharf, with not another human being in sight. Well, what now? I thought.[18]

It was a question many an arriving remittance man was asking himself. And one to which the answer was pretty obvious. Having come all this way there was nothing to do but set out on the grand adventure.

CHAPTER THREE

WESTWARD HO

Once in Canada most remittance men headed directly to the Canadian west. The best of eastern Canada, they had been assured by numerous guidebooks, had been tamed into pastoral farms and rustic communities. There was, therefore, scant opportunity for adventure and economic profit in Ontario, Quebec, or the Maritime provinces. The lure of the west was irresistible, so they bundled steamer trunks and boxes of supplies onto the Canadian Pacific Railway trains and rolled west from St. John, from Quebec City, from Montreal. So hasty was their exit from these cities their first impressions of Canada were acquired by gazing out the windows of a passenger coach chugging relentlessly westward.

Daisy and Jack Phillips spent only four hours in St. John before taking second-class passage on a train to Winnipeg. St. John was the first of Daisy's disappointments with Canada. There is "such a mixture of the finished and unfinished and certainly a great impression of dust and dirt," she wrote, "and the painted wooden houses in a fair-sized town look strange. The roads are all dust and not paved."[1]

Already the Phillipses were feeling plagued with money troubles, hence the second-class berths. It was not an experience Daisy recommended. She did, however, find the journey's monotony somewhat alleviated by the company of a "Mrs. Young," who with her three children was also bound for Windermere. Mrs. Young's husband, a retired army captain, had come out earlier to prepare the way and she was en route to join him.

"It is nice to know somebody nice on the train as most of the folk are of the farmer order, and the carriages, etc. are not at all luxurious."[2] But Daisy's optimistic spirit and sense of humour sustained her even amid this apparently trying company.

> The whole thing is really great fun, and we shall laugh at it all later on. There are cooking stoves at the end of each car and the folk camp out and fry sausages, and bacon and eggs, etc., and a good many of the women put on overalls and tackle things....The sleeping arrangements are really most amusing as the seats are made into beds and curtains are let down, but you see a leg going into a trouser suddenly come out under the curtain or a lady doing her hair is suddenly exposed to view. Jack chuckles and thinks it very primitive, but I feel with him I am well protected, but when Freda [Daisy's sister] comes out she must come 1st class, where it is quite nice.[3]

Arthur E. Copping, making the same trip a couple years before Daisy Phillips, would have agreed with her assessment of the first-class section. Copping was quite glad to be in first class: it kept him well separated from the cars full of emigrants from Eastern Europe, many of whom he thought terribly poor and wretched looking. After a quick glance in the second-class cars that brought up the train's rear section, Copping didn't again venture beyond the first-and tourist-class accommodation.

He found train travel in Canada very different from that in Britain due to it "being like a gliding ship." He enjoyed the open corridors between cars. His ramblings took him through drawing rooms, parlours, lounges, kitchens, and sculleries. There were stately dining rooms "shimmering with silver flowers and glass." He delighted in a stall that sold peanuts, candy, and chewing gum. In the same car as the candy stall was a post office and a barber shop. The elegant restaurant car served fine meals of roast turkey, chicken salad, and "excellent coffee."[4]

Copping was also impressed with the stewards who "were only less sharp than naval officers." The negro attendants, he remarked, wore grey uniforms and "had your boots already blackened in the morning when you arose."[5] They were also waiting attentively to brush your clothes.

Such luxury didn't come cheaply and Copping found the rates throughout the train obscenely expensive. He discovered, however, that it was possible to keep costs at a manageable level by not paying for a bed. In first class, for example, Copping found he could sleep very well in the "handsomely upholstered seats."[6] Tourist-car berths were also cheaper and not much less comfortable than the first-class berths, although not as luxurious.

The Phillipses, too, found the train prices high. Throughout the journey, Daisy reported, Jack and she drank only tea, as the beer, at one shilling a bottle, was more than Jack thought he could afford. "We have breakfast and an evening meal in the dining car," she wrote, "but we feel we must be economical."[7]

Easily disillusioned, J. Ewing Ritchie paid little mind to the accommodations or facilities aboard the train during his 1885 journey. Instead he stared glumly out at the landscape passing his window seat. He found Canada

> a land that must have been made by God well before he tried his hand on Great Britain and Ireland. It is true some part of it has an exquisite combination of wood and water and rock, but the greater part was either forest or gigantic plains or valleys of stone — which seemed to shut all hope from the spectator. In Canada — that is, along the railway lines — there is little life in the forest, few flowers display their loveliness, and no song-birds warble in the trees. All is still — or would be, were it not for the peculiar croaking of the frogs, to be heard like so many hoarse whistles from afar. You go miles and miles without see-ing a farm or even a log-hut....The train every now and then stops, but you see no stations, and why we stop is only known to the engine-driver. We take no passengers up, and we set none down, or hardly ever.[8]

What to Ritchie was a dismal and discouraging journey, Daisy Phillips initially found invigorating.

> It is very wonderful to see these immense tracts of land and so few houses and people....We are nearing Lake Superior and the country is hilly....There are fir trees everywhere, and what look like silver birch....We continually pass rivers, very wide as a rule and all frozen, and many lakes; all of them are very broken in shape and have many little islands about. There are huge stone boulders of white and reddish stone in all the country we are now passing through. We go miles and miles with no sign of a

hut or house and no people, but the sun is shining and the vastness of everything is wonderful after the size of England....I shall be glad to get to Golden and see what our part of the country is like.[9]

Jack Phillips was less impressed with the attentiveness of the black porters than was Copping. When they failed to waken him Phillips filed an indignant complaint only to have one of the men tell him, "I call you early, Massa, but you was in dreamland!"[10]

Even Daisy's unceasing good cheer came to be tested by hundreds of unbroken miles of timber and lakes. "I am sure we should rave about the scenery if we had a few miles, but when you get hundreds you somehow get used to it," she wrote.[11] Most of the travellers were quite relieved when their train finally steamed into the station at Winnipeg.

In Winnipeg they were poised on the threshold of Canada's vast west, which had so captured their imagination back in Britain.

Charles Holliday, entering the west at the port city of Victoria almost three decades earlier, found this west-coast community perfectly created to suit the disposition of a British gentleman. After passing through a customs inspection, performed "by a friendly little man with a bushy beard," who spent as much time showing an interest in Holliday's plans and background as he did searching through his trunk, Holliday was directed by the customs inspector to the moderately priced Occidental Hotel. It was still early morning and what Holliday craved more than a bed was a "large breakfast."[12]

Accepting an offer from the customs inspector to stow his trunk in the small customs shack until he was settled, Holliday set out from the docks to the town. Along the way he passed the old "Bird Cages," as the province's Parliament Buildings were called because of their domed roof line. Walking over a long plank bridge supported on piles driven into the mud below he passed the "muddy smelly slough" where the Empress Hotel, a bastion of Colonial British style, taste, and standards, would be built in 1908.[13]

It was midmorning, not yet nine o'clock. For sleepy Victoria this was early and the streets were mostly deserted. "I met very few people, and only one vehicle, which to my astonished eyes was a real English four-wheeled cab — the sort we used to call a 'growler' — cabby and all; he greeted me with a cheerful 'Good morning,' and a flourish of his whip. Soon the smell of coffee led me into a snug little restaurant; there was a large picture of Queen Victoria on the wall, and the white-aproned waiter might have been imported from an Old Country inn. It all felt very homey."[14]

Walking in any direction, Holliday found, he could leave the city behind and be instantly among fields, or wandering rough country roads that passed rose-covered English-style cottages.

Victoria, he later wrote,

> had that peculiar British atmosphere of unruffled tranquility....The people I met in the ships and on the streets were the most leisurely I had seen, yet there was a great deal of business transacted there: they just did things without unnecessary fuss. And they were all so kindly, these so English people; it was as if the warm sun of the Pacific had melted their starched shirt exteriors and exposed the natural friendliness that lay beneath. After California they seemed almost indolent; the Englishman considers everything at length before he does it — often an unconscionable length; the Californian says, 'Oh heck, let's do something, anyway; we'll see whether it was necessary when we've done it.[15]

Holliday wasn't the only Briton to feel that Victoria was like a replication of a small, ideal British town. With its South Downs-like climate of mild winters, gentle rains, and warm summer sunshine, its seaside location, and its pleasant grass meadows and Garry oak forests, Victoria reminded them of the best of Britain's summer resort communities. Victoria was automatically assured a British nature because nearby Esquimalt Harbour became the home port of the Royal Navy's Pacific Squadron in 1865 and nineteen years earlier Victoria's townsite had been selected as the Hudson's Bay Company's Pacific coast headquarters.

By the early 1870s the community was a sleepy, predominantly British-populated provincial capital. The decision to terminate the Canadian Pacific Railway transcontinental line at Vancouver in 1885 determined that Victoria's port would always be of less commercial importance than that of nearby Vancouver. Most British immigrants saw this as a rather happy event, for it guaranteed that Victoria would remain small, pristine, and cultured, rather than becoming an industrial, commercial, and shipping hub for western Canada's resource-based economy. Author, sportsman, and lawyer Clive Phillipps-Wolley summed up the British attitude toward Victoria after visiting the community in 1884. "I came across no place in America in which I would be so content to stay as in Victoria...there is time to rest for a moment, and fancy...that there is something else in the world to live for besides the accursed dollar."[16]

Holliday, ever one to shun the formal trappings of British social conventions and institutions, stayed away from Victoria's thriving Union Club. Founded in 1879, the club was patterned after London's aristocratic Pall Mall clubs, where oak panelling surrounded plush upholstered chairs and male exclusivity was assured. Members, and their male guests, sipped properly prepared gin and tonics, sampled single malt Scotch, and perused recent issues of the *Standard*, the *Field*, or *The Times*. Many a retired India Man, as soldiers and bureaucrats who made their careers in colonial service in India were known, had opted to make Victoria his retirement home. These men dominated the Union Club's membership list.

The club was also a popular hangout for the adventurers Warburton Pike (known in the club as "Pikey") and William Adolph Baillie-Grohman. Pike arrived in Victoria in 1884 and was to use the city as a home base from which he launched various expeditions into the Canadian wilds and cooked up mining and land development schemes with Phillipps-Wolley and other like-minded British gentlemen who loved the outdoors, sportsmanship, and the accumulation of riches based more on lofty plans and speculation than applied labour.

"Pikey," however, was a bit of an oddity in Victoria and the Union Club's lounges. Prior to coming to Canada he had shocked his family by consorting with whores and gambling wildly at the casinos and clubs of London's East End. As was true of Baillie-Grohman, he came into an independent income upon reaching his maturity and almost immediately set out on a series of hunting expeditions that would take him to Scandinavia, Iceland, and through many American states, and ultimately land him, at the age of twenty-three, in Victoria. His years spent abroad hunting and exploring wilderness country left him with little inclination toward propriety and conformist behaviour.

Shortly after arriving in Victoria he bought land in the community and on the nearby Gulf Islands. One plot of Gulf Island property contained a sandstone quarry which soon made him one of the wealthiest men in Victoria. Yet he rarely carried money with him, was often seen wandering around barefoot, wore ragged clothes, and usually lugged around a scarred and worn rucksack. This behaviour led to his routinely being turned away from theatres and other social events, but earned him a reputation for being an eccentric that most of the Union Club's

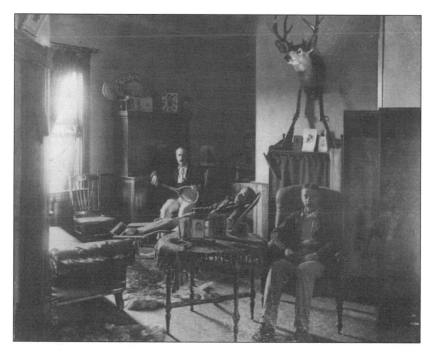

Even public schoolmen turned bank employees still dedicated themselves to the pursuit of sport and games. Bachelor quarters, Vernon branch of the Canadian Imperial Bank of Commerce. Greater Vernon Museum and Archives, #507.

membership found quite endearing. Only when he tried to bring a native Indian woman into the clubhouse did they politely chastise him for his behaviour (and, one can assume, closed the doors firmly against the woman's entrance).

Politeness was common coin in Victoria it seems. Holliday was amazed at how friendly and kind people were to him during his two weeks there. At the Occidental Hotel he was paying a dollar a day, which was quickly burning a hole in his meagre savings, but with the help of the customs inspector he was able to rent a room in an elderly lady's home for a dollar a week. The woman took a motherly interest in him when he told her his burgeoning plans to venture into the British Columbia interior. She asked him to provide her with the address of his family in Britain, as "'so many people go into those awful mountains and are never heard of again!'"[17]

For Holliday this kind of comment was all the encouragement he needed to venture out beyond the confines of Victoria's genteel setting. While Holliday found Victoria pleasant indeed and even speculated on retiring there some day (a dream he would fulfil many years later when he retired from the Okanagan to Victoria), he saw little in the way of prospects for a young man of very limited means. This was a conclusion that many Britons were reaching. Victoria's business community was well established and more or less static. By 1890 *The British Colonist in North America: A Guide for Intending Immigrants* was advising young men coming to Victoria to not "depend too much on something 'turning up.' Some young men who have tried it in Victoria, have come out with empty pockets. It is no place for an idler, without plenty of cash, and the immigrant must have a settled purpose, and 'turn something up' for himself."[18]

There was another drawback to Victoria that many of the young men who ended up there encountered. Herbert Edmund and Richard A. Church came to Victoria in April 1887 after spending little more than a year on a farm near Barrie, Ontario, being trained as farmers. Church's father had invested one hundred pounds apiece on this farming education for his sons, but they found the experience mostly wasted, as the farmer wouldn't allow them to operate any machinery or handle the horses. They did learn to milk cows, and the many long hours in which there was nothing to do greatly improved their tennis serves and returns. After only a few weeks in Victoria they were so bored by the quiet lifestyle they set out for Calgary with a mind to make it as cowboys.

Holliday, too, was growing restless after only a couple weeks in Victoria. Using yet another of his Uncle Willie's letters of introduction, Holliday presented himself to a Major Wilson, a well-known early resident of Victoria. Holliday expected to meet a typical retired major, which he regarded as being usually "rather important and pompous sort of persons." So he was surprised to find "this one in a pokey little office which seemed to be full of sacks of flour and oatmeal....He was taking things very easy in a swivel chair, with his feet on the desk, smoking his morning cigar; a perfect example of the Victoria businessman of the day."[19]

Major Wilson introduced Holliday to the engineer C.E. Perry, "as a young friend who was hard up and wanted a job (quite true, for I only had a very few dollars)." Perry offered him a job with his surveying party, which was soon leaving for the B.C. interior to run surveys for a projected railway. "The Interior of British Columbia," said Holliday, "sounded romantic and suggested adventure. Naturally I jumped at the job."[20]

In Winnipeg many of the young men getting off the train were also hearing the call of the Canadian west's heartland; in this case the call was that of the Rocky Mountain foothills and Alberta badlands country. Winnipeg, gateway to the west, often proved disappointing. They had anticipated streets teeming with horses, cowboys, and wild Indians, and saloons full of women who were wilder yet. But by the 1880s Winnipeg and most of Manitoba had been developed into farmland. This was a land of wheat fields; the city a place of refinement and stoic Protestantism.

By 1885, reported J. Ewing Ritchie, Winnipeg boasted many churches, banks, schools, manufacturing plants, and a mercantile class that was well established and thriving. Twenty-six thousand people lived here. There were three daily newspapers and one weekly.

The only drawback to Winnipeg, Ritchie found, was the mud — gummy, deep, sucking mud that worsened with every rain or with the spring snow melt. The streets "I fear in wet weather...must be almost impassable," he wrote. "As it is, the sides are now dried up, as if they were ploughed, and carriages seem to make their way with considerable difficulty; but there is a magnificent broad wooden side walk to all the streets, while in the middle sufficient smoothness has been attained for the due working of street railways."[21]

Despite the muddy streets, however, Ritchie found walking the city streets "amusing." Everywhere he turned there were grand shops and soundly constructed office buildings. "Ladies in the latest fashion meet you one minute, and the next you jostle a swarthy Indian, half-civilized, and his squaw, still less civilized than himself. Odd fur-skins are exposed for sale, while a stuffed bear adorns the main street, up and down which run all day long the newsboys with the latest telegrams from London or Paris, or New York."[22]

Undoubtedly the city underwent many changes between Ritchie's 1885 visit and that of the Phillipses in 1912, but Daisy and her husband passed through Winnipeg so quickly her only impression of the city was based upon the "magnificent" railway station. Although the stationmaster singled out the couple for news of the Old Country, his offer to take them over to the station hotel, "a wonderful place and well worth seeing," had to be turned down for lack of time.[23]

Not everyone hurried through Winnipeg on their way into the western heartland. Some found here a civilization and British atmosphere that suited their natures and expectations. The Garry Club was Winnipeg's equivalent of Victoria's Union Club. Club members organized polo matches, hockey games (Britons quickly became enamored of this manly sport, which was unheard of in Britain at the time), club fights, and boat racing. The newcomers, who could afford the club dues and the living costs of Winnipeg, lounged away the hours in the club-house's expansive rooms or steamed in the Garry's Turkish baths. They drank, they ate, they languished, and all too soon many of them were broke, with little to do but eye the mail in hopes that their next remittance would soon arrive. When it did, many of them headed farther west in search of opportunity, adventure, and a less expensive lifestyle.

Canada was surprisingly expensive for a colony. "If I were to lecture on Canada I should call it the 'Land to the Little Dollar,'" Ritchie lectured his readers. "A dollar here is of no account. This morning I went into a shop and had a bottle of ginger-beer, and the cost was one shilling; and this, too, after I had been administering a little 'soft sawder' to the fair American damsel who waited on me, in the mistaken hope that she would be a little reasonable in her charge."[24] Disillusioned and baffled by his apparent inability to charm Winnipeg's women with his wit and good manners, Ritchie joined the throngs of young men heading westward by train.

Ishbel Aberdeen and her husband passed through Winnipeg during a grand rail tour of Canada in 1890 and were much impressed with the people of Winnipeg. They were surprised, however, by the layout of the town. "The houses are sort of scattered pell mell as if you had thrown them down in a handful, a big one and then a little old log hut by the side of it, and then a store and so on and of course weeds everywhere," Ishbel wrote in a letter home to Britain.[25]

Winnipeg had another surprise waiting for Ishbel and Lord Aberdeen. No sooner had they disembarked from the train than Ishbel's younger brother, Coutts Marjoribanks, intercepted them. He had ridden up from the Dakotas to meet them, bringing a sad tale of his difficulties trying to make a go of it as a Dakota rancher. Despite the start-up capital of six thousand pounds it was rumoured Ishbel had given him and an annual allowance of four hundred pounds, his 960-acre ranch was foundering. The land was excellent, with abundant water supply, but Coutts had elected to make the ranch a specialized breeding operation in the middle of a cattle market recession that left few ranchers interested in upgrading their herds with a bloodline as rarified as that of Coutts's stock. Coutts also had quickly established himself as the leading socialite of the Dakota Territory. He and a number of British acquaintances became infamous for their heavy spending and relaxed lifestyle, which included riding to the hounds, long hunting trips, and heavy betting losses at local horse-racing tracks. By the time Coutts tracked Ishbel down in Winnipeg he was heavily in debt, his grand ranch house remained unfinished, his cattle stock was unsalable, and Coutts could see no future for himself in the Dakotas.

"He has had a bad time of it," Ishbel confided to family friend John Sinclair, "between droughts and losses of stock generally....His neighbours are not nice people to associate with, and everything is mortgaged....we are going to get a report on the profitability of selling the place and then try to get Coutts over into Canada into some civilized part, probably British Columbia."[26]

Coutts returned to Dakota and packed up; leaving for British Columbia that October. The ranch, however, would not be sold until February 11, 1901. Until then it stood abandoned; there were rumours in the Dakotas for years that his British friends took over the cattle without compensating Coutts at all. When Coutts sold the ranch to Andrew A. Will for $7,001, he realized a capital gain of $3,961 over the purchase price of $3,040. Whether Ishbel even knew of this sale and Coutts's profit is doubtful as she never mentioned it in her correspondence. By 1901 Coutts was firmly and disastrously ensconced in the Okanagan with the duty of managing the Aberdeen's ranching operations there — ranches that in many ways seem to have been established primarily to give Coutts some semblance of having a legitimate occupation.

While Coutts returned to Dakota, Ishbel and her husband headed out into the prairie surrounding Winnipeg to see how British emigrants were settling into their new land. Ishbel was appalled. "May heaven preserve us from ever being fated to banishment to the far-famed wheatlands of Manitoba! Oh the inexpressable dreariness of these everlasting prairies! Wooden shanties, most of the size we would put up for a keeper's shelter at home, but here inhabited by farmers owning some hundreds of acres and some half-dozen children....Nowhere yet on the prairie have we seen even a geranium pot, or a young tree planted."[27]

In her observation of the mean condition in which many western Canadian settlers lived, Ishbel echoed the opinion of many of the young, educated, and privileged Britons coming into the west. Once they stepped beyond the relative comfort of Winnipeg or Victoria they were often shocked to see just how rough life was in the rugged west. It was hard for them not to look askance at the people among whom they were now expected to live, or face with trepidation the lifestyle they were supposed to embrace as their own.

It was equally difficult for hardened Canadian settlers to feel anything but scorn for these people, who were flooding into the country and bringing with them all manner of odd equipment, expectations, attitudes, and so little ability to cope in a harsh land. Having raced across the eastern part of Canada in great haste to get to the west, it was now time for the remittance men to come to know Canadians, and try, in turn, to be understood by them. For both it would be a difficult, frustrating, often impossible, and usually, despite everything, mutually entertaining and amusing experience.

CHAPTER FOUR

BY JOVE! THIS WILL BE WIZARD!

Canadian Dick Templeton first saw Bob Murray in the waiting room of the Winnipeg rail station. One glance told Templeton the tall young man was just in from Britain: his pants were flannel, his jacket tweed, his hat a straw boater. "In his hands he carried a couple of port-menteaux....He then made his way to where the freight had been dumped, and I found he also possessed a large cabin trunk.

"'Now where on earth can he be going,' thought I, 'with all that stuff. If his luggage consists of clothes he's got enough to furnish a moderate store.'"[1]

As much out of curiosity as anything else, Templeton walked over to the man and offered to help him move the heavy trunk and bags to a nearby hotel. The newcomer introduced himself as twenty-year-old Bob Murray, and after glancing about in vain for a porter to handle his luggage for him, accepted Templeton's offer. Staggering under the weight of the trunk and bags, they crossed to the hotel and got Murray settled, then the two men went for dinner.

"After dinner when our pipes were going smoothly I asked him for an account of himself. He said...he was a native of Dublin, Ireland. He had been sent to Canada by his father as a last resort, because of his inability to pass even one of the many exams for which he had sat."[2]

The young man's start-up money was running out at an alarming rate and he was desperate for a job to carry him through to when his first remittance cheque was expected to arrive. Templeton took a liking to the young man and the next day they went together to the Standard Employment Bureau, where Templeton used his influence to get Murray a job as a teamster at a logging camp owned by a man named Joe Sullivan. Templeton worked at the camp, which was located near Willow Bluff in Manitoba. Knowing Murray would "look ridiculous" if he showed up at the camp with so much gear, Templeton convinced him to leave many non-essentials, including a tennis racquet and elegant dinner jacket, behind. Murray, having no experience working with horses or doing any manual labour, faced enough problems fitting into the rough work camp without being obviously singled out as a remittance man.

Initially Murray found life in the camp almost more than he could bear. "At first he was horrified at seeing all his food on one plate but resigned himself to eating from it," Templeton recalled. Murray also faced some vicious bullying from one large, tough teamster. "Every greenhorn has to put up with a lot of rough treatment at first," Templeton told him. "If you're made of the right stuff you'll weather it out. If not, you'd better go in for some gentler occupation." Murray proved his mettle when he finally beat the bully up. He went on, Templeton later wrote, to become "a fine teamster in the course of things."[3] Despite the arrival of regular quarterly remittance cheques from home, Murray was still working at the camp when Templeton quit the job a couple of years later.

Not all remittance men were lucky enough to have someone like Templeton to lend a helping hand and sound advice. And not that many of them would likely have listened anyway. Their public school education, their upbringing, their family, and peer role models disinclined them to staying quiet, blending into the background, and learning the lay of the land before asserting themselves.

Philpot, in his guidebook to Canada, warned against the British upper-class attitude of superiority.

> Another class of persons apt to fail at first as emigrants are those self-opinionated people who think no one has a good idea in their heads but themselves, and who refuse to be guided by those who are wiser; their prejudices and self-conceit will soon lead them into trouble and misfortune, and when they have sacrificed their last shilling they begin to see their error, and are better and fitter men to recommence than when they

had money in their pockets, and no experience to guide them in the use of it.[4]

As was true of most of Philpot's warnings, few took heed. Instead they came to Canada assured that the society they had just left was superior to all others and that if there was a British way to do something then it must assuredly be the best way, or if there was a British way of thinking about a subject it must be the superior way. As the Rev. T. C. Papillon said, "The graduate of a British public school brings away with him something beyond all price — a manly, straightforward character, a scorn of lying and meanness and fearless courage. Thus equipped he goes into the world and bears a man's part in subduing the earth, ruling its wild folk, and building up the Empire."[5]

These attitudes were reinforced when they looked upon the land and the lives of its inhabitants. As Ishbel Aberdeen was horrified by the homes and country outside Winnipeg, many young remittance men were shocked and dismayed by all they saw during the train ride across the prairies.

"The scene, as I sit," wrote J. Ewing Ritchie,

is not cheering. Far as the eye can reach there is the prairie. It was the same all the way from Winnipeg. It will be the same all the way to Calgary, some 400 or 500 miles hence. It is intensely hot, and men and women sit in the open air, under such shade as the wooden houses afford. It is intensely cold in the winter. Not a tree is to be seen, or a hill, or a farmhouse; nothing to relieve the monotony of the sea of grass land on every side except here and there a prairie fire — the first step to be taken before a farmer commences the cultivation of the soil; and I must own a prairie fire by night is rather a pretty sight.[6]

Stumbling off the train at a stop near Moose Jaw, Ritchie found himself on the brink of despair. "It is now noon on the prairie, and I am dying of heat," he lamented.

Oh, for the forest shade! Oh, for the crystal stream! Alas! the water here is not good for the stranger, and I fear to touch it....What am I to do? The beef here is so tough that you can't cut it with a knife, and must have belonged to the oldest importation from my native land; and I have to pay a price for which I can have a luxurious repast in London....I have been out on the prairie under the burning sun. It is cracked, and parched, and bare, and the flowers refuse to bloom, and only the gigantic grasshopper or the pretty but repulsive snake meets my eye. That dim line, protracted to the horizon east and west, is the railroad. That far-off collection of sheds is the rising town of Moose Jaw. That blue line on the horizon, which makes me pant for the sea, is a mirage.[7]

By the time the train finally steamed into Calgary, Ritchie was nearly inconsolable. But he soon stoically rallied and set out to get a firm grasp on the social milieu of this young community in the heart of the Canadian west.

The Calgary of 1885 was a ramshackle place, growing rapidly. Huts and wooden houses were, as with Winnipeg, scattered with apparent randomness across the plain. Most bordered Bow River, which was lined with poplars; the foothills and Rocky Mountains formed a pretty backdrop. After the dreariness of his train ride across the prairies, Ritchie found himself inclined "to think well of Calgary...and of its shops, all well stocked; but these shops are little better than huts, and the hotels certainly don't throw the shops into the shade."[8]

Ritchie checked into the leading hotel (unnamed), which he thought was located too far from the railway station. The hotel contained an open room with a dark dining room on one side; on the other was "a little row of closets, which they dignify by the name of bedrooms." Each room contained a narrow bed, a row of pegs for clothes, a little shelf on which stood a wash basin, and a mirror that "reflects very poorly the looker's personal charms, whatever that may be," and a small window. The hotel, like all the other Calgary buildings, was one-storey. "What we call in England a gentleman's house, I should say, does not exist in the whole district. A gentleman would find existence intolerable here, though the air is fine, and the extent of the prairie unbounded."[9]

After meeting a few Calgarians Ritchie became concerned about personal safety and fretted about leaving his roll of cash stashed under his pillow. There was no lock on the window of his room and he could easily imagine some ruffian crawling in during the night and pilfering the money while he slept.

Not that he anticipated the cash lasting for long.

Calgary, he discovered, was even more expensive than the rest of Canada. "The price of fruit is prohibitory; cucumbers, such as you in London would give three-pence for, are here at Calgary as much as a shilling. Eggs are four shillings a dozen; meat and bacon and ham are as dear as in England and not a quarter so good. I am appalled as I see how the money goes; I fear to be stranded at the foot of the Rockies."[10]

Being stranded would mean having to cope with the wild men of Calgary, whose behaviour he found even more appalling. "Last night, for instance, as I was sitting in the cool air, smoking on one of the peculiarly bad cigars in which the brave men of Canada greatly rejoice, and for which they pay as heavily as if they were of the finest brands, a half-drunken man came up, abusing me in every possible way, threatening to smash every bone in my body, and altogether behaving himself in a way the reverse of polite."[11] This incident began when the cowboy was thrown from his horse after galloping up dramatically to the hotel entrance. Ritchie, who made a quip to a companion at the cowboy's expense could see no reason his comment should have precipitated such a strong reaction. The man's friends calmed him down and Ritchie consequently avoided a beating. One of the friends told Ritchie that "this drunken insulting ruffian was one of the best fellows in the place. If so, Calgary has to be thankful for very small mercies indeed."[12]

Not all young British men coming into Calgary found the community threatening and ramshackle. For a good many it was the gateway to a fine adventure — for in the open plains of southern Alberta were found ranches. And ranches needed cowboys. Presented with the chance to become a cowboy, one remittance man was heard to say, "By Jove! This will be wizard!"

Before even securing a job as a wrangler the young men had usually added a cowboy costume to the repertoire of outfits, such as formal dinner wear, polo uniforms, and croquet party wear, that they kept stowed in their steamer trunks. This new outfit was assembled after consulting in the hotels with cowboys who had come in from the range for a night on the town. The first and most serious acquisition was a cow pony, although these small, rangy horses were a bit of a disappointment to men used to thoroughbreds, or the even larger hunting and polo horses of Britain. Even if the young man had brought with him a saddle, its lack of a horn would make roping cattle and horses difficult, so there was a need to purchase a highly ornamented western-style saddle and equally fine bridle. Having attended sensibly to the needs of his horse, it was now time to put together a suitable cowboy kit for himself. This, based on the advice again of working cowboys, consisted of boots with a good high heel, woolly chaps, spurs at least two inches in diameter, a woollen shirt worn well open at the neck so that a brilliant pink or violet silk handkerchief could be knotted at the throat, and a wide-brimmed Stetson with a fancy braided leather band around the crown. A leather shoe lace served as a chinstrap to hold the hat on. It was a garish outfit and such was the naiveté of many a remittance man that he didn't realize the cowboys were putting him on. The remittance men strode manfully, and, considering the large spurs, noisily, up and down the boardwalks of Calgary, swaggered in and out of the bars, and generally made themselves a constant source of amusement to the hard-bitten Canadian cattlemen.

Coming into Calgary in 1905, H. R. Whates found many remittance men wandering the streets in these garish cowboy outfits. "Calgary is a ranching city, and the Mecca of the superfluous son," he wrote.

> Thither go the young gentlemen from England who cannot, or do not, pass their examinations; or cannot, or will not, sit on a stool in father's office or who have neither the capacity nor the will to make for themselves acceptable careers in the Old Country. They go to Calgary, usually with some capital, to 'raunch.' When they have lost their money, as they sometimes do, they still 'raunch' — as 'cowpunchers,' for somebody else, at from twenty dollars to forty dollars a month, according to their skill as stockmen. If they have not the grit to do this, and keep at it, they write home for money. Many of them have regular allowances. The remittance men form a notable element of Albertan society and Calgary is their headquarters. They abound in the lounges and bars of the hotels, clad in breeches and Norfolk jackets, and wearing round, soft felt hats, with enormous brims.[13]

Some emulated the behaviour of the hardened cowboy. Having come from a society in which the consumption of alcohol was rampant, they had little problem with the hard drinking that cowboying seemed to necessitate. Indeed many a Canadian cowboy was awed by how these British gentlemen could knock back one whiskey after another. The ability of remittance men to drink, and their fondness for alcohol, would constitute a vital ingredient of all Canadian tales about remittance men.

The ever-snobbish Ritchie, however, was not to be one of the young men who would fit into the Calgary lifestyle. He was scandalized by all he saw. After a few days of hard drinking in what he found to be the most drunken community he had ever experienced, he decided it was time to leave. Almost as if fearing for his soul, he announced his intention to return to Britain.

> I begin to doubt whether I am not relapsing into the wild life of those around me. Fortunately, I have not yet acquired the habit of speaking through my nose, nor do I make that fearful sound — a hawking in the throat — which is a signal that your neighbour is preparing to expectorate,... but my hands are tanned. I sit with my waistcoat open, and occasionally in my shirt-sleeves. I care little to make any effort to be polite; I am clean forgetting my manners, and feel that in a little while I shall be as rough as a cow-boy, or as the wild wolf of the prairie. It is clear I must not tarry at Calgary too long.[14]

While some remittance men never got much closer to cowpunching than discussing the possibility in the Calgary bars, the majority did find work on neighbouring ranches and set about learning the trade. A few even came to Alberta with a position already guaranteed.

William Robert Newbolt arrived in Canada in 1884 at the age of eighteen. His father had served alongside General Thomas Bland Strange at the British Army's St. Helena garrison and had secured for his son a shareholder position in the general's Military Colonization Company (M.C.C.). General Strange had acquired a large tract of land that followed the shores of the Bow River with the intent of creating an immense ranch.

After arriving in Canada, Newbolt met up with General Strange in Kingston, Ontario, and the general immediately dispatched him as the head of a three-man party that was to link up with a cattle drive of stock being brought from the U.S. Great Plains country to the M.C.C. ranch by cattleman Tom Lynch. Newbolt caught up to Lynch's trail herd at Deer Lodge, Montana. Apparently General Strange had considerable faith in Newbolt, as he entrusted the young man with a bank draft to pay for both the cattle and the cost of the cattle drive.

The men on the drive were tough American cowboys who had been on the move for hundreds of miles through weather that had included blistering heat, a snowstorm, and long drenching rains. Newbolt showed up among these men wearing his fine English tweeds, puttees, and a bowler hat. According to the legends that grew out of this experience the cowboys greeted Newbolt by galloping past the young man and riddling his bowler hat with bullets fired from their revolvers.

When things calmed down and they could think of no other fun to be had with him, Newbolt was given the all-night herd watch. The shift was supposed to last four hours but Newbolt was none the wiser so they left him for the whole night.

Worn out from a night in the saddle, Newbolt's harassment continued the next morning when the cowboys presented him with a temperamental outlaw horse to ride that none of them could even manage. They were in for a surprise. Newbolt had been around horses since he could first walk, had ridden countless hours to the hounds in England, and was an experienced horse man. He slipped easily onto the saddle, stayed on during the horse's first energetic bucking, and then set out

Robert Newbolt had this portrait taken in Montreal just before he headed west to meet the M.C.C. cattle drive in 1884. GAI NA-1046-5.

60

galloping the horse across the countryside until it came to an exhausted, sweat-lathered, broken standstill.

Having proven himself to the cowboys, they backed off and even helped him assemble a sensible cowboy kit (as opposed to the woolly chaps and other regalia many a remittance man was simultaneously purchasing from outfitters in Calgary). By the time the herd arrived at the M.C.C. ranch, Newbolt had been accepted as one of the cowboy gang and they reportedly respectfully considered him "a man amongst men."

As an M.C.C. shareholder, Newbolt could either choose to take a section of land from the ranch's holdings for his own or work for wages. Newbolt soon chose to go into ranching for himself and selected for this purpose a plot of land close to the Bow River, east of De Winton. Before the onset of winter Newbolt had put up a small log cabin and was ready to start ranching. He purchased ten head of breeding cows from General Strange and registered his cattle brand as D.I.O., which stood for Dammit I'm off! And so he was. Newbolt went on to turn his ranch into one of the most profitable in the area and became a respected cattleman and member of the southern Alberta community.

Charles Sturrock arrived in Calgary in 1903, having been sent out to western Canada by his family in Jedburgh, Scotland. At the time Calgary had a population of four thousand and a police force of seven. After drifting around the town for a few days, assembling what everyone assured him was the appropriate cowboy outfit, and meeting many other remittance men in the various bars and hotel lounges, Sturrock got a job on a ranch owned by Pat Burns. He spent two years with Burns learning the ranching trade. Among the many other remittance men that he met was an Englishman named Eric Buckler. They decided to throw in their lot together by investing in adjoining quarter-sections. Each quarter-section cost ten dollars. "That's 160-acres each, by Jove, we ought to make it," Buckler said. (15) Their land was near Millarville on the slopes of Sheep Creek, facing the peaks of the distant Mist and Storm mountains in the Rockies, and about fifty miles from Calgary.

Sturrock and Buckler spent several days in Calgary outfitting for the trip to their new land. They bought a team of workhorses, which they named Biddy and Buck, harness, a wagon, and an emergency feed supply of oats. To provide them with a shelter while they built the two cabins (one on each quarter-section) required by the settling regulations, they bought a large tent. Other items purchased included a stove, large quantities of food, cooking utensils, bedding, lanterns, barbed wire, spikes and axes, and copious amounts of Scotch whiskey. To this supply they added the rifles, shotguns, fishing rods, and other gear they had both brought with them from Britain.

It took two days to reach their land. In the distance they heard the running water of Sheep Creek. Far off a coyote called. The air blowing down from the mountains was fresh with the feel of ice but a hot sun burned down from a blue sky to warm the two men. Everywhere in the long, wild grass they saw prairie chicken, spruce partridge, ruffed grouse, and rabbits. Sturrock bounded off the wagon almost immediately upon their pulling up and shotgun in hand hurried into the grass. Minutes later he returned grinning with several dead chickens and two rabbits stuffed in his game pouch. "This is the life," he told Buckler. "At least we won't starve."[16]

Buckler meanwhile had been taking stock of the land they had bought. He was awed by it all. "Look at all the grass," he said to Sturrock, "and the timber. It won't be hard to start up here."[17] While Buckler skinned the prairie chickens and rabbits for dinner, Sturrock strode off again — this time with fishing pole in hand to the creek. He soon returned with several rainbow trout. By the time they finished their feast it was nearly dark and they had to struggle to get the tent set up on top of a hill overlooking Sheep Creek. While the view was excellent, neither man had considered the tent's exposure to wind. During the night a strong gust came up and knocked the tent down upon them. They spent the rest of the night sleeping under the wagon.

Next morning they breakfasted on trout, coffee, and Scotch, following which they moved the tent to a more sheltered location farther down the hill amid a clump of trees that stood next to a running spring.

Sturrock and Buckler decided to build their homestead cabins where their two quarter-sections joined. They separated them by one room's width. This way, they reasoned, if one of them decided to quit his land the other could buy him out and easily link the two cabins together to expand his housing. In what seems a surprisingly practical manner, the two men spent the first day planning what to do by way of land development and establishing the order in which tasks should be completed. Sturrock even suspended further hunting operations for the day. The first thing, they decided, was to dig a hole and build a privy astride it. They finished off the day by constructing a lean-to to shelter their team. In subsequent days they cut fence posts and strung wire around their property and set down logs for the foundation to their houses. But it would take them two years of fumbling and fussing about before the houses would finally be built; for those years they would continue living in the tent. They decided to work their quarter-sections together as one ranch, which they named the Buck Ranch.

The decision to set up on their own rather than working as hired hands for the larger cattle ranches that had been established in the early and mid-1800s was common for remittance men. Land was inexpensive and many of these would-be ranchers were blissfully unaware of the costs involved in buying stock and feed, drilling wells, building a home and barn, and other expenses which made it difficult for many a cowboy to start up a ranch with only the resources of his cowpuncher's wages. A remittance man had an advantage over his Canadian or American counterpart in that he received money from home or had been given a sizable chunk of seed money upon his departure from Britain. The fact that these young men, who often seemed so foolish and inept, could afford what they could not was to be a source of much ill will between Canadians and remittance men. But it was largely a one-sided rancour. For the most part remittance men seemed to treat everyone they came upon with a cheerful friendliness and innocent trustfulness that sometimes exasperated their Canadian contemporaries as much as it amused them. In the skits, satires, yarns, and tall tales that Canadians created to mock remittance men, it is their naiveté, incompetence, and absurd manners that were emphasized more than any scandalous behaviour.

CHAPTER FIVE

OH I SAY! HOW DEUCEDLY UNSPORTING!

He went by the nickname Buck and few of his Canadian settler neighbours knew his real name. His parents owned a profitable engineering and implement firm in Lincolnshire. They had hoped that after a short apprenticeship he could rise to a position of managerial influence within the company. Buck, however, quickly established a reputation for coming to work drunk or staying home to nurse a crippling hangover. Finally, fed up with his antics, Buck's father put him on a boat for Canada.

Buck came well financed with two thousand pounds in hard cash and the guarantee of a quarterly remittance of fifty pounds to cover operating expenses and provide pocket money. His parents instructed him to buy a farm near Calgary. They promised that if he operated it viably and proved himself, they would continue to financially support his efforts. Buck, happy to escape from the sternly watchful eye of his parents, gleefully set out for Canada. Looking back from the stern of the ship, he sighed, "Peace, perfect peace, with loved ones far away," as Britain faded from sight. After landing in Montreal he caught a train to Calgary and was soon well ensconced in the city's best hotel — the same one Ritchie had so loathed.

After decking himself out in the requisite cowboy garb, Buck started looking for a ranch. He had quickly noted that Canadian farmers were much like their counterparts in Britain — people who grubbed in soil and so had dirt under their fingernails and grimy clothes — but cowboys rode horses, carried guns, and wore colourful outfits. This, Buck decided, was the life a young man of good family should lead when he came to Canada.

He found a small operation south of Calgary that to his completely inexperienced eye looked viable. Prairie stretched this way and that, several rough buildings were grouped around a couple corrals, and it was only a short gallop from the bars of the city. A gnarled-looking Canadian with skin so darkly browned by sun and wind that Buck thought him at first to be an Indian was selling out. The cowboy told Buck he wanted only a fair price. Buck considered the purchase price carefully and made an offer he thought quite shrewd. The broken-down cowboy accepted glumly and Buck was certain he had struck a bargain that would make even his father proud of him.

There was, however, Buck realized, another bargain to be driven. Just when the cowboy thought the deal concluded and was reaching his hand out for the gentlemanly handshake, Buck pulled himself up to his full height, cocked one eyebrow in the direction of the nearest shack, and said: "And now, what do you value the buildings and improvements at?" While toasting the incredible good luck of his having had a British gentleman come his way, the cowboy related his reaction later to some buddies in a Calgary hotel: "When I heard this Englishman say that, I was just agoin' to holler — 'Well of all the damned fools!' An' then I seen all at once who'd be the damned fool an' I got my trap shut in time! An' that simp paid me over again for all the fixtures."[1]

Needless to say, by the time Buck purchased some livestock from the equally wily owner of a breeding farm and hired a foreman to manage the ranching operation, precious little remained of the two thousand pounds. In short order the stock started mysteriously disappearing and Buck found himself unable to pay the always well dressed and apparently prosperous foreman. The man told Buck he would take his wages that were in arrears in the form of an interest in the ranch. The sum in arrears multiplied at a rapid rate. Buck stared at the records of indebtedness presented to him by the foreman, but could make no sense of the logic behind the arithmetic. Figures had never been his strong point in school and he thought it too rude to question the foreman directly about the meaning of all the numbers written into a maze of different columns. Finally one day the foreman pointed out to Buck that he now owned greater equity in the ranch than Buck and that there really was no profit in the young man remaining there. Buck had to agree, for he had none of the start-up capital left and the fifty-pound quarterly remittances were insufficient

Englishman Osborne Brown built this log cabin on his Elbow River homestead in the early 1890s. He was a charter member and president of the Calgary Polo Club. GAI NA-3913-1.

to support him. As he rode off to try his fortune elsewhere, Buck wished the foreman the "jolly best of good luck." It is said the foreman didn't laugh out loud until Buck was just a dimple of darkness against the skyline.

From here Buck was reported to have gone on to become a camp cook for one of the big ranching operations near Calgary. For a time Buck deceived his parents about the loss of the ranch by sending home posed photographs of himself standing next to pedigreed bulls. The fine ranch buildings visible in the background were actually those of his employer, as were the bulls with which Buck posed. Ultimately, however, Buck was found out by his parents when the father came to see his son's fine stock-breeding ranch. Enraged by Buck's deceptions, his father cut him off entirely and the young man never heard from his parents again.

It was typical of these stories that little sympathy was shown for the fact that Buck had been bilked out of his money by at least two Canadians. The prevalent attitude was that remittance men received the fate they deserved.

The popular Canadian folklore that grew up around the presence of British remittance men in the Canadian west represented them as fools, drunkards, louts, scoundrels, and snobs who refused to fit into the evolving Canadian society. The British gentleman was derided in bars, satirized on stage, lampooned in books, savaged in music halls, and generally treated with scorn.

In *The Range Men*, L.V. Kelly sums up the western Canadian attitude toward remittance men. They were looked upon by westerners, Kelly writes, "with the scorn that a capable man feels for the unfit — the scorn that men who had made their own way with nothing to start on but a sound constitution feel for the failures who commenced life with the proverbial silver spoon. For years the doings of the remittance men, their misfortunes, characteristics and errors of omission and commission, served as the sauce and dessert over many a camp-fire."[2] They arrived in Canada, he writes, with "leggings, monocles, caps, accent, and habits, and proved everlasting sources of enjoyment and personal gain to the hard-headed settlers and cowboys. A remittance man in any particular district was a local pride and his doings were magnified and improved upon for the edification of the inhabitants of other districts, who, if they too owned such a person, listened in superior silence and then came back with more outrageous doings of their own man."[3]

So intently did Canadians concentrate on the behaviour and antics of failed remittance men that the designation of who was or wasn't a remittance man soon became twisted in the popular mind. No longer was it strictly anyone who came from Britain and was sustained by, or given a start with, cash from parents or family at home in the Old Country. By the 1890s remittance man was a term of derision applied to the British gentleman who was considered a failure. Other British emigrants who had arrived and prospered with the help of remittance money from Britain took pains to distance themselves from this group and often denied any connection to their less capable brethren. They took to joining in with their Canadian neighbours in regaling each other with stories of remittance men, while carefully down-playing the point that they were in fact products of the same culture, society, and remittance system as those they joined in scorning and labelling with the moniker of remittance men.

William Walker came to the Okanagan Valley to learn farming. His parents had intended him for a clerical vocation. In public school he studied theology, Greek, Latin, and the classics, but Walker was little interested in these studies and scored poorly on tests. Instead he concentrated on sports, playing football and cricket almost incessantly. Later, when he was nineteen, Walker rebelled against his parents' wish that he enter the clergy. "Well," said his father, "it'll have to be the colonies then." And so to the colonies Walker went. He arrived in Penticton at the south end of the valley on August 8, 1894, and travelled to a farm in the nearby Similkameen Valley. His father had paid the owner five hundred dollars a year for him to learn farming. When Walker came into the valley he was decked out like the typical remittance man: tweed Norfolk coat, knickerbockers, wool stockings, and a tweed cap.

After he spent a year-and-a-half learning to farm, which as far as he could see appeared to entail mostly weeding and picking onions, his father sent him enough money to buy land for an Okanagan fruit farm. Walker had a grander scheme. In the southern part of the valley was a wild gold-mining boom town called Fairview. Men were dragging gold out of narrow, deep shafts dug all over the western hills surrounding the Fairview townsite. At the time Fairview boasted the largest hotel north of San Francisco and looked to be a town with a prosperous future. Walker joined in the quest for gold, investing money in mining operations and property around Fairview. But Fairview's gold strike was small and not especially good; soon the mines dried up and the miners were lured away by the stories of the vast Klondike gold strikes being discovered in the Yukon. The hotel burned down and Fairview was abandoned as quickly as it had been built. Walker was left with no money and nothing to show for his investments except some sagebrush-choked desert in the middle of nowhere that could support little in the way of life other than throngs of rattlesnakes.

Undaunted by this turn of rotten luck and even worse business acumen, Walker headed north to Kelowna, worked on an orchard for his friend W. D. Hobson, and eventually saw a chance to buy some land from the local diocese of the Roman Catholic Church. Asking Hobson to assemble the purchase of 385 acres of land for him, Walker hurried back to Britain and convinced his parents to advance him further financing. With his parents' backing, Walker returned to the Okanagan, bought the land, and proceeded to build a successful orchard. Walker eventually married Dorothea Thompson and the two became stalwart members of the Okanagan Valley community.

From their position of social prominence they joined the rest of their equally prosperous and successful British peers in looking with some disdain upon other remittance men who had not fared as well.

Dorothea Walker in later years recalled with great vividness remittance men like Richard Tidmarsh. Tidmarsh, she would say, was a Greek and Latin scholar who used to send chess problems home to the *London Times*. He lived in a shack and was known for wearing the same old brown corduroy suit from the time he arrived in the Okanagan to the day he died. "I don't know if he ever washed," Dorothea said. "Tidmarsh used to go on benders. He often had a keg of whiskey in his shack and just sat in bed and drank."[4] He was a remittance man, she gravely pointed out: sufficient explanation for both his alcoholism and poor hygiene.

Conversely she remembered ten young public schoolmen who also lived in shacks up in the Okanagan hills. "They were nice young fellows, though, not remittance men." The remittance man, she insisted, "was a waster who got an allowance to keep him out of the way; many were younger sons. They would work sometimes for men who owned land. I knew some of them. You didn't take them seriously as you knew they couldn't buy bacon and beans without the little income they got from Britain."[5]

The fact that Walker himself had only succeeded due to the financial intervention of his parents on two separate occasions, and that he had been sent to the colonies because his parents could see no future for him in Britain because of his poor showing at school and refusal to enter the clergy, seemed to have entirely escaped the Walkers. The distinction between themselves and remittance men was that they had succeeded, whereas the remittance men had not. And the young men in the shacks who were "nice young fellows" were also not remittance men apparently, for the simple reason that they were "nice," and good company for riding to the hounds or playing cricket.

This effort of British immigrants with a public-school background to blend in with Canadians by eschewing their own didn't always work, for many Canadians were quite ready at this time to paint all Britons, especially the English, with the same tarry brush. Among English-speaking Canadians, loyalty to the United Kingdom was still deeply ingrained and few would, as proven at the beginning of World War I, hesitate to hasten to her defence. But there was in Canada, too, a growing nationalism that stressed economic, cultural, and social independence from Britain.

This was especially strong in the Canadian west, where men and women with British roots were finding they could shuck the class distinctions and rigidity that restricted the freedom and economic opportunities of many of their relatives still in Britain. Canada was a land of opportunity, a place of the clean start. The arrival of the British public-school boys, with all their affectations of social superiority and their often extravagant funding from home, threatened this new-found freedom from the class system that so stifled Britain. British nobility in Canada could expect neither the respect or the subservience they would automatically receive in Britain. It was a circumstance many British gentlemen proved incapable of adapting to and their inability to reshape their behaviour to fit that of the new country only further alienated them from their neighbours; it also reinforced the Canadian popular perception of them and fuelled the resultant disdain.

Although remittance men came from all parts of Britain and were as likely to be of an Irish, Scottish, or Welsh background as English, the average western Canadian was most likely to assume such men were English. To some degree this had to do with accent, and partly it was simple prejudice on the part of the Canadian westerner. Public school boys, no matter if they were Scottish or English, all assumed manners of speech that set them apart from their fellow citizens. A Scottish remittance man was unlikely to have a rumbling brogue for an accent, nor would an Irish remitter sound like a Derryman. The accents that Canadians thought of as Scottish or Irish were mostly the accents of the common classes, so when they heard a public school boy talking they paid scant attention to what part of Britain he called home and simply labelled him an Englishman. The English, saddled now with the sins of all British remittance men, had a heavy burden to carry. "Whatever prejudice exists against Englishmen is due to the fact that they assimilate less quickly than do the Scotsman and the Irishman and members of certain other races," wrote A.G. Adshead in "The British Emigrant in Canada: The Bright Side," an article published in the June 1909 issue of *Travel & Exploration: A Monthly Illustrated Magazine.*[6]

Englishmen were seen as being too self-important to get their hands dirty farming. They also, the common belief was, expected a good, solid Canadian to kowtow to them and jump at their beck and call. Stories proliferated of Englishmen assuming themselves to be better than Canadians. One of these involved an English aristocrat hunting for ducks near Calgary, who employed a local settler to serve as his guide. The guide led the imperious, snobbish fop to a marsh. With great gusto the aristocrat shouldered his shotgun and dropped a large drake with a perfectly delivered wing-shot. But the duck fell into a slough on the other side of a barbed-wire fence.

"Ow, my good fellah," called the aristocrat to the settler, "just climb ovah theah and fetch that bihd, like a good fellah."

For the Okanagan remittance men, any wild game might prove a proud kill, even a rat-tlesnake. BCARS 66566 D-4216.

The guide snapped back, "Pick up your own damn bird!" and stomped off, leaving the bemused and distraught aristocrat with no option but to scale the fence and slog into the slough himself or abandon his kill.[7]

Another story that made the rounds of the Calgary hotel lounges and bars told of an English greenhorn who went to the Calgary land agent and applied to "prove up" (get title to) his homestead. "How many acres broken?" inquired the land agent. "What do you suppose I am? I'm not a blasted sod-buster; I'm a rancher" retorted the young remittance man. "Well, in that case, what stock have you got on the place?" asked the land agent. "We-ell, there's the cayuse...and there's the dog," replied the prospective rancher, who needless to say didn't have a prayer of getting title to his homestead.[8]

English-baiting became a refined art in the Canadian west. This consisted of taking advantage of the naiveté of young remittance men to get them to believe the most outlandish things or undertake bizarre behaviour in the belief that it was what a cowboy or seasoned westerner did to cope with a situation. The absurdly impractical, but garish, cowboy garb favoured by the remittance men of southern Alberta resulted from assurances by Canadians that this was how a cowboy dressed.

Many tales focused on the perceived inability of Englishmen to figure out the simplest of things. One story related how a young remittance man wanting to buy some horses for his new ranch visited a livery stable where he saw two huge mules placidly munching oats from nosebags. Turning to the livery-keeper, he asked, "I say, do you always have to keep them muzzled?" The liveryman reportedly sincerely assured the man that it was a necessary safeguard or they might rip a cowboy's arm off with their enormous teeth.[9]

Peter Briggs, a remittance man who settled in the High River country in the 1890s, insisted on galloping his race horses across the Alberta prairie. Inevitably one of his horses, named Randel, stepped in a badger hole causing horse and rider to suffer a bad tumble. Randel regained his feet first and trotted off, leaving Briggs to limp home on foot. Arriving at the nearby ranchhouse of George Ross, he muttered to Ross that nobody ever "told me about those blasted badger holes."[10]

Perhaps, however, someone had told him about the squint — a two-headed turtle seen only by moonlight. The squint's spiral spring-shaped tail enabled the creature to travel by somersaults. The squints, cowboys advised gullible British gentlemen, lived chiefly on alkali soil, whistled in their sleep, and were weak-minded. If remittance men wondered why they never saw squints, the cowboys explained that the turtles were shy and always somersaulted away from newcomers.

Equally uncommon was the denturia, an animal about the size of a jack-rabbit that was twice as big in front as it was behind and suffered toothaches whenever Texas was struck by a hurricane or it rained in Omaha. The denturia taunted cattle by making faces at them and hissing from their ears. If an Englishman expressed any doubt as to the animal's existence, the cowboys were known to produce a denturia hide. This usually looked quite similar to that of a jack-rabbit that might have suffered a bad mauling from a coyote.

In British Columbia's Cariboo country Englishmen were often told about the snoohook — a bird that looked like a vulture but was larger and more repulsive. The snoohook spent most of the year in the Arctic, where it fed chiefly on muskeg moss and whale oil, a diet that gave the bird an unpleasant, rancid odour. Snoohooks, Cariboo ranchers and miners maintained, always wore monocles of clear ice over their left eyes, and screeched meaninglessly with a decidedly English accent.[11]

As early as 1880, books satirizing British upper-class visitors to Canada started appearing. *The Englishman in Canada* by a writer identified only as "Mac" was a spoof of the sort of travelogue, such as that written by J. Ewing Ritchie, that was so popular in Britain during the late 1800s. Mac's English character is so uninformed about Canada that he plans to begin his trip by landing at St. John's, Newfoundland, and walking to Montreal. Along the way he is certain that he will have to fight savages, wild beasts, and face "other unknown terrors." After braving the wilderness surrounding Montreal he hopes to come out at Toronto, board a streetcar, and set out on a short, diverting tour of Manitoba and British Columbia. Upon arriving in Canada the young bachelor, who is Mac's protagonist in the tale, seems oblivious to his own boorish manners and inability to comprehend that the self-confident, capable Canadian men and women he encounters have no need of his British ways or civilization. The story ends with his going to Ottawa, expecting to be offered the post of Inspector General of Curling and Skating Rinks for the Dominion of Canada. He figures the appointment should be worth at least one thousand-pounds per annum, as nothing less would be sufficient for a gentleman of his calibre.

These counter-travelogues were common throughout Canada until World War I, as were plays satirizing the British gentleman. In Toronto music halls sell-out crowds laughed uproariously at the antics of English characters who strode about wearing monocles and outlandish tweed costumes, stammering and ranting such lines as "don'tcher know," "I say!" and "deucedly clever," or in one case of apparent insight at some plight that had befallen the character during his attempts to deal with shrewd and capable Canadians, "Oh I say! How deucedly unsporting!"

Sometimes the satire was used as a podium from which to take shots at other favourite targets of scorn. Such was the case with the tale of Geoffrey O'Connell, which became a local legend in the Assiniboia District of the Northwest Territories (now part of Saskatchewan) in the 1890s. O'Connell was reported to be the failed son of a family deeply involved in British politics. For many a year he lived in the Assiniboia region and availed himself of the generosity of the homesteaders there, while more or less going around in a constant state of inebriation.

Eventually he returned to Britain after promising his parents that he was a changed man and ready to make a serious effort to pull his life together. He didn't, of course, and embarrassed them terribly with his drunken antics. One day, when he was still bleary with drink, they bundled him on a ship back to Canada. But times had changed in the Assiniboia area while he was gone and the people no longer would take him in and look after him.

Finally, goes the tale, he was brought before a judge to answer a charge of being drunk and disorderly, which led to the Crown petitioning to make him a permanent ward of the state due to his inability to care for himself. The judge asked the defendant about his family and O'Connell mentioned that he had a brother. "I suppose he's a worthless charlatan, too?" queried the judge. "Yes, your honour," O'Connell replied in a downcast voice. "What does he do?" O'Connell is said to have cast the judge a rogue's smile. "He's a lawyer, sir." The quip didn't save O'Connell from a harsh fate, however, for legend has it that he was sent to a mental institution where he lived until his death.[12]

Satires such as this easily turned to invective. Calgary's *Tribune* of July 2, 1895, railed against young remittance men, calling them dudes. Dudes, it said, "dress themselves up in the garb of cowboys, [with] spurs the size of small cart wheels...hats cut with a scissor and covered with mud to look old and tough." They do little, the paper went on, "but ride round the country on a half-starved cayuse. Too lazy to plough, and too shiftless to own cattle, they eke out an existence on the remittance plan. Their only redeeming quality is that they do not marry and are not therefore likely to perpetuate the breed."[13]

The *Tribune* and other western Canadian papers increasingly lambasted remittance men for their ways and reported on their many shortcomings with regard to work. Remittance men no longer seemed a sufficiently damning phrase so they were tagged with a series of others. Remitters, tenderfoots, greenhorns, mud-pups, cheechakos, bronchos, were all terms intended to single them out. John Sandilands' *Western Canadian Dictionary and Phrase-Book*, published in 1912, defined broncho as referring to an "Englishman who still clings to Old-Country manners and speech; so called because he requires 'breaking in.'" Once broken in, Sandilands continued, the bronchos might be considered by their western Canadian counterparts as "Improved Britishers."[14]

Fewer Canadians, however, were willing to undertake the effort of breaking in an English broncho. Across the prairies and throughout British Columbia, job postings placed in such locations as the Farm Help Register in Winnipeg bore the notice: No Englishmen Need Apply. In 1910, when Harry Aldred was trying to find work in the Okanagan Valley, he was met with the same situation. Aldred tried vainly to talk the farm owners into giving him work despite the dead giveaway of his English accent. "I worked hard to get my English accent under control," he said, "but I never could."[15]

Aldred was unique in that he was willing to hide his Englishness to fit into the Canadian workplace. Most British gentlemen would never have considered such an approach. They were proud of who they were and not about to change for the sake of appeasing what they saw as rough, uncouth Canadian sentiments.

Perhaps no story so well symbolizes this refusal to conform than that of the British gentleman supposed to have lost his way in the dense forests on the British Columbia side of the Rocky Mountains. Lacking any knowledge of wilderness survival, he wandered aimlessly before finally, half-dead from thirst, being found by some Canadian woodsmen. Considering the presence of several mighty rivers in the area, all running high with spring melt, his rescuers were puzzled by his dehydrated state. "Why didn't you drink some water?" they asked. "Why," he replied, "I didn't have a bally drinking cup, don'tcher know!"[16]

Hearing of this tale, Rudyard Kipling marshalled to the fastidious Englishman's defence. Of the Canadians' decrying of the remittance men, he said:

> It is true that in his own country he is taught to shirk work, because kind, silly people fall over each other to help, and debauch and amuse him. Here, General January will stiffen him up. Remittance-men are an affliction to every branch of the Family, but your manners and morals can't be so tender as to suffer from a few thousand of them among your six millions....The Englishman is a born kicker. He kicks on principle, and that is what makes for civilization. So did your Englishman's instincts about the glass. Every new country needs — vitally needs — one-half to one per cent of its population trained to die of thirst rather than drink out of their hands.[17]

CHAPTER SIX

CIVILIZING WILDERNESS — THE BEAUTIFUL ART

In the fall of 1882, William Adolph Baillie-Grohman and his friend Theodore Roosevelt, then a member of the New York State Assembly, were tracking a mountain goat in the Kootenay highlands. They had been on the trail for hours and, given the mountain goat's lead, expected the hunt to continue for many hours more, possibly even into the next day. This was the kind of challenge on which the two acquaintances — and avid outdoorsmen — thrived: hard days on the hunting trail, cold nights spent in darkest wilderness with the stars a silvery blanket overhead, the promise of a good kill at the end of the trail.

The two men broke out of a dense forest and stared down upon a wide valley stretching south from the bottom of a long glittering body of water that the maps denoted as Kootenay Lake. In the fall the valley bottom land was at its best with fields of wild hay interspersed with shallow marshes. Baillie-Grohman surveyed the land below him and promptly forgot all about tracking the mountain goat. Instead he dragged Roosevelt down from the hills into the valley and soon the two of them, both having an eye for grand engineering projects, were discussing how this land could be transformed from flooded bottom land into an agricultural paradise.

Roosevelt soon returned to New York State and Baillie-Grohman to Victoria. Whether Roosevelt ever thought again of the possibilities of developing the East Kootenay bottom land isn't known, but Baillie-Grohman became obsessed by the land's potential.

Beneath the reedy grass covering was rich black loam, hundreds of acres stretching from the lake to the American border. Baillie-Grohman envisioned the vast area being developed as an entirely British colony, where all that was finest about the British character could flourish in splendid isolation from the lesser races and nationalities. Chinese immigrants might have already established North America's second-largest Chinese community in the very heart of British Victoria, but here in this valley, with Baillie-Grohman's influence, there would only be British residents.

There was just one hitch that Baillie-Grohman could see hindering the transformation of vision into reality. The land spent much of the year underwater, flooded by overflow from the lake to the north. In fact the flooding was so bad that the Kootenay bottom land was really a vast

Avid outdoorsman William Adolph Baillie-Grohman envisioned transforming B.C.'s
East Kootenay bottom land into an agricultural paradise for British gentlemen.
BCARS 4801 A-1974.

swamp, cut into a maze by the meanderings of the Kootenay River. It was an uninviting place for most of the year, infested by mosquitoes and overgrown along the river banks with thorned crab-apple trees. In 1865, trail-builder Edgar Dewdney explored the area in an effort to find a path for a trail the British Columbia colonial government had contracted him to build from Osoyoos to the East Kootenay mining operations. The seasoned woodsman and his Indian guide, known only as Louis, wandered lost and starving for several days before finding their way out. Dewdney came back later with a trail crew and built a route to the mines through the swampland, but much of the year it was flooded and impassable. Dewdney, and other engineers, could see no economically viable way to construct a trail through the bottom land that would be free of flooding and resultant closures. They undoubtedly never conceived of the land being an agricultural mecca.

To Baillie-Grohman, however, such a vision was as obvious as his own genius. Equally obvious was the prospect of a fortune to be reaped by the visionary who succeeded in developing this valley. In 1883 Baillie-Grohman convinced two land promoters, Gilbert Malcolm Sproat and A.S. Farwell, to accompany him to the valley to investigate its development potential. The two men were dismayed to learn they had travelled all the way from Victoria through harsh country to explore a valley awash with spring run-off.

But Baillie-Grohman was undaunted, for by now he had divined the solution. It was simple. The source of Kootenay River, which fed the lake, was only about four miles from Columbia Lake, lying to the west of Kootenay Lake. Columbia Lake was happily a good six feet lower than Kootenay Lake. Baillie-Grohman assured the two promoters that if a canal was constructed between the two lakes, enough water could be diverted from Kootenay Lake into the Columbia River system to drain the bottom land and allow its agricultural potential to be realized. A four-mile canal and a bit of work widening the river's mouth would do the trick. Baillie-Grohman spun his visions before Sproat and Farwell and by the time the three men returned to Victoria the two promoters were converted to the cause.

Now all that was needed was money and provincial government approval to proceed with the canal's construction. It would take four years of financial negotiations, political intrigues, and unceasing court battles before Baillie-Grohman's Kootenay Land Syndicate Company started construction of the canal. Three years later the canal, complete with locks to control the flow in order to prevent flooding of land already being profitably farmed on the shores of Columbia Lake, was

Although his East Kootenay development was intended to be exclusively British and free of the taint of other races and ethnicity, Baillie-Grohman relied on the labour of Chinese immigrants to construct the canal intended to drain the land for development.
BCARS 50648 C-4284

completed. The cost was also more than the fifty thousand pounds raised in Britain by the Kootenay Land Syndicate Company; Baillie-Grohman apparently covered the extra costs out of his own reportedly substantial wealth.

Although Baillie-Grohman's grand design had been realized, the control of water flows into Columbia River rendered the canal a costly failure. The canal's allowed flow levels proved insufficient to drain the Kootenay bottom land. The hoped-for British Eden remained a swamp covered by three feet of brackish water. Soon Baillie-Grohman's claim to the land was rescinded because he had neglected to carry out a required property survey, and another development company won the right to press ahead with reclaiming the rich soil from the grip of flood waters. This company proposed to achieve the drainage by diking the river and lake to prevent flooding. They had no plans to create an exclusively British agricultural community: anyone who had money to buy land was welcome. Many of the farmers came north from the United States.

So ended Baillie-Grohman's grand venture to civilize the wilderness of eastern British Columbia and make a fortune. Although Baillie-Grohman's plan was grander than most, such plans were by no means unique to the well-known sportsman and adventurer. Throughout

British Columbia's interior, and to a lesser extent in other parts of the Canadian west, such land development projects flourished. The goal of all was to make a fortune by opening land up for settlement and development by British immigrants. The Okanagan Valley, the Comox and Cowichan valleys of Vancouver Island, and Windermere in the northeast Kootenays were all developed primarily through land promotions that advertised the availability of fertile farmland in new British communities being formed in the heart of the Canadian western wilderness. Some, such as Walhachin in B.C.'s Thompson River Valley and Cannington Manor in southeast Saskatchewan, went further and offered prospective upper-class British settlers the opportunity to live in exclusively British agrarian utopias.

In 1890 Lord and Lady Aberdeen arrived in Vancouver and encountered George Grant McKay, who back in Scotland had once carried out road-building projects for Ishbel's father. Ishbel Aberdeen had only recently met her brother, Coutts Marjoribanks, in Winnipeg and there had learned that his ranch in the Dakota Territories had failed. She had promised "Couttsy" that she would try and find an opportunity for him in Canada, speculating at the time that British Columbia seemed a probable location. When the Aberdeens met McKay, the problem of what to do with her brother was very much on Ishbel's mind. McKay was sympathetic to her trouble and, having spent some time in the Okanagan Valley, suggested that this was the place for the Aberdeens to invest in some land that would be guaranteed to prove a profitable venture.

McKay was known in the Okanagan as Gee-Gee and was considered by all who knew him to be a smart, smooth-talking operator. He was also an aggressive land promoter. Charles Holliday, who had only arrived in the Okanagan the year before, heard it joked in the bars there that when McKay died "and the gates of heaven opened up for him, he would seize St. Peter by the lapel and say to him, 'How are the chances for laying out a townsite here?'"[1]

In 1890 the Okanagan was just opening to settlement. The economy was still based on ranching and large tracts of Okanagan land were held by individual ranching families, such as the Vernons after which the largest northern Okanagan town was named. The Okanagan Valley is narrow; the bottom land is mostly under lake water, above which shelves of bench land are backed by mountains. Although prior to 1890 a number of British settlers had planted fruit trees, few viable orchards were in operation.

One of the problems hampering agricultural development in the Okanagan was the lack of good railway connections: the nearest station on the CPR trans-Canada line was at Sicamous, a good day's travel from Vernon. Travel from Vernon to the rest of the valley was by boat or overland by rough tracks that could hardly be rated as roads. McKay assured the Aberdeens that it was a matter of a few years at most before a railroad spur was constructed to connect the central part of the valley to Sicamous. Based on McKay's supposed local knowledge the Aberdeens entrusted him with ten thousand dollars to buy 480 acres of land near an Oblate missionary outpost run by Father Charles Felix Adolph Pandosy, who was reputed to have planted the first apple tree in the Okanagan. The property was close to a lakeside landing where a hotel and some other buildings were being constructed. This site would become Kelowna. McKay told the Aberdeens that when the railway came to Kelowna the land's value was bound to increase tenfold.

Relieved to have at last found Marjoribanks a good home, Lord and Lady Aberdeen returned to eastern Canada. Marjoribanks soon arrived in the valley with a footloose companion, Eustace Smith, who was appointed foreman. The pair commissioned the construction of an extravagant ranch house that when completed sported gold Japanese wallpaper, seven chimneys, and no insulation. From the base camp of their ranch house Marjoribanks and Smith sallied forth on shooting expeditions, whiled away the nights in various taverns throughout the Okanagan, and stalwartly avoided undertaking any agricultural development of the farmland.

McKay meanwhile purchased large chunks of land bordering the Aberdeen's property, laid out a townsite called Benvoulin, and capitalized on the Aberdeen's good name in Britain to start promoting his lands throughout the Old Country as a farmer's paradise waiting to happen.

In 1891 the Aberdeens travelled to the Okanagan to see their estate for the first time. They found the property had no access to the nearby lake, lacked its own water source, and contained farm buildings that were dilapidated and flea-ridden. Ishbel was undaunted, however, and fancying that the land was similar to that of her Scottish home in the highlands country called the estate Guisachan. Although Marjoribanks was obviously indifferent to the idea of actually farming the land Ishbel decided, with some prompting from McKay, that they would grow fruit there and make from it jam and preserves for export. "It would be nice to see poor old Coutts a rich man after all," she wrote friends in Britain.[2]

Coutts Marjoribanks (seated) and foreman Eustace Smith, circa 1890.
The Kelowna Museum #12303.

Ishbel rather liked the brand name "Premier preserves," and the Aberdeens decided that to realize a fortune from jam manufacture they needed some substantial orchard operations. It was obvious even to them that the Okanagan did not produce enough to support such a venture. The ever-helpful McKay, however, had a solution. McKay had become friends with Forbes George Vernon and was also a main shareholder of the Okanagan Land Development Company. This company was involved in buying up land tracts, subdividing them into small acreages, and then marketing them in Britain as prime orchard properties.

McKay convinced the Aberdeens to invest fifty thousand pounds in the 13,000-acre Coldstream ranch, which was being offered for sale by Forbes Vernon. The land was to be subdivided into small holdings and sold to settlers who would plant orchards. From the orchards would come fruit which the Aberdeen's preserve company would turn into jam at a factory built in Vernon exclusively for this purpose.

Ishbel was enthusiastic about the plan and saw in it the beginnings of a fine community in Vernon. The land, she wrote, would be sold to settlers "of a very good class...a good nucleus for the future: — we ought to get in time a really high-class little community here."[3] Ishbel's predictions were to come true but not in time to save the Aberdeen's investments in the Okanagan. By 1894 Ishbel was despondent about the whole adventure. "The fruit at Guisachan was a failure, owing to alkali," she wrote. "It has been a big loss to plant all those trees down there."[4] The Coldstream venture, meanwhile, fared little better. Originally the ranch had been stocked with two thousand head of cattle but by 1894 this figure had dwindled mysteriously under Marjoribanks' management to eight hundred and Ishbel reported that after costs the cattle sold for a large deficit. No jam was ever produced in the factory, which had been optimistically constructed before hardly any fruit trees were even planted, let alone ready for harvest. Eventually the Aberdeens sold their Okanagan properties. "Neither the purchase money nor all that was spent on development ever came back," Ishbel later admitted, "and the results of our investment in B.C. have been very sad."[5]

Despite the Aberdeens' personal losses over the Coldstream and Guisachan developments their efforts to create viable farmland in the Okanagan attracted a lot of attention to the valley. By the time the Aberdeens gave the area up, settlers from Britain were pouring in — lured by promotional literature that promised opportunity, profit, and the chance to live a gentlemanly existence to all who had the money, the character, and the desire to succeed. The words of Albert Henry George, the Fourth Earl Grey and Canada's governor general from 1904 to 1911, were often quoted by the promoters. Earl Grey owned a small fruit farm in the Kootenay Valley and thought himself quite the gentleman farmer. He imagined that virtually all the valleys of B.C.'s interior could be transformed from wilderness into prime orchard land.

In 1905, in a speech delivered to the Royal Agricultural Society at the New Westminster Exhibition in British Columbia, he opined:

Fruit growing in your province has acquired the distinction of being a beautiful art as well as a most profitable industry. After a maximum wait of five years, I understand the settler may look forward with reasonable certainty to a net income of $100 to $150 per acre after all expenses of cultivation have been paid.

Gentlemen, here is a state of things which appears to offer the opportunity of living under such ideal conditions as struggling humanity has only succeeded in reaching in one or two of the most favoured spots upon the earth. There are thousands of families living in England today — families of refinement, culture and distinction, families such as you would welcome among you with both arms — who would be only too glad to come out and occupy a log hut on five acres of a pear or apple orchard in full bearing, if they could do so at reasonable cost.[6]

From 1890 to the outbreak of World War I the B.C. interior was to undergo a fruit-farming bonanza that would make many a land developer wealthy and leave far more remittance men and other British gentlemen destitute. Everywhere promoters were hastening to stake out land for subdivision into orchards. They created advertising pamphlets and brochures for distribution in Britain. Virtually any valley or open plain was deemed appropriate for fruit farming. As had been the case with Baillie-Grohman's plan to develop the Kootenay bottom lands, no

AN "OLD-TIMER'S" BUNGALOW AND GARDEN.

The cover of the Columbia Valley Irrigated Fruit Lands promotional brochure portrayed a Windermere valley that bore little resemblance to its reality. BCARS collection.

problem was seen as a deterrent — swamps could be easily drained, deserts irrigated, ground that was only pebbles would bear fruit if the belief was there, severe winter cold was blithely discounted as being nothing more than a bracing tonic for the spirit.

Holliday, who by now had become a permanent resident of the valley after spending a short time working his way inland from Victoria, reported that there were droves of "real-estate men and company promoters...for there were many suckers and the fishing was good....the fortunate ranchers from whom these speculators bought their land for subdivision shrugged their shoulders and took their unearned increment with a tolerant smile." And the British came flocking.

> Retired officers of the army and navy, retired Indian civil servants; men who had gone broke growing oranges and tea and thought apples and peaches might put them on their feet again; English school boys whose parents sent them to the "colonies" with their blessing because they would not fit into anything at home; professional men, fed up with their profession, who with dreams of a life of ease longed to be farmers; shrewd shopkeepers looking for business openings, ladies looking for husbands, ladies of easy virtue, cardsharpers, just plain bums and then sisters and cousins and aunts of men who had come out ahead of them...they were all there.[7]

Communities sprang up throughout the valley, townsites with whimsical names: Peachland, Summerland, Naramata, Kaledan. A developer by the name of J.M. Robinson was involved in creation of all four of these south-Okanagan farming towns. He was alleged by the locals to have come to the valley seeking gold because a clairvoyant had guaranteed that in the mountains just above what would be Peachland there was gold aplenty waiting to be discovered. Robinson found no gold, but he did stumble across two withered peach trees struggling for life in the thin, sun-baked soil on the slopes leading up to the mountains. An ideal peach-growing country he surmised and staked out a claim to all the land there. He then parcelled it up into small acreages and promoted his community of Peachland in Britain.

The development was a huge success, although the orchards mostly failed. One prospective orchardist arrived to find the soil of his ten-acre plot clung tenuously to the side of a hill. Robinson reputedly assured the dubious landowner that the angle of slope was ideal for drainage.

Another developer sold his orchards already planted. He would pack the property with two hundred or more seedling apple trees planted a mere six inches apart, have a photograph taken of this lush-looking property, and then sell the farm to British gentlemen who were tiring of trying to make a go of it on the Canadian prairies. The farmer to be would, of course, shortly find that the seedlings, with no space to grow, and lacking any water for irrigation, soon withered.

By this time, however, the developers had moved on to other parts of the valley or British Columbia to again spin their dreams. As Holliday said there was always another sucker ready to buy into a well-promoted land speculation.

Despite the sleaziness of many of the Okanagan land promoters the valley did eventually prove a viable fruit-farming region. Okanagan fruit was winning prizes, including a gold medal for apples awarded annually from 1906 to 1909 by the Royal Horticultural Society in London. Slowly the settlers banded together and developed co-operative irrigation systems to solve the riddle of how to grow fruit in land that, although overlooking blue lakes, was eternally water poor. A railroad line was extended from Sicamous to Vernon; the rest of the valley was tied to the railroad system by stern-wheelers that plied the length of Okanagan Lake and offered a faster means of travel than the valley's crude road system. New varieties of hardy fruit trees were developed capable of surviving Okanagan weather and soil conditions. By 1908 land that had been selling for a dollar an acre ten years earlier would fetch one thousand dollars.

What was true of the Okanagan, it was reasoned by developers and British settlers alike, must be true of the other valleys of the B.C. interior. Developers poured in. Townsites and adjoining farm acreages were staked out, brochures printed, and droves of British upper- and middle-class citizens were convinced to invest their money in starting a new life — a life befitting a gentleman. Even the B.C. provincial government pitched in to help promote fruit farming throughout its largely unsettled mainland. Despite all the rapidly accruing evidence to the contrary — frost damage, orchards dying inexplicably, unknown blights breaking out where they had not existed initially, and the ever common problem of inadequate irrigation — the provincial government claimed in its *Handbook of British Columbia*: "It is now an established fact that apples of excellent quality will grow as far north as Hazelton on the Skeena River between 55 and 56 degrees north."[8] By 1911 when the handbook was published, such a claim was obvious fraud, for few areas outside the Okanagan were proving viable for fruit farming.

An area that was only somewhat more plausible as a fruit-farming paradise was the Windermere Valley, to which Jack and Daisy Phillips were lured by the promotional efforts of Robert Randolph Bruce. A mining engineer, land promoter, and former CPR land agent who would eventually become a lieutenant-governor of British Columbia, Bruce first saw Windermere in 1897. It was a valley with benches quite similar to those that were just beginning to prove successful fruit farming land in the Okanagan. Bruce, who could claim no agricultural experience or knowledge, declared the Windermere benches were similarly ideal for farming, formed the Columbia Valley Irrigated Fruit Lands, acquired a large tract of land from the CPR, arranged advertising in Britain through the CPR's Land Department, and set out to attract prospective farmers.

The promotional material hit Britain in late 1911, and by the spring and summer of 1912 more settlers came than Bruce had anticipated in his wildest dreams. The brochures pictured gentrified British men and women living in a green, bountiful land, surrounded by beautiful mountain peaks. "Windermere, British Columbia: Orchards, Sports, Homes," read one brochure headline. Bruce, deciding to shuck off all false modesty and honesty, represented himself as being a Windermere old-timer, one of a small group of miners who came to the valley seeking gold and through inadvertent plantings realized that Windermere's real wealth was to be found in agriculture.

"We felt," he wrote,

we were wasting time in the valley, but yet we could not tear ourselves away from it. We tried strawberries and found them luscious and plentiful. We tried hens and turkeys, pigs and sheep, to find a fatter purse and a better table. We gave up buying canned vegetables, and raised our own tomatoes, asparagus, celery, and green peas, and when we were not busy we would go off back into the hills and replenish the larders with deer or bear, blue grouse or partridge, or get a boat and go up the lakes hunting the wild duck and geese amongst the bulrushes at the southern end of Windermere Lake.

When the cold weather began to set in in November, and just after we got the first fall of snow, that was when we went back after deer; and a glorious time we had when we would gather round the camp fire at night after a big day's hunt. Then on the Windermere Lake after the frost came, we had a beautiful sheet of ice for skating and ice-boating. We found that though the temperature would go down to 20 or 30 below zero, the air was dry, and kept the system tingling with life. We were full of energy and bustling over with health, and just had to be doing something. Then we would get a fall of a few inches of snow, and the jingle of sleigh-bells would be heard all through the valley. Perhaps a week or two later the great Chinook wind would begin to blow, warm and soft, and would lick up the snow and leave all bare and open again. In the spring we would all be busy in our gardens and fields, and the open, park-like country would be carpeted with wild flowers.[9]

To this land of bountiful harvests, thronging wildlife awaiting the sportsman's gun, and misplaced Chinooks, Bruce claimed settlers were coming who had hunted tigers in India and enjoyed playing polo on the newly laid-out polo field. Irrigation canals had been built so an irrigated acre of land could be had for prices ranging from ten to thirty pounds per acre. A railway spur line was soon to be completed that would allow farmers here to be the first in B.C. in terms of proximity to the prairie and eastern markets for exporting their fruit. All this could be had for an approximate investment per settler of about one thousand pounds. Jack and Daisy Phillips raised the money and bought into Bruce's dream machine.

"Yes, it is a beautiful valley, with its mountains and its glaciers, its rivers and its lakes, its beautiful sun-lit glades shortly to be perfumed with apple and cherry blossom, and may those new to it find in it as much pleasure in the future as this 'old-timer' has experienced in the past."[10]

Bruce's pamphlets were nothing more than the marketing tip of a preposterous con. The valley was virtually unsettled; no development had been undertaken at all. The irrigation canals, which the pamphlet described as built, were still on the drawing boards. No one, least of all Bruce, had any idea if commercial orcharding was feasible. All the evidence indicated that, given the harsh winter temperatures, cherry or apple trees would have a hard time surviving, let alone bearing marketable fruit. And before even the first seedling could be planted the settlers were going to have to break the land, which meant falling hundreds of densely packed fir trees and removing the stumps. Then they would have to build houses and barns, till the soil, purchase and plant fruit trees, dig irrigation channels and wells, and construct roads to connect their farms to the outside world. Any time for leisure was going to be brief at best.

Yet the Phillipses and countless other middle- and upper-class Britons bought into the dreams being woven by the land promoters' assurances that somehow this rough, wild land could be quickly tamed and transformed into a rural utopia where they could work a bit on the land and enjoy a lot of leisure. The venture was a fantasy with little basis in reality. Few Britons in the late 1800s had any background in agriculture. By 1890 less than 8 percent of the population of Britain made their living through farming.[11] The ever-decreasing number of upper-class families who still owned landed estates hired foremen to run the operation and had become distanced from day-to-day operations. Most of the growing middle class lived in the towns and cities; their incomes dependent on manufacturing, mercantilism, professions, or transportation businesses. Agriculture was seen as a pristine, spiritual, and utopian activity that would allow one to escape from the overcrowding, pollution, class struggle, and generally sordid conditions of the modern British city. It was this idealization of the agricultural lifestyle that the promoters capitalized on so expertly, demonstrating a keen psychological and sociological shrewdness.

Anyone who knew the slightest thing about agriculture would have seen through the lie being foisted by the land promoters. It is for this reason, perhaps, that the Windermeres and Peachlands attracted precious few of the many Irish, Scottish, or Welsh farmers immigrating by the thousands to Canada and the United States. Even had the promoters allowed these lower-class Britons to buy into their developments, it's doubtful many of them would have been as naive as the gullible middle- and upper-class British who were the developers' chief marketing target.

Naiveté was not the only reason the developers focused their promotional strategies on the upper classes of British society: more compelling was the rapidly increasing market demand. Starting in the late 1800s and continuing to World War I, the number of what Canadian immigration officials sometimes termed "higher-classed migrants" exceeded all expectations. This designation was applied to the upper class and professionals. Poor immigration record-keeping practices and the absence of detailed ship manifest records make it impossible to accurately determine how many British upper-class citizens came to Canada in any given year, but records clearly indicate that the numbers were climbing.

In 1880 the number of Britons sailing in the cabin class to non-European destinations totalled 56,734. By 1900 the number jumped to 86,914. From 1900 to 1912 Britons who could afford to emigrate by sailing cabin or first and second class, as opposed to travelling in the steerage, rose to a 1912 high of 266,145. Some of these numbers were undoubtedly tourists or business travellers, but even with fast steamships overseas travel was still relatively rare except for immigration purposes; the majority of these upper-class travellers were leaving Britain to try their luck in a new country.[12]

By the late 1890s almost 27 per cent of adult male immigrants coming into Canada from Britain fit into this "higher-class migrant" group, despite the fact this same group constituted less than 22 per cent of the adult male population in England and Wales. Between 1906 and 1913 Canada's percentage share accelerated from 23 per cent to about 40 per cent; this gain was realized at the cost of the United States and South Africa, both of which experienced equivalent decreases.

Upon arrival in Canada many of these immigrants headed west to pursue the life of an agricultural gentleman. Most gravitated toward regions where an upper-crust British population was already established or where such a community was being promoted for settlement. The result of this movement of like toward like was development of a series of enclaves where British values, traditions, and customs determined community tone and identity. These communities were, especially as western Canadian immigration accelerated in the late 1890s and early 1900s, intermixed with other racial, ethnic, and social-class populations; but their British character was stridently promoted by the residents and the presence of non-British gentlefolk amid their ranks was monitored with wary unease.

In Victoria, British gentlemen relaxing in the posh London-style environs of the Union Club were within a few minutes' walk of the opium dens of western North America's second-largest Chinatown. On the small city's streets blacks, Indians, eastern Europeans, Slavs, Americans, and hundreds of Britons from the lower classes jostled past British gentlemen dressed in the tweeds and knickers that earned them the nickname "Longstockings." The Okanagan Valley was home to a growing number of Italians, Orientals, and Germans, as well as the British settlers who constituted the valley's majority population. On the prairies, Germans, Swedes, and Norwegians were common — even in southern Alberta where members of the British upper classes had established a dominant presence. In the late 1890s and early 1900s, as federal minister of immigration Clifford Sifton's promotion of central-eastern European immigration to the west brought Ukrainians, Poles, and other groups into the prairies, formation of a culturally diversified society was ensured. Although many of the British settlers lamented Sifton's opening of the prairies to settlement by "stalwart peasants in sheep-skin coats" there was little they could do to hold back the tide.

They did, however, strive with extra vigilance to sustain a British way of life and attempt to ensure the maintenance of their values and customs. The upholding of British social traditions, retention of close connections to the Old Country, and the idealization of everything that was British distinguished these communities from areas of western Canada where British settlement was less pervasive. Remittance men were also attracted to these communities and their presence added to the British identity.

When new communities, such as Windermere, were created out of the wilderness, every effort was made to ensure that only people of British background, and of the right social class, were admitted. This intent was carefully underscored in the marketing literature and was well received by the immigrants who invested in the communities. However, this desire to remain isolated resulted in whole communities of people who had little idea of how to break new land, operate a farm, or even in many cases how to cope without the assistance of servants and hired help — help which didn't exist throughout much of the Canadian west.

Of this group Jack and Daisy Phillips were classic examples. Jack knew nothing about farming. Daisy had no experience in housekeeping. "I shall have to wash," Daisy reported with some surprise in her first letter from Windermere, "so will you see if you can find me a handbook, a small one, on the subject, and ask Mrs. Lakewood how to wash handkerchiefs. I have soaked them but they will not come quite clean. Do you soak in cold or hot water, and do you use salt in the water?"[13]

In many of Daisy's subsequent letters the lack of domestic servants in Windermere was lamented. Daisy, daughter of Frederick Oxley, owner and publisher of the *Windsor and Eton Express*, had prior to coming to Windermere lived all her life with servants who attended to virtually every aspect of daily chores. Although resigned to doing without servants initially, it was with increasing dismay that Daisy recognized she would likely never again have servants to do her work for her.

The lack of domestic servants was a complaint many echoed. They were usually surprised to discover this shortage of domestic labour despite the many warnings offered by most of the popular guidebooks to settling in Canada. *The British Colonist in North America: A Guide for Intending Immigrants* counselled in 1890: "Domestic servants are very hard to obtain, and families should learn to do their own work....Families emigrating, who desire the service of domestics, can bring out elderly people of unattractive appearance."[14] Given the shortage of young, single, and attractive women in Canada the guidebook warned that such servants would quickly elope with some young Canadian, leaving the family with no help after paying to bring the domestics to Canada with them.

Upon arriving in Windermere Jack met a Mr. Bowden who said he had farmed a bit in England. Mr. Bowden suggested Jack might be well advised to buy the land next to his so the Phillipses could benefit from his knowledge. Jack, being a little fuddled by all the contradictory reports he was now hearing about the farmability of the land, quickly agreed. Haste to buy land was necessary Jack thought because so many (about sixty) people had arrived already that year. "I regret not having come out a week earlier as some of the best plots have been taken up," he wrote in a letter to Daisy's mother. "It is impossible to give any opinion of the place. One man you meet says it's a terrible place where fruit trees won't grow and where nothing that was advertised in the pamphlets is ready. Another will say the soil is excellent but it will be a good time before profitable farming will take place." With what might have been forced good cheer he added: "The scenery is certainly splendid and all that is written in those pamphlets will be true in about a year's time."[15]

Whatever his hesitation about the development, he was favourably impressed with the quality of the people coming to Windermere. "There will be plenty of people all round who are more or less financially situated as we are, but servants, white or yellow are quite out of the question. There aren't any and we shall have to do all our housework ourselves, but everybody is in the same boat and the only two ladies I have heard of here at present...both undertake it cheerfully. I take it Daisy will too."[16]

As it turned out Mr. Bowden's experience in farming had been quite limited and he was in poor health. Both he and his wife shortly died, among the first casualties of the attempt to civilize the Windermere wilderness. There would be more casualties: some would die, most would simply lose their investments and see their idyllic dreams fade and be replaced by an experience that left them embittered. In a few years a Settlers' Association would be formed to fight against Bruce's Columbia Valley Irrigated Fruit Lands Company which so miserably failed to deliver on any of its promises.

Were all of the promoters charlatans and crooks? Or were many — like Baillie-Grohman — misguided visionaries? Certainly some were of this latter ilk. Holliday recalled a man he knew only as Snodgrass, who laid out the townsite of Okanagan Falls in the southern part of the valley. Okanagan Falls was at the foot of Skaha Lake, then known by the less charming name of Dog Lake. On a townsite map Okanagan Falls was a grand-looking place. It had railroads running through it, park reserves, a hospital site, a space blocked out for a city hall, and several hotels bordering its boulevarded streets. Wharves extended from the shore onto the lake, fronting industrial areas. Surrounding the town were small farms. For one hundred dollars with ten dollars down and the balance payable when such money came available, an acreage could be had by the aspiring British gentleman farmer.

Of Snodgrass, Holliday wrote, "The old chap himself undoubtedly believed that his vision would materialize; he went to live there himself and made strenuous efforts to get things going, but it was one of the many schemes of the day that petered out."[17] Years later Holliday passed through Okanagan Falls and stopped by a little tumble-down store with a gas pump outside. From the store emerged Snodgrass, still the only inhabitant of his townsite. "'If I can get some capital interested,' said he in the course of conversation, with the dreamy far-away look of the visionary in his eyes, 'I'll have a good town here yet.'"[18]

Eventually Okanagan Falls would, along with all the available bottom land in the Okanagan, become developed and prosper. The same was true of Baillie-Grohman's swampland in the East Kootenays. Other communities envisioned by dreamers every bit as inspired as Snodgrass and Baillie-Grohman would, however, not fare as well. Among these would be the remarkably ill-conceived British utopias of Cannington Manor and Walhachin.

CHAPTER SEVEN

CANNINGTON MANOR

In the summer of 1882, Duncan Pierce, the eldest son of Edward Michell Pierce, journeyed into the largely unsettled Moose Mountain area of southeastern Saskatchewan — then part of the district of Assiniboia. The young man was enchanted by what he found — an expanse of gently rolling parkland with rich, unbroken soil. Sprinkled across the prairie were myriad wildflowers. The occasional wild fruit tree was in blossom or already showing the first signs of the fruit that would be ready for fall harvest. On the nearby low hills were thick stands of birch, poplar, ash, and maple. In the distance, several small lakes sparkled in the bright sunlight.

Duncan Pierce hastened back to the nearest civilized outpost of Moosomin, then known simply as Fourth Siding, and telegrammed for his father to join him. The fifty-year-old retired British Army captain and broken-down gentleman hurried out from Toronto. After taking only a quick glance at the country that had so impressed his son, Pierce decided this was the place that would make him once again a wealthy and respected man. Cannington Manor was about to rise from the fertile loam of Saskatchewan prairie.

Pierce, like so many British visionaries in the late 1800s came to Canada down on his luck, but full of hopes, dreams, and an unshakeable belief in his own abilities to create something good and British out of the raw, unformed clay of the western Canadian wilderness.

No one could deny that Pierce's British blood was of good lineage. The arms of the Pierce family had been granted and patented by the Heralds' College of England in 1560. One Pierce had been Keeper of the Wardrobe for Queen Elizabeth I, James I, and Charles I. The name of Lord Admiral Duncan, later Viscount Duncan of Camperdown, appeared on the Pierce genealogical chart. So, too, did that of Captain John Miller, commander of the ship *Theseus* upon which Lord Horatio Nelson led the botched raid against the Spanish at Santa Cruz on July 24, 1797. Nelson, wounded by grapeshot, had a mangled limb amputated on the ship's deck while Miller directed the British withdrawal. A family member whose name was redeemed in the later Protestant England of the 1800s was that of Richard Pierce, one of the few British gentry to support the claim of James Scott, Duke of Monmouth to the throne in 1685 over Catholic upstart James II. Monmouth's rebellion ended disastrously when his peasant army was summarily destroyed in a battle on the plain of Sedgemoor in Somerset by an army loyal to the king. Pierce was hanged, drawn and quartered; Monmouth beheaded.

The Pierce family, however, had prospered in the nearly two hundred years since Robert Pierce's grisly end. Edward Pierce was born into a life of luxury and wealth. His father had extended the family's fortune through marriage to Elizabeth Michell of Devon. The Michell family had many land holdings in London, Hertfordshire, and Somersetshire — among them the Manor of Cannington, near Bridgewater.

For many years Pierce's British home was Taunton Castle in Somerset, a grand estate with turrets, ivy-coated stone walls, vast grounds, and dozens of drafty rooms. Pierce was involved in banking and shipping enterprises. He and his wife Lydia had eight children: four sons and four daughters.

Pierce was a typical bulwark of the British upper class. He was well educated, served as a captain in the yeomanry, and was a pillar of the Anglican Church. Tall, heavy-set, with an imposing bearing, he was reportedly ever-optimistic, charming, and graciously urbane. Optimism was to prove vital for Pierce, for in the late 1870s or early 1880s, a bank failure wiped out much of his fortune. What was left, according to one of his sons, was lost due to a disaster at sea. Pierce had invested in a shipping company which owned three ships sailing from Britain to Africa and various Asian ports. With mercantilism so profitable in those years the company shareholders invested all their capital to buy, equip, and float a modern steamship. During either the second or third voyage the ship was wrecked and all hands lost. The shipping company was bankrupted, along with its shareholders, including Pierce.

Faced with the prospect of a life of impoverishment and social disgrace in Britain, or rebuilding his fortune with a new start in Canada, Pierce bundled up his family and caught a fast steamship to a new land. He had been attracted to Canada by British newspaper advertisements which offered, as an incentive to immigration by British citizens, especially those with an English ethnicity, 160 acres of free land to any male aged over eighteen. After settling his family in temporary quarters in Toronto, he and son Duncan began their search for the right package of land.

The advertisements offering land to British citizens had been placed by the Canadian government in response to Prime Minister John A. Macdonald's deep concern that immigration by non-British citizens threatened the national unity of Canada. If British heritage and predominance in Canada were undermined by a tide of European, Slavic, and, worst of all, Asian immigrants, Macdonald and his cabinet worried, Canada would soon become a melting pot as diluted of ethnic identity as was the United States. Were that to happen, Macdonald fretted, would it not soon follow that Canada would be swallowed up by its much stronger, more populous southern neighbour? If, however, the nation's British heritage could be sustained through continued British immigration, and immigration from other ethnic groups could be constrained, Canada's independence could be assured through the maintenance of close political, economic, social, and cultural ties with Britain.

By taking advantage of the free land offer, Pierce expected that he and his four sons could all lay claim to adjoining quarter-sections, giving them eight hundred acres of property. When he tried to register the claim to the land he and Duncan had selected, however, Pierce was told the plot was closed to settlement. The land agent was unable to satisfactorily explain why the land was unavailable. Situated in the immediate shadow of the Moose Mountains (really a series of hills never exceeding three hundred feet in altitude) the land may have been withdrawn because it was immediately adjacent to the White Bear Indian Reserve. The entire reserve was situated on the mountain itself and eventually development of the surrounding prairie would leave nowhere for the Indians to eke out a living by hunting. In the future the reserve's borders might need adjustment to enable the native people to eventually change their economy from hunting and gathering to agriculture.

96

But Pierce was determined to get the land they had selected: some bureaucratic plan was not going to stand in his way. He travelled to Ottawa and sought an interview with Cabinet Minister David Macpherson, soon to be appointed Minister of the Interior. At first an interview was denied but Pierce refused to leave until his calling card was delivered personally to Macpherson. Within minutes Pierce had his interview. Macpherson, as Pierce was undoubtedly well aware, was a friend of Brigadier-General Edward Michell, after whom Pierce had been named. The meeting went well but Macpherson didn't have the authority to overturn the ruling that had withdrawn the land from settlement. He was, however, impressed enough with Michell's namesake to arrange an appointment for Pierce with the prime minister.

In his interview with Macdonald, Pierce played well upon the prime minister's anglophile leanings by promising that his intention was to bring British citizens of good class to western Canada as part of an English colony. This, he said, would help ensure that western Canada remained linked to a British heritage and was not drawn towards the United States and American ways. The prime minister quickly agreed to bend the rules and make the land available for the posting of a settlement claim for one day only. Pierce immediately registered claims for himself and his sons: the land was theirs. As no one else knew of the one-day opening there was no competition.

Until his death Pierce would swear that Macdonald also promised that when the community was established he would personally intervene on Pierce's behalf to get a branch line of the CPR built to link his English colony to the rest of Canada. Pierce knew that a rail link was vital to the future prosperity of any community he created in the barren prairies, where, especially in winter, traversing a distance of forty-five miles could require three or more days of hard travel by wagon. Without a rail link, access to markets for farm produce and livestock sales would be difficult, perhaps even impossible. With the promise of a rail branch line and the deeds for the land in his pocket, Pierce returned to Toronto a happy, confident man. His happiness was somewhat dampened when a few weeks later Annie, his second daughter, died of typhoid fever in Toronto before the family departed for the prairies. She was twenty-seven.

Soon after the funeral Pierce moved his family to Winnipeg. From there Pierce and his sons set out to build a house and prepare the way for the women. It was November when the Pierce men arrived at their new home. Pierce, unlike many of his British upper-class compatriots, was wise enough to immediately hire a local Canadian settler named

Sam Whitlock to advise them of the measures they should take to brace for winter, and on the best type of house to construct. Whitlock took one look at the darkening sky and got the bemused Englishmen digging a large hole in the ground. By the end of the day the hole was dug out and a rough plank covering built over top. The men spent the night huddled in the shelter of the hole. In the morning they woke to find almost a metre of snow blanketing the plank roof. Temperatures quickly plummeted and the ground froze so that further digging was virtually impossible. It didn't matter; the hole dug the day before was large enough to serve as the future cellar and an interim shelter until a house could be raised over it.

Pierce sensibly realized that building a house in winter would prove a difficult job for inexperienced workmen like himself and his sons. He hired additional settlers to work under Whitlock's direction. The house they constructed was a strange affair — really two log houses, with a passage between, connected by one roof covering both houses and the passage. Before the building was completed Pierce deemed it suitably equipped to house his family and in January sent for his wife and daughters.

After a harrowing trip that took two days to cover the forty-five mile distance from Fourth Siding southwest to the homestead, the women arrived. Lily Pierce was relieved to arrive safely. "The sight of our brothers in overalls, mitts and queer fur caps amused us girls immensely," she later wrote.

> The left half of our house was only chinked and plastered just in time for our arrival. We girls had one bedroom and father and mother the other upstairs. The large sitting room was downstairs. Entrance to the cellar was in the passage, one half of which was used for our stores, the other for the kitchen, which also served as a sleeping place for our boys and any visitors, all lying on the floor in rows like sardines. Sometimes when the visitors were numerous they were so tightly packed that if one turned over the whole row had to do the same.
>
> It was all such a change from our luxurious life in England, but we were young and full of life, had the great joy of being all together, and everything seemed a joke, and so we were very happy.[1]

After weathering the winter the Pierces got down to the serious business of creating an English colony. The first task was to attract other British citizens of good class. Pierce wrote letters to English newspapers describing the country in which his settlement was located and the opportunities to be found there. He weighed these against the troubles facing those trying to sustain a respectable lifestyle in Britain. It is possible on the Canadian prairie, he wrote, "to live like princes on the money required in England just to pay taxes."[2] Waxing ever more nostalgic, he claimed that a gentleman "could lead and enjoy an old English squire's existence of a century ago."[3]

The letters achieved their purpose and by the end of Pierce's first year several families joined him on the prairie. Pierce now had the seeds from which would grow his English community. It was time to found a townsite. Pierce named his community Cannington, after the family home in Somersetshire; later, at the request of postal officials, this was changed to Cannington Manor.

Cannington Manor founder Edward Pierce. Saskatchewan Archives Board R-A49.

Men of vision, of course, take charge of important affairs themselves and so Pierce personally laid out the townsite. Collaring Canadian carpenter Charles Pryce to assist him, Pierce paced out the village streets, Pryce pounding in wooden pegs along the route wherever Pierce directed. By the time the townsite was blocked out with pegs, Pryce had taken to calling Pierce "the city contractor" because throughout the exercise Pierce kept telling him that some day a city would stand on this spot.[4]

The entire townsite was situated on a section of Pierce's land holding, which he quasi-donated with the proviso that he would automatically receive a one-third share in all businesses constructed in the village in exchange for their use of his property. Pierce's land was virtually his only asset, so for start-up capital he took in as partners Ernest Maltby and the brothers Harry and Robert Bird. Together the four formed the Moose Mountain Trading Company to act as a holding company for ownership of all the village's buildings. Only the church, vicarage, and school were to be exempted.

Much of the social, religious, and cultural life of British communities in the late 1800s was focused on activities of the Anglican Church. Pierce was a staunch High Church Anglican, so one of the first buildings erected at Cannington Manor was a church. In keeping with his grand vision, however, it was not the usual crude log shack that served the spiritual needs of most prairie villages. Raised in June 1884, the church was built in the form of a cross. Appointments were furnished by gifts, solicited primarily from relations living in Britain. The cross on the bell tower, porch, front doors, and pews were all hand- carved. Pryce proved his talents as a carpenter went beyond driving pegs into the ground by handcrafting the choir stalls, Bishop's chair, and faldstool out of birch wood brought down from Moose Mountain.

A year later when Bishop Anson of the Diocese of Fort Qu'Appelle came to officiate at the church's opening, he was so struck by its completeness and fine quality that he consecrated it instead of merely opening it as had been planned. This made Cannington Manor's All Saints Anglican Church the first in the Qu'Appelle diocese to be consecrated.

Pierce's village was growing but the same was not true of his economic fortune. He and his sons were having little success as farmers and the work was not Pierce's idea of how men of culture should live. Farm labour, Pierce felt, should be done by hired Canadian help who were better suited to lives of hard physical toil than gentlemen such as himself. The trouble was that although the Canadians were quite willing to dirty their hands this way, they wanted to be paid for their labour. Again the problem of being land-rich but cash-poor dogged Pierce's plans.

There was, however, a solution that would firmly cement the British nature of Cannington Manor and also bring in much-needed cash. Soon advertisements were posted in British newspapers, such as the *Manchester Guardian* and the *Yorkshire Gazette*. They read in part:

> young men with a little capital looking about for something to do, I especially counsel to join their countrymen here. They should, however, before launching into business on their own accord, place themselves with an English gentleman settler abroad for a time, and acquire a thorough and practical knowledge of farming generally, as peculiar to this country, the old world style being of little or no avail in the Great Northwest. This is an English colony, English manners and customs being rigidly adhered to. I shall take pleasure in providing the fullest information and advice, and will secure land and locate young men, if they will correspond with me.[5]

It was, of course, mostly fathers of young men who communicated with Pierce. For one hundred pounds a year, Pierce assured the interested parent, he would take a son off their hands and make a gentleman farmer of him. The sum covered room and board and the cost of farm training. At the end of the year the young man could continue his training if the family forwarded an additional annuity. Alternatively, the young man could set up his own farm near Cannington Manor, where he would be a welcome member of a well-established British community. The advertisements and subsequent responses to inquiries from Britain proved very successful and soon the first of what was to be a steady stream of remittance men arrived at Cannington Manor. Some families sent as many as three sons to Pierce's grandly described Agricultural College. The advertisements also attracted older settlers, who arrived complete with families, maids, servants, and possessions to start a new life in Canada. The population of Cannington Manor was growing, a community was evolving, Pierce could see his dream being fulfilled.

Pierce's advertisements for farm pupils proved successful beyond even his rather inflated expectations. Between 1884 and 1888 about sixty young men were sent to Pierce to learn the Canadian art of farming.

The Canadians who lived at Fourth Siding and on nearby farms had never seen anything like this invasion. Off the train scrambled a host of impeccably dressed young men bound for adventure and excitement at the puzzling entity that was Cannington Manor. They unloaded from the baggage cars trunks stuffed with tennis rackets, cricket bats and stumps, guncases, books, paintboxes, easels, musical instruments, evening dress, and riding habits.

Among the first to come were Charles Steedman, Gerald Napier, and eighteen-year-old William Beckton with his elder brother Ernest. The Beckton boys were typical of most. They came from Manchester, had been well educated, but failed to apply themselves to anything other than having fun and partying among the city's social elite. Their maternal grandfather, Sir John Curtis, was a three-time mayor of Manchester and a wealthy cotton magnate. He was also a man of rigid religious and social standards who was little impressed by the boys' antics. His solution was to pack the Beckton boys up and ship them to Pierce. From Fourth Siding the Becktons and other remittance men travelled by jolting ox-carts driven by hired Canadians over the rugged track to Cannington Manor.

Pierce meanwhile had been busily preparing for the arrival of his first paying pupils. He had an additional room added on to the back of his odd-looking two-in-one house. The room was small but when divided into eight cubicles would rather handily, he surmised, allow him to fulfil his obligation to provide room and board. Many of the new arrivals spent little more than a week or so in these cramped quarters before hiring a Canadian carpenter to build them a "bachelor's shack" near Pierce's farmland.

Steedman and Napier threw their lot in together and had one shack constructed. The Becktons bunked together in another shack.

The Steedman and Napier shack was so elegantly finished that it resembled an English drawing room. Eventually the two had a beautiful English-style garden planted outside. Steedman also proved to have a touch for the culinary arts and soon earned himself the nickname "Cookie" because of the many sumptuous meals he served up to the other remittance men.

Most of the farm pupils, including the Becktons, however, subsisted on salt pork, game, and eggs. Some paid a farmer's wife a dollar to bake up weekly installments of bread and buns from a hundred-pound flour sack. A few followed Steedman's directions and learned to make their own dough by first kneading it in a wooden grocery box, then, after tossing a buffalo coat over it, allowing the dough to rise overnight.

Charles (Cookie) Steedman in the kitchen of his bachelor shack.
Courtesy of Saskatchewan Provincial Historic Park.

Despite Pierce's supposed commitment to provide room and board, those living outside the cramped quarters soon found themselves covering their own food and lodging costs. None of the young men appear to have resented Pierce's failure to deliver on what was promised. Who would they complain to? If they wrote home about the true state of affairs at Cannington Manor, their families might order them home or curtail the remittances that kept flowing in. Life at Cannington Manor was too much fun to take such a risk.

If the young men had been criticized at home for taking their leisure and enjoying life, such was never the case at Cannington Manor. Pierce, in deteriorating health and having no real competency as a farmer, quickly lost interest in trying to educate his pupils — who were soon known among the area's Canadian residents as Pierce's pups. He built a small house on his property and hired a local farmer, Scotty Bryce, to live there and both run the Pierce farm and teach the young Britons. When Pierce and some of the other British gentlemen, who were cashing in on Pierce's idea by acquiring British farm pupils of their own, did try to educate their wards, the effort was greeted with amusement by the pupils. "We laughed and made fun of these men trying to teach us farming when it was evident that they knew so little about it themselves," one pupil later wrote.[6]

Bryce's presence on the farm failed to alter this situation. The Canadian farmer had two tasks running at cross-purposes. To teach the utterly inexperienced workers how to farm would require taking time away from operating the farm itself. Bryce quickly realized if he wanted something done it was simpler to do it himself than entrust any of the pupils with the task. "I was glad when the young gentlemen took to tennis," he confided to his Canadian brethren, "so I could get on with the work."[7]

So the young men collected their remittances, set up cricket matches amid the wild prairie grass, tried to play gentlemanly rounds of tennis on impromptu courts laid out on soft prairie soil, galloped about on horses in pursuit of baffled coyotes, and slaughtered game birds by the hundreds. On Sunday evenings they joined with the more staid elements of the community at the Pierce home for evensong. One reported to his family that evensong at the Pierces' was a favourite event for the gentlemen as it restored a sense of civilization to them. It was a formal affair, and the young men would put the evening clothes they had carried in the trunks from Britain to good use by donning their black coats and white collars and pristinely white shirts. (The practice of boiling the shirts to make them white led to the shirts being called "boiled rags.") With Michell Pierce directing, they would group around his wife and three daughters to sing hymns. "Father had a very beautiful voice and dearly loved all the old hymn and psalm tunes, which we would sing in harmony," wrote daughter Frances of the occasions.[8]

Other cultural and social events became cornerstones of the life at Cannington Manor. Residents formed a glee club, had a small band, and put on plays that ranged from bawdy comedies to Shakespeare.

Cannington Manor's fortunes seemed on the surface to be improving steadily during this period. By 1887 the Moose Mountain Trading Company had erected a general store and post office, as well as a grist mill powered by a wood-burning fifty-horsepower steam engine. The mill, as was true of most other business ventures undertaken by the British residents at Cannington, was built by Canadians. They also trained the Britons to operate the equipment.

Soon the Mitre Hotel was erected. About six of the farm pupils hastily moved into the premise's rooms. During the periods when the

Cannington Manor residents in front of the Mitre Hotel. Left to right: Herbert Beckton, Bob Baker, G. Dicking, Jim Williams, Paul Bray, Ernest Beckton, William Beckton, and Bob Bird. Saskatchewan Archives Board R-A6785.

Assiniboia District wasn't burdened by a prohibition law against alcohol consumption, they provided the hotel's best customers. After the hotel came a blacksmith's shop, a sawmill, a shoemaker's shop, a land agent's office, two cheese factories, and a pork-packing factory.

When prohibition wasn't in effect the liquor flowed copiously at the Mitre Hotel. A glass of whiskey was ten cents and the bar was self-service. After a hard day of play the remittance men sprawled about the lounge and proved they were typical members of the British Victorian era by drinking themselves under the table. On one occasion hotel owner Jim Williams, a former member of the North West Mounted Police, was struggling to restore order among a boisterous group of young drunks. When they ignored his shouted commands he pulled a rifle out from under the bar and shot down the stove-pipe. The Mitre Hotel didn't burn and the smoke drove the patrons out into the blowing snow.

Assiniboia's periods of prohibition barely dented the alcohol consumption rate at Cannington Manor. Manitoba remained "wet," so it wasn't hard to acquire bootleg whiskey. Smugglers rolled in regularly and farm pupils and gentlemen farmers alike were quick to buy up their stock. A haystack conveniently positioned behind the Mitre Hotel was so riddled with stashed bottles of whiskey that pushing a hand into the hay anywhere would usually turn up a bottle. One remittance man always had a whiskey bottle stowed on his buckboard; he kept it inside a tin kettle and for some reason known only to himself used a potato to bung the spout. The Becktons, always having a taste for the stylish gesture, maintained a rough cabin on the shores of Cannington Lake. The site was dubbed "Whiskey Camp" and had been established specifically for drinking parties that were interspersed with waterfowl hunts.

Once a couple of smugglers hit town and sat down with a group of Cannington residents in one of the bachelor shacks. The purpose of the meeting was to sample the product and negotiate a purchase price. Glasses were raised, toasts made, and soon smugglers and townsmen alike were slurring their speech and weaving tales. The smugglers, so willing to provide samples to prospective customers, confided that their cache of liquor was huge and stored near Cannington Manor. A couple of the men subtly pressed the two bootleggers for more details about the location and from the resulting hints guessed where the whiskey was hidden. They slipped away from the meeting and spirited the liquor away. Far too gentlemanly to insist on anyone in Cannington Manor paying for their ill-gotten loot, the two men gave out bottles freely to all who were in need. One former resident was rumoured to go misty-eyed at the memory and intone: "We had enough to float the whole village. And we did."[9]

Between playing and drinking it was hard to find time for serious development of the surrounding lands for the purpose of farming. But some of the men were growing tired of the directionless life they were leading and, more to the point, the crude conditions in which they existed. Among these were the young Becktons. The two reasoned that with sufficient capital they could build an appropriate estate at Cannington. All that stood between them and realization of this idea was, typically enough, money.

They sat down and wrote their grandfather asking for money to start a farm. Sir John replied by sending them a few shares in an old Spanish iron mine. The brothers were stung by this apparent rebuke — it was a little too clever a prank by far for the upright Sir John. But perhaps Sir John knew more than he ever let on, for within months a new ore vein was struck at the mine and it became one of the most profitable iron mines in Europe. The Beckton boys were suddenly rich men. That wealth multiplied even more just a few months later when Sir John died and they were among family members to inherit part of a

200,000-pound estate. Although the bulk, according to the necessity of the primogeniture law, went to Sir John's only son, there was still a good deal of cash for the grandchildren. The Becktons booked passage to Britain in 1887 to spend the winter and claim their share.

In the spring of 1888 the two young men, accompanied by their younger brother Herbert, returned to Canada aboard the *Circassian*. They had a plan for Cannington Manor — a plan every bit as grandiose as that of the community's founder. Cannington Manor would be the home, the Becktons had decided, of the finest horse-breeding ranch in Western Canada; perhaps in time even the best of its kind in all of North America.

It was this vision that made the Becktons the rightful heirs to leadership of the Cannington Manor community. With the kind of dramatic closure seldom seen outside fiction, no sooner had the Becktons returned from Britain with wealth of which Pierce could only have dreamed than the founder of Cannington Manor died. Equally laden with dramatic symbolism, Pierce died at the age of fifty-six on June 20, 1888, exactly six years to the day from when he had left England for Canada. He was buried in the centre of the churchyard next to his beloved All Saints.

Before his untimely demise, June 20 had been designated as a sports day in Cannington Manor. Despite the sombre news the day went ahead as planned, and some said that it was the best day of its kind at Cannington Manor because the crowd seemed so gaily dressed and festive. Perhaps it was the presence of the handsome Becktons that contributed to making the day so fine.

The Becktons were "typical good-looking blonde Englishmen," according to their contemporaries. They were also a family profoundly proud of their Englishness. Wrote one of the Beckton's sisters, "I think we are as pure Norman Saxons as English people can be. I don't think we have either Irish or Scotch blood but we are north country."[10] Their mother's Curtis line traced its English roots back to the thirteenth century. The Beckton side had similar lineage.

Attractive, educated, and wealthy in a land where cash was hard come by, the Becktons were held in awe by even the most well off of their neighbours. They soon established themselves as an economic cornerstone of the community.

It was their intent to import thoroughbreds and greatly improve Canadian horse-breeding practices. To do this, the young men decided, they needed a truly magnificent and modern breeding ranch. The estate was named The Didsbury Stock Farm after their home town near Manchester. It soon became shortened to either Didsbury or simply The Ranch.

No sooner had the Becktons finalized their plan than Ernest married Pierce's youngest daughter, Jessie. He and his brothers commissioned construction of an estate house. Didsbury took the better part of a year to build. The house was constructed of coloured stone dragged out of the dry bed of Antler Creek a mile from the building site. It had twenty-two rooms, a verandah, French windows, a ballroom, and servants' quarters above the back staircase. Later, a wing consisting of a hall with stairs leading up to the quarters for bachelors was added. This six-bedroom section was known as the "ram's pasture." Below the ram's pasture was a large, well-equipped billiard room, where the Beckton brothers liked to lounge in leather chairs by an ever-stoked fireplace and entertain a dozen or more remittance men at a time. While the young men enjoyed billiards, conversation, and drink, the estate's permanent valet, known only as Harrison, scurried about fetching and packing.

The Cannington Manor hunt club in front of Didsbury.
Courtesy of Saskatchewan Provincial Historic Park.

Didsbury's outbuildings were almost as grand as the estate house. They included a stone construction foreman's house, bunkhouse, stone racing stable, brood mares' barn, cow barn, kennels for foxhounds and other pure-bred dogs, hog house, a shed for cockfighting (it was never used as the roosters froze to death the first winter), and a driving shed which housed cutters, buggies, imported surrey, and a special dogcart made by Cannington Manor's English wheelwright.

The horse stable was finer than most of the Canadian settlers' homes, or those of the Becktons' British neighbours for that matter. It measured 120 feet by 24 feet and the inside walls were completely panelled with mahogany siding. Each thoroughbred had a polished brass name plate above its stall. As the horses began to bring home racing honours the trophy room filled with gleaming silver trophies and rows of ribbons. The glass cupboards in the harness room housed polished saddles and harnesses.

Building and maintaining this luxurious operation continuously fuelled the local economy. Local carpenters, masons, plasterers, and other artisans found near-steady employment at Didsbury and wages higher than they could earn elsewhere. Some Canadian farmers left their women and children to take care of the homesteading and went to work fulltime for the Becktons or the contractors providing materials for the estate's never-ending appetites. For some of the hardworking settlers it was the first time they had real cash in their pockets instead of merely exchanging crop yields for supplies.

Jessie Pierce thought the life at Didsbury a fairy tale come true. The Pierces's Canadian experience had been continually marred by an absence of capital. The daughters and Lydia had worked hard to keep the big household functioning. Now, wrote Jessie, "I had nothing to do but to enjoy my liberty from the monotonous chores, my pretty rooms, books, and unrestricted leisure."[11] She became renowned for her management of the Becktons' household. Seldom did Ernest and Jessie dine alone and the food was always plentiful. More than one hundred pounds of meat alone was consumed at the estate on a weekly basis.

Didsbury Game Pie was favourite fare. Jessie's recipe for this dish read: "Line a good large round milk pan with a good crust of venison steak. Fill to the brim with prairie chicken, mallard ducks, teal, snipe. Season to taste, cover with crust and bake from two to three hours."[12]

Almost immediately upon their arrival back at Cannington Manor the Becktons had initiated the building of a race-track, intending it to be the focal point of their thoroughbred breeding operations. The track

The Cannington Manor race track in 1889 during Race Days.
Saskatchewan Archives Board R-B994.

had a judge's box and grandstand. Typical of anything the Becktons undertook, the track was one of the best in western North America. By 1889 it had become the centre for the annual sports days, renamed and expanded to become Race Week.

Horses were brought in from across North America to compete on the track. During the races the Becktons and other thoroughbred horse owners placed extravagant side bets, and rumours started to circulate that the Becktons were more often losers than winners in these betting sprees.

To improve their horse stock, the Becktons toured the United States buying up horses wherever they went. The most famous acquisition was Jase Phillips, a stud with two Kentucky Derby winners in his pedigree. In addition to the races at Cannington Manor, the Becktons took their horses to events throughout the Canadian and American west. Their horse colours, orange and black, were soon well known on the racing circuit. Bettors everywhere must have been hard-pressed to keep from laughing with glee when the Becktons rolled into town. Wherever they went they gambled on the races and lost heavily.

Still the Becktons' horses performed well and won respect throughout the region. Imogene II won the Queen's Plate in Winnipeg and at the 1895 Show Fair in Regina, Beckton horses were in the money during every race.

Despite the betting losses the Becktons' money seemed inexhaustible and there appeared to be always a fortune left over to enjoy the many pleasures life had to offer and to shower gifts upon the neighbours. The Becktons formed the Cannington Manor Hunt Club. Foxhounds of Isle of Wight stock were shipped up from Iowa. Every fall the British residents allowed their crops to languish in the fields for a week while they hunted and played polo. Men and women alike rode to the hounds. Given the profusion of badger and gopher holes covering the prairie the wild dashes across open terrain were dangerous, but few were intimidated. Amazingly, although many horses tripped and fell, there were few serious accidents.

The hunting was followed by a Hunt Dinner and Dance at the town hall, hosted by the Becktons. Formal attire was required and the ever-faithful Harrison was on hand to serve the drinks. In the morning breakfast was accompanied by champagne fetched from the Becktons' well-stocked wine cellar.

Their Canadian neighbours looked with tolerant bewilderment at these people who risked a harvestable crop by allowing it to wait upon their completing a week of hunting and partying. The Canadians and the British lived side by side in the Moosomin area of which Cannington Manor was a part but they mixed little and they were destined to never understand each other.

Neither the Pierces or the Becktons ever encouraged the British community to integrate with the Canadians. They viewed non-British settlers as a source of labour, a source of income if they could sell things to them, and sometimes as a nuisance as necessary and exotic as the nearby White Bear Reserve Indians. The rest of the British community shared their views. One woman described the Canadian settlers as "respectable labouring folk."[13]

For their part, the Canadians largely dismissed the British as ludicrous novelties when they weren't in the position of being able to earn a dollar by working for them. Pierce's pups was their derisive term for the farm pupils. Drawing-room farmers was the label by which they dismissed the British residents who maintained agricultural operations.

By 1890 it was evident that the Cannington Manor community was beginning to show some structural weakness. The pork-packing house was losing money and would soon close. A first cheese plant had failed, and the one that replaced it was merely limping along. The general store never had been profitable because it couldn't compete with the prices of mail-order firms and too many British customers were extended credit they were unable to pay off. As the 1890s progressed, the economic position of the community worsened but it seemed all were too busy having fun to notice what was happening.

Horse racing began to obsess the community. At one Cannington Manor race day a Beckton horse known as Miss Tax was heavily favoured to win because she had never been beaten. Betting by community members was heavy and all on Miss Tax. The Becktons led the betting, supporting, as was their habit, their own horses.

During a neck-and-neck race Miss Tax stumbled and the opposing horse bolted past to win the race. British gentlemen swore and cried foul; British ladies just cried. The Becktons paid up their betting losses as they always did, and if they noticed the deteriorating condition of their bank accounts they never let on. But the money was running out. Because too much attention had been spent on racing and not enough on improving the breeding stock or marketing it, there was also no new source of money to be tapped.

It wasn't just money that was giving out. The enthusiasm and sense of purpose, which may have been nothing more than to be British on the prairies and live a British gentleman's life, was fading before harsh reality. In 1895 William Beckton had gone to England and returned with a bride. But the woman hated the brown prairie and missed the green countryside of her English home. She urged William to take her back to England and in 1896 he acquiesced and departed. He was the first of the major British figures in Cannington Manor to leave, but within a year the other two brothers simply abandoned Didsbury and followed. Jessie Beckton wrote: "For another year the other brothers carried on as before, but a broken atmosphere and divided interests brought about the inevitable break."[14]

Other families soon departed. The Bird brothers sold out their share in the Moose Mountain Trading Company to partner Ernest Maltby. Maltby shortly abandoned the store and moved to nearby Manor. At last, in 1900, the long-awaited rail line came through the area, missing Cannington Manor by about ten miles. The cheese plant closed. James Humphrys, owner of the pork-packing plant, folded shop and then moved away in 1903. With the Becktons gone and the Pierce farm-pupil system in collapse, there were no young men to replace those who left. And many were leaving. As early as 1899 some of the young men were returning to Britain to join units shipping out to do battle in the Boer War. Others joined locally formed units and departed for South Africa.

In 1903 a number of the remaining men joined Pierce's sons, Harvey and Jack, in heading off for the Klondike Gold Rush. Still trying to restore the family fortune, the two sons hoped to strike it rich. Neither Pierce was ever heard from again and at last the remaining members of the family had to accept that, as inexperienced as miners as they had been as farmers, they had probably frozen or died of starvation in the Yukon wilderness. Some families became so disillusioned with the crumbling lifestyle at Cannington Manor that they followed the Becktons back to Britain. Most, however, moved away to other parts of Canada where there might be jobs for educated men in public service or as teachers, or where the starting of a new business might be possible.

Pierce had dreamed that Cannington Manor would eventually become a major city. In truth, the community never thrived and had existed in a precarious relationship with the neighbouring Canadian settlers. After the last British residents left, a farmer tilled the roads up between the houses and sowed wheat. Soon the buildings were stripped of their glass and anything else that could be put to use by other homesteaders. Pierce had hoped his community would survive millenia — it lasted just twenty years. But of all the utopian British communities raised in the Canadian west it was probably the most successful. Others, such as Walhachin in the British Columbia interior, would have a shorter, even more quixotic history.

CHAPTER EIGHT

WALHACHIN

About thirty-five miles west of Kamloops, in the British Columbia interior, two narrow benches of land run along opposite banks of the Thompson River. Tightly pressed between a line of low hills and the river, the benches cover about five thousand acres. In 1907, bunchgrass, cactus, and sage was about all that grew there. Snakes, gophers, plenty of grouse, the occasional hawk, and a few stray coyotes constituted the local wildlife. In fall, before the snow came, cattle brought down from the highland range found only meagre graze. With winter, the stark landscape was further hardened by bitter, freezing winds that blew out of the Cariboo region to the north and howled down the tunnel-like Thompson River Valley. Spring brought mud; summer temperatures routinely cracked one hundred degrees Fahrenheit.

The local Indians called the benches Walhassen, a Shuswap Indian word meaning "land of round rocks." Indians and cattle ranchers alike had little use for the place. The land was mostly owned by a rancher named Charles Pennie who thought it bloody awful rangeland. But in 1907 these wind-blown, sunbaked benches became the unlikely setting for the last of Canada's British utopian communities.

Starting in the late 1800s, and reaching a feverish pitch by the early 1900s, British Columbia underwent what was for the province an unparalleled land boom. Property prices, especially in interior regions such as the Okanagan Valley, skyrocketed. To provide the vital link of an unbroken railroad running from sea to sea, the CPR trans-Canada line had followed the Thompson River valley into the Fraser Canyon and then on to the coast. A few years later the Canadian National Railroad also laid its main Canadian track through the Thompson River valley. In theory, farms and communities situated near the railroad were bound to prosper; with two railroads to choose from, the future was considered immensely promising for the Thompson region.

Just a short distance from the Thompson River, the Okanagan Valley was proving good country for fruit farming. By 1907 land that fifteen or twenty years earlier had sold for a dollar an acre fetched a thousand dollars or more. Looking at the broad, blue Thompson River, and seeing the open benches bordering its shores, developers began to imagine this land blanketed by fruit trees rather than bunchgrass and sage. In the Okanagan, bench land above the valley's lakes was the most productive and suitable land for fruit farming. So why couldn't the benches of the Thompson Valley be similarly transformed?

Among those having such thoughts was Charles E. Barnes, an American land surveyor conducting surveys of the Thompson Valley from a base in the nearby community of Ashcroft. Wherever Barnes went he was well-liked because of his amiable, intelligent, and always optimistic character. Barnes believed nothing was ever too difficult. He believed unfalteringly that where there was a will to achieve something, a way would automatically follow. Barnes also didn't plan to spend the rest of his life as a surveyor at other people's beck and call — he was a man looking for an entrepreneurial opportunity.

Eventually his surveying activities brought him to Charles Pennie's ranch; there Barnes saw something that left an indelible impression on his mind. Pennie had a small apple orchard that was barely two acres in size. The trees, and fruit harvested from them, were in excellent condition. Barnes looked at the bench land surrounding this orchard and saw in his mind's eye a land sprouting with fruit trees — enough trees to provide a livelihood for a community.

Barnes was so struck with his own imaginings he apparently didn't look carefully at the small plot or question Pennie closely about the site. Pennie's orchard, as was often the case on local ranches, had been planted purely to provide fruit for his family. The orchard, however, had been sited with great care. This was the most arable chunk of land on Pennie's ranch. Drawing water from a nearby creek, he had constructed an irrigation ditch to provide the trees with a controlled water supply. The trees were also planted in a slight depression, which protected them from the worst of the winter winds. As Barnes was already enthusing about the potential of the benches and was obviously interested in buying them from Pennie, the rancher understandably didn't volunteer any opinion on their suitability for fruit farming.

The first thing Barnes needed to establish a thriving orchard-based community was financial backing. He could have gone back to the United States and sought money from development companies there, but such firms were well acquainted with the difficulties inherent in land development in western North America and would likely balk at a proposal that was as long on vision as it was short on hard horticultural data. Barnes decided the best source for money would be found in Britain, especially from companies already active in the booming British Columbia land market.

There was possibly another reason Barnes opted to seek British capital over American or Canadian financing. Barnes admired the British, especially upper-class Britons. In later years the residents of the community he created would remark favourably on how Barnes, despite being an American, was in his manners and habits every bit as much a gentleman as they were. He even dressed like them, striding around the settlement in tweed knickers and cap.

Barnes approached the British Columbia Development Association (BCDA) and pitched his plan to the local agents at their Victoria office. The BCDA was already heavily engaged in developing the province. Its projects included: the two-thousand-acre 111-Mile House Ranch and Hotel on the Cariboo Road and the Nicola Land Company Limited. The company also held shares in the Alaska and North West Trading Company and the North Pacific Wharves and Trading Company.

Its memorandum of association described the BCDA as being precisely the type of company that was capable of attracting the kind of "top drawer" colonist Barnes envisioned harvesting the fruits of the community he wanted to build. Barnes wanted higher-class Britons to share in his vision, and he imagined himself easily blending in with them. Within the memorandum of association was the proviso that BCDA would "promote, organize and conduct the colonization of British Columbia by the introduction of suitable emigrants from Great Britain."[1] Further, BCDA was dedicated to establishing villages that would carry on agricultural enterprises.

Barnes was duly impressed when he saw a list of the BCDA's shareholders. Seventy per cent of them stated their occupations as being either gentlemen or knights. A further 28 per cent listed themselves as barristers, solicitors, or holding military rank. Among these shareholders was Sir William Bass, the brewery baronet, who, after receiving a proposal from Barnes, came to inspect his development site in 1907.

On his way to Walhassen, Bass dropped by Lord Aberdeen's Coldstream estate in the Okanagan and enlisted the services of a local agriculturalist and an engineer — who were respectively referred to in company documents simply as Palmer and Ashcroft.

After the four men conducted a brief tour of the bench lands the two supposed experts declared that Barnes's plan was sound and a fruit-farming community here would prosper. Bass accordingly recommended to the London-based BCDA board of directors that they raise the necessary capital to purchase the land from Charles Pennie and proceed with development of a settlement.

On January 21, 1908, C.H. Wilkinson, BCDA managing director, and E.E. Billinghurst, BCDA's provincial manager, based in their Victoria office, bought Pennie's ranch. They also purchased the adjacent J.B. Greaves ranch. *The Ashcroft Journal* reported the full purchase price as being about two hundred dollars per acre for a total price of $229,400. Included in the purchase price were all outbuildings, livestock, and the ranchers' additional land leases.

The train station at the Pennie ranch had been designated simply as Pennie's, but the BCDA immediately took up the Indian word

Unlikely setting for a British-agrarian utopia. Walhachin in 1910. BCARS 68566 D-529.

Walhassen and had the train station redesignated as such. In 1909 they altered the spelling to Walhachin.

BCDA appointed Sir Talbot Chetwynd to oversee the Walhachin project. At the time, Chetwynd was BCDA's cattle manager at 111-Mile House Ranch. He was descended from the "ennobled house of Chetwynd," which suitably impressed Barnes but did nothing to qualify him as a manager of either cattle or land development projects.[2] Chetwynd had attended the Wellington public school. He fared poorly in his schooling and failed the Sandhurst Military College entrance examination even though Wellington was specifically established to ensure graduating students could pursue military careers. Unimpressed by his academic failure, Chetwynd's family dispatched him to Australia as a farm pupil. He reportedly had not done well in Australia and it was rumoured to have been family influence that at last secured him a position with the BCDA.

With Chetwynd at the helm, the BCDA created two companies to specifically operate Walhachin. British Columbia Horticultural Estates Limited, with Barnes as manager, would conduct agricultural development. The suitably named Dry Belt Settlement Utilities Limited would proceed with townsite development. Barnes worked quickly to add more land to the project by purchasing the additional 3,265 hectares that encompassed the bench on the north side of the river. He paid a dollar per acre to the Dominion government and warranted that the company would provide water for irrigation to ensure the agricultural development of the northern bench.

From the outset Walhachin had one advantage other utopian British communities, such as Cannington Manor, had lacked — hard cash accompanied grand vision. There was also a plan and a commitment on the part of the BCDA to actually come through on its promises to prospective residents. In this way it differed greatly from the Windermere development in which Jack and Daisy Phillips were about the same time investing their capital and hopes. The BCDA management, drawing upon the experiences of farming operations in the Okanagan, realized there would be anywhere from a three- to five-year growth period in which the settlers' newly planted fruit trees would yield little financial return. BCDA factored this delay into its development plan and the company's own expectations of profit. After duly considering the realities of developing such a piece of totally raw land, the BCDA put together an extensive marketing and development plan; it was now time to start attracting settlers.

First plantings of fruit trees. BCARS 64048 D-3183.

The Walhachin promotion was similar in tone, design, and misleading rhetoric to that of the Columbia Valley Irrigated Fruit Lands Company at Windermere. Among the members of BCDA's advertising design team was journalist John Fitzgerald Studert Redmayne, who in 1909 would author *Fruit Farming on the "Dry Belt" of British Columbia.* This book became an often-quoted source of information on the pros and cons of fruit farming in areas such as the Okanagan Valley. Redmayne was a man of many hats: journalist, advertising writer, promoter, Fleet Street connections man, and a member of the staff of the British Columbia Information Bureau and Agency. It was while in this capacity that he authored his dry-belt farming guide.

By 1910 BCDA had raised the capital and started sufficient initial development at Walhachin to begin promoting the venture. It did so from its offices in Waterloo Place, which were conveniently situated next to British Columbia House from where Redmayne wielded his pen and creativity to bolster interest in B.C. interior fruit farming.

It took thirty pages for Redmayne and his associates to satisfactorily extol the many virtues of Walhachin. No longer did Walhachin mean "land of round rocks"; no, the word was now "an Indian word signifying an abundance of food products of the earth."[3] And from the fertile, well-irrigated soil of Walhachin would grow the finest apples, the ripest peaches, the juiciest cherries. Between the trees, potatoes, onions, and vegetables of all sorts would be planted and yield bountiful harvests. Settlers arriving at Walhachin would find houses awaiting them. These would not be the crude shacks that new settlers such as the Phillipses in Windermere were forced to erect in a race against oncoming winter storms. Walhachin's settlers would move into ready-made homes as pleasant and well appointed as any to be found in Britain. Stores, a hotel, rail stations, and a community of like-minded and positioned peers would provide a complete sense of place to the settlers.

The costs were reasonable and fair. In the Okanagan an acre of land was running one thousand dollars. At Walhachin five-acre and ten-acre blocks were offered for sale. A ten-acre block, already planted with fruit-tree seedlings, started at thirty-five hundred dollars. Unplanted ten-acre plots went for as low as three thousand dollars. A painted four-room house, with hot-and cold-water bath, could be had for eleven hundred dollars. If additional bedrooms were required they cost a mere $125 per room.

To sweeten the deal, BCDA offered payment terms. This was an important consideration because, although the target market was the upper classes, many of the settlers would be young men living on a remittance from home. There was seldom enough cash available for them to buy land and a house without some form of financing. BCDA invited purchasers to divide the total price into four yearly installments with an annual interest fee of 6 per cent to be applied against the outstanding balance. The BCDA also offered to manage any acreage for an additional fee. This allowed absentee owners to get their land started on the path to tree maturity before they were able to conclude affairs in Britain and move to Walhachin.

The BCDA even arranged transportation for the settlers. Steamship fare from Liverpool to Montreal was quoted at ninety dollars for first class, forty dollars for second class, and twenty-five dollars for third class. Rail fare from Montreal to Walhachin was eighty dollars for first class, thirty-five dollars for colonist class. The BCDA was also successful in getting Canadian customs to waive duties or tariffs against the settlers' personal effects. This allowed them to bring their china, silver, linens, Chippendale furniture, pianos, and artworks without having to pay the usual import duties.

As was common with fruit-farming promotions in Britain, the Walhachin campaign was a roaring success. Applications flooded in, were vetted for the appropriateness of the settler, and were approved with haste. Among those buying in were scions of such British luminaries as Prime Minister Lord Asquith, Lord Nelson, King George V, and Cecil Rhodes. The latter sent his nephew packing to Walhachin after the young man allegedly, and unintentionally, precipitated a revolution in Costa Rica.

Among the early arrivals in Walhachin was an Englishman with a less noble background named B. C. Footner. Happily for Barnes, Footner was an accomplished builder. Barnes immediately drafted Footner to start building houses for the other arriving settlers. Typically, no work on the promised houses had been undertaken until the matter was of extreme urgency — such urgency taking the form of settlers literally stepping off the trains with the expectation that a house awaited them. Footner, who spent the next few years doing more carpentry than farming, watched the arriving Walhachin residents with a jaundiced eye. In later years he described Walhachin as "a catch-all for rejects."[4] This seems a little harsh; mostly the settlers were simply naive, utterly unprepared, upper-class flotsam hoping to find in Walhachin a life of comfort and elegance.

Although the bulk of the settlers were dependent on money from family or personal investments in Britain they were a different breed of remittance men from those living in shacks throughout the nearby Okanagan Valley or raising hell as cowboys around Calgary. The residents of Walhachin lacked any trait of rebelliousness. They gloried in their class traditions, manners, and expectations. Walhachin's residents, even the formerly rambunctious Rhodes nephew, went out of their way to behave as British gentlemen. They rigorously adhered to the maintenance of class systems within the community, insisted upon dress appropriate to each social occasion, and held themselves aloof from the surrounding communities. Within weeks of the first settlers' arrival their neighbours throughout the Thompson Valley took to calling Walhachin "Little England."

Only one-sixth of those who eventually came to Walhachin were dependent on their farms for a livelihood. The main group of settlers seldom worked their farms at all, relying instead on hired help to do the bulk of the labour. This is evidenced by Walhachin's population figures. In 1914 the population peaked at 150 settlers. Also listed as citizens of Walhachin were 110 workmen and 40 Chinese domestics. There was a precise one-to-one ratio of hired labour to residents. Of the 150 British settlers, about 40 were women. Most of the males were aged from twenty to forty.

The primary attitude of the residents toward work was well reflected in the following comment on western Canadians. "The western scheme of life, a know nothing worship of hard work and dollars...is not the life's ideal of the majority of the enlightened and cultivated people of the earth's surface today, nor will it ever be."[5]

But a willingness to work hard and invest money in the working of the land was an absolute necessity at Walhachin. An area so ill-suited for agriculture needed unceasing labour to make even some of the soil capable of supporting the growth of fruit trees and vegetables. Everything worked against the possibility of the land being agriculturally viable.

Walhachin's annual rainfall averaged a scant 7.55 inches. Summer temperatures routinely exceeded one hundred degrees Fahrenheit. In winter, when wind chill was factored in, temperatures could drop to between twenty-five and thirty-five degrees below zero. Winter winds blew almost unrelentingly up the valley.

Between the two benches was an inexhaustible source of water that the settlers could only watch flow uselessly past their water-starved land. The hydraulic lift technology necessary to pump river water the eleven hundred feet up to the benches did not yet exist. Even before the first settlers arrived, Barnes was deeply concerned about how Walhachin would overcome the absence of a sufficient and dependable water source.

On the south shore were three creeks — Brassey, Jimmie, and Upper Ranch — and a small lake. They provided enough water most of the year to irrigate lands immediately adjacent to the creeks and to pipe water into the townsite. But the primary land designated for agriculture was on the northern shore, the lands acquired from the Canadian government. Here there was no readily available water. Barnes searched the northern shore country for a water source and finally discovered Deadman's Creek, which was fed by underground springs. The water flowed strongly and would, Barnes surmised, more than meet Walhachin's needs. Standing between the creek and Walhachin farmland was twenty-two miles of rugged terrain cut with gullies and rock bluffs.

The only way to move the water from Deadman's Creek to Walhachin was via a flume or trough. After little deliberation the settlers and BCDA management jointly commissioned construction of a combined trough-flume system that would be six feet wide by thirty inches deep. The system had to move water by gravity flow, so an intricate network of trestles was required to maintain a constantly descending angle. Once the water arrived at the Walhachin farmland it could be diverted into ditches dug between the rows of trees to provide trickle-irrigation.

Until the flume could be constructed, however, those trees already planted on the northern shore were in danger of dying and there was little sense in further plantings. Clearly the flume had to be built quickly, and just as evidently, given the lack of finances available, it had to be built cheaply. The project was completed in a surprising six months at a total cost of under one hundred thousand dollars. Speed and economy had been achieved. On April 29, 1910, the flume was opened. At first water bubbled down the flume, rising quickly to full capacity, and everyone looked on with optimism. No sooner had maximum flow been reached, however, than it

Although the vital flume-system at Walhachin looked impressive upon its completion, it proved incapable of supplying the community's irrigation needs. BCARS 64055 D-3190.

was noted that the flume was shaking on its foundations, and joints were popping and rupturing. The water entering the flume was hastily turned off. After much trial and error it was finally determined that the greatest depth the flume could support was a meagre six inches.

There is a right way and a wrong way to build just about anything and the Walhachin flume had been constructed by methods that were about as ill-considered as is possible. No engineering study or plan was completed beforehand. The 1.35 million board feet of lumber used was all reject material from a local sawmill. The boards varied from a thickness of one inch to 1 3/4 inches. This wasn't thick enough to prevent the wood warping under the twin assault of moisture on one side and intense drying by sun on the other. It was also too thin to block seepage and the seams couldn't be effectively caulked.

The boards were also a hodgepodge of lengths. A properly built flume is constructed in sections from boards of an equal length. If one section collapses or needs repair, the uniformity of length allows a crew to dismantle only a short section and replace it without disturbing the rest of the flume. At Walhachin the boards were just nailed together as they were handed to the workman, consequently the flume was one continuous section.

Then there was the problem with the trestles upon which the flume was supported. Determining the load-bearing capacity of lumber is a precise science and building a trestle bridge is an involved and complex

The Walhachin Hotel just after construction in 1910. BCARS 64057 D-3192.

undertaking. At Walhachin the trestles were built with no regard for the load-bearing tolerances of the wood used. Primitive footings were cemented in place here and there for the timbers to rest upon; in other places the trestle was footed on an available stone or just dug into the thin dirt. The finished trestle support system barely held up the weight of the trough itself; when a full load of water was added it began to wobble and self-destruct.

After settling for a weight load of only six inches water depth, the settlers failed to ensure that even this precious water all reached the fruit trees. A wooden trough should be lined with a gravel bed or a thin coat of cement to keep the water moving and prevent seepage. The sections of canal dug into the earth that linked trough sections together should certainly have been gravel or cement-lined. But only small parts of either the troughs or the flumes were so prepared. The rest was left unlined and all along its journey from the creek to the orchards, the water seeped away with disheartening haste. Leakages in the flume sections poured down onto the already spindly footings and undermined them. As a result, sections of flume were continuously collapsing and, because of the interlocking construction, when one footing gave away it could take down hundreds of feet at a time. When the system was operating, up to 40 per cent of the water flow was lost to seepage before it reached the orchards.

A year later this already inadequate system was further taxed when it was decided to divert some of the water across the Thompson River to the southern bench. The creeks on that side had proven incapable of supplying enough water for the three hundred acres of orchard on the southern shore and the townsite. In April 1911 a steel pipe was laid across the river, but it was soon swept away by debris during spring run-off. A new six-inch pipe was then slung from a suspension bridge. This time the pipe held and was used for the next four years until it was replaced with a twelve-inch pipe.

Despite Walhachin's critical water shortages, Barnes saw to it that the townsite remained adequately serviced year-round with hot and cold running water. The Walhachin Hotel offered patrons fully appointed bathrooms and most of the homes were similarly equipped. Walhachin's residents showed not the slightest inclination to forego any physical discomfort to ensure that their crops were adequately irrigated. In fact they didn't let the demands of an agricultural life infringe much upon any aspect of their standard of living.

The British settlers enjoyed a good life, not all that different from that which they might have had back in the Old Country. In urbanized

Britain they would have had a greater variety of diversions to enjoy, but they made the best of the limited resources available.

At the centre of Walhachin's community life stood the hotel. Completed in the spring of 1910, the hotel featured a large dining room overlooking the orchards. From a wide, open balcony that fronted the building's second storey, the view of orchards and the Thompson River was excellent. The hotel boasted separate billiards and card rooms, and ladies' and gentlemen's parlour rooms in its east wing. There were also two separate beverage rooms — a formal one where suitably attired gentlemen and ladies could gather and another where workmen could get a drink. Surrounding the hotel was an English-style garden. Several horse-drawn Democrat wagons were kept on hand to take residents and their guests on tours of the orchards.

In the middle of the desert, the tone set by the hotel struck everyone but Barnes and his British settlers as being singularly bizarre. Evening dress rules were in effect at the dining room — attire was as formal as it would have been at a downtown club in London. For the regular balls, men wore dinner jackets, top hats, and white gloves, and carried canes. The women donned fashionable evening dresses. One woman, who travelled from a nearby community called Ashcroft Manor to attend such an evening ball, was dismayed to find that she had neglected to pack any long white evening gloves in her overnight bag. She agonized over whether she should remain hidden in her hotel room rather than create a social gaffe by going bare-handed and bare-armed. Then she realized that the strict rules of etiquette by which the residents guided their lives would prohibit them from openly snubbing her by either word, gesture, or behaviour. Having reached her decision the woman stiffened her lip and brazened out the evening.

The Canadian settlers living in Ashcroft, Savona, Kamloops, and on the neighbouring ranches found Walhachin steeped in its own exclusivity. When they passed through the community they were confined to the workmens' bar and were never invited to formal functions. Even nearby British settlers, such as those who lived at Ashcroft Manor, were similarly snubbed because it was construed they had "gone colonial." Invitations for this group were rare.

While Walhachin's British settlers looked askance at their Canadian neighbours, Canadians were often scandalized by the behaviour of the residents. Women were accepted at all times of the day into the formal beverage room and need not be accompanied by a man. At the weekly card parties, where the high stakes astounded the Canadians, women anted up right alongside the men. Since the early 1800s women in

Walhachin resident proudly displays eight potatoes weighing 12 pounds. Growing vegetables between the fruit trees, however, depleted the soil of vital nutrients and promoted the spread of blights. BCARS 74379 D-8200.

Britain had been able to go into many exclusive clubs and were able to gamble, so the residents of Walhachin saw nothing unusual about such behaviour. British women also smoked, something few Canadian women did.

All this shockingly wanton behaviour was only a small part of what differentiated them from the surrounding communities. More important, they did little to integrate their economy with that of the region. The residents of Cannington Manor had also held themselves aloof, but at the same time they had drawn upon the labour and knowledge of their neighbours to survive. This fostered an atmosphere of mutual tolerance. At Walhachin the labour force of Chinese domestics and casual labourers was largely brought in from elsewhere at the time the BCDA began development. The Walhachin orchardists never bothered to seek advice on how to proceed with their fruit-farming operations. Lacking any practical farming experience they either relied on the knowledge of hired labourers or, in the rarer circumstances where they worked their own fields, blundered along independently using a precarious system of trial and error.

Had they consulted with the locals they might have realized the mistake inherent in planting vegetables between the rows of fruit trees. Although the vegetable plantings did yield good harvests and allowed the settlement to realize some immediate income, they also depleted soil nutrients that the fruit trees badly needed. When the residents decided to allow potato plants to rot into the soil as further fertilization rather than dig them up at the end of season, it promoted the spread of blights and fungus and attracted gophers and moles to the orchards. Given the problems, the income realized from the vegetable plantings made the effort hardly worthwhile.

Walhachin's total property included about five thousand acres. By 1913 only about 20 per cent had been cultivated. Virtually no further agricultural expansion within the settlement was possible as the residents could find little land that showed the slightest promise of being agriculturally viable. The simplest tests revealed soil that could support no plantings, or soil that was so thin against the bedrock that nothing of worth would grow there. It was obvious that it was impossible for the community to support its lifestyle on the basis of an agrarian economy.

Nevertheless, until the calamity of World War I, Walhachin had the appearance of a prosperous and thriving community. Between early 1910 and the summer of 1912 numerous business ventures were opened by residents and newcomers. A livery stable, a laundry, a butcher shop, a general store, haberdasheries for both women and men, two restaurants, an insurance and real estate office, a drapery and millinery shop, and other businesses all boasted a thriving trade. But it was a trade that drew principally from the residents themselves who were, of course, mostly financed by family and business income from Britain.

The first sign that the community was in trouble came on June 12, 1912. Without warning, BCDA announced that it was withdrawing financial support from the Walhachin development project. It advised shareholders to sell their shares and attempt to recover what they could from original investments. A ripple of anguished dismay passed through the community but was almost immediately alleviated by the arrival of an apparently benign saviour.

The somewhat unlikely hero was Charles Henry Alexander Paget, recently risen to the title of the Sixth Marquis of Anglesey. The twenty-eight-year-old peer arrived in Walhachin in the summer of 1912 and immediately commissioned construction of an estate he named Anglesey. Built about three miles west of the townsite and situated on the north side of the river, Anglesey featured a large British-style home that included among its many lavish features a cement-lined swimming pool and a music room in which he installed the grand concert piano that the classical pianist Pederewski had left in Vancouver upon completion of a North American tour.

As he had no sooner arrived at Walhachin than the BCDA pulled out, the marquis summarily bought out the company's shares. Much of Walhachin was now owned lock, stock, and barrel by one man. Fancying himself to be of an egalitarian bent, the marquis decreed that henceforth the hotel would no longer have one bar for commoners and one for people of class. Among the resident British this didn't go down well, but there was also very little they could do about it — the marquis owned the hotel and was also Walhachin's ranking nobleman.

The community had more than its share of nobility — there were several knights, counts, and earls. But in noble ranking a marquis is above all these, being subordinate only to dukes, princes, kings, or queens. The class-conscious residents could hardly lead a revolt of gentry against the decrees of a marquis who also rightfully owned the community's favourite drinking establishment.

Besides, it was soon evident that the marquis was not about to force everyone to mix with unwashed commoners at all occasions. His lovely swimming pool and the surrounding patios were instantly a favourite place for summer parties and were thankfully barred to anyone lacking a titled lineage.

The marquis's scrapping of social class conventions on one side and insistence on their maintenance on another was symptomatic of his own contradictory nature. He was described as being friendly and even shy by some; yet others found him to be overbearing and insistent upon things being done according to his ideas. By day, dressed in workboots and overalls, he took to the fields and toiled alongside his hired labourers. Yet he maintained rigid class barriers regarding who was welcome in the estate's formal rooms.

The marquis was also a man in debt. Before his death, his cousin, the Fifth Marquis of Anglesey, was rumoured to have racked up crippling debts against the family business operations in Britain. The newly minted marquis was now responsible for these debts. Although never displayed publicly, perhaps it was an inner sense of desperation that drove him to make several major investment forays into the then unproven oil fields of Alberta. By 1915 these investments would bring the young man to the brink of financial ruin.

In the meantime, however, the marquis bestowed upon Walhachin his social leadership, his modestly proclaimed knowledge of agriculture, and his inspired sense of engineering principles. Early in 1914 the marquis acquired a lot on the south shore of the Thompson River, which he decided was ideal for fruit farming if only it could be irrigated. But the six-inch pipe bringing water across the river from the north shore couldn't supply any more land. The marquis, with what most British considered suitable pluck, didn't believe in the words "cannot be done." The solution was obvious — all that was needed was a bigger pipe across the river. He invested $7,250 to purchase a twelve-inch wooden pipe to replace the steel one. But neither the marquis or the other British residents considered whether the steel suspension cable could support the extra weight of a water-burdened wooden pipe.

No sooner was the pipe filled with water than the suspension cable sagged so badly the new pipe almost dropped into the river. For the many weeks in spring that the river was swollen by spring run-off, the pipe had to be emptied in order to keep it from being swept away by the current. Even when the pipe could carry water, the gravity feed angle was so poor due to the sagging of the cable that less water was borne across the river than had been carried by its steel predecessor.

Throughout all these troubles the play went on unabated. By day the residents played tennis on specially prepared grounds, golf on a small course they had constructed, and cricket at the local pitch; rode to the hounds after harried coyotes that were rounded up to fill in for the absent foxes; shot grouse by the dozens until hardly anything took to the wing on the benches; and whiled away the hours with formal tea parties on the hotel's decks. At night they attended classical performances by their community music group, put on plays, danced at weekly formal balls, played cards, drank robustly, dined on exquisite and extremely lengthy meals, and shunned business discussions. During town meetings the debates revolved around building or not building a church (they didn't), allowing women suffrage (75 per cent of those attending this December 1910 debate voted against the idea), and taking up a collection to appropriately attire a local polo team (this too foundered).

When the neighbouring communities sponsored meetings to discuss collective agricultural issues, there was seldom anyone from Walhachin in attendance. Only two of the residents ever accompanied other area agriculturalists on trips during the winter non-growing season to Pullman, Washington, where a small American university offered horticultural courses that could have vitally contributed to the ability of the orchardists to improve their farming operations.

Instead, many from Walhachin headed for Europe — especially home to Britain. The Chetwynds and the Barnes families embarked annually on tours of France and Italy. Those who stayed behind whiled away the days and dark nights in their homes, at the hotel, or in trying to assemble hockey and curling teams that could compete with the same success against their neighbours as did their cricket, polo, tennis, and other British-tradition sports teams. "Walhachin," declared the first and only edition of the Walhachin Times, "for its size and population is one of the most sporting villages in this country or any other."[6] As was typical of the public-school traditions of the time, participation in sports constituted a peculiar mania for the residents of Walhachin.

But another sport was now looming that appealed every bit as much to the character of the residents of Walhachin. By early 1914 it was evident that Europe teetered on the brink of war. Walhachin's British were loyal to the core to the needs of Mother England. Since the summer of 1911, the Walhachin company of the 31st British Columbia Horse had been drilling three times a week in the fields surrounding the town. Every summer more than twenty of the young men abandoned any pretense of farming to attend the annual summer training camp of "C" Company in Vernon. When war broke out in August of 1914, the men of Walhachin lined up to embark for service. Within a month forty-three of the young orchardists left for active service; by 1916 when the call for Canadian volunteers would reach a peak — no one believing at this stage that a quick, decisive victory was any longer possible — no English orchardists of military age would remain and there were only a handful of older men.

The women left too. Everyone was in such a rush to get back to Britain that most of the women departed with only what could be fitted into a suitcase or trunk. Furniture, china, valuable pictures, personal mementos were all abandoned. The puzzle that has never been explained was whether they were escaping a dying community or whether they believed the war would only last weeks and that they would soon return.

By 1918, when the guns fell silent in Europe, only fifty British residents remained in Walhachin. They presided over a community in collapse. The marquis's debts had caught up to him and he was desperately trying to get the British Columbia government to accept his holdings at Walhachin as a donation, which might assure the community's continuance. With few men to maintain either the orchards or the irrigation system, everything was in disrepair. In April 1918 a severe two-day rainstorm struck. Gale-force winds ripped trees out by their roots and stripped the branches from hundreds of others. The rains washed out the foundations of many of the trestles supporting the irrigation flume and a one-mile section collapsed. The storm damage was the final blow. The few returning veterans could find neither the capital or the determination required to reconstruct the irrigation system.

The marquis's last-ditch effort to get the provincial government to take the land and use the Walhachin settlement as the basis for a new agricultural community for returning soldiers met with icy rejection by B.C. premier John Oliver, who was known to have little use for uppercrust Englishmen. Before turning the marquis down, Oliver commissioned a survey to determine what it would cost to put the irrigation system back on its feet: $240,000. Neither the financially strapped marquis or the remaining residents could possibly raise that kind of money in the postwar economy.

Almost as quickly as most of the families had decamped with the outbreak of war in 1914, the remaining families and men of Walhachin started to pack up and leave their land, their investments, and their dreams. Canadian labourers and CPR rail personnel were able to grandly appoint their own homes with the abandoned belongings of the departed residents. By 1921 faltering efforts to keep the irrigation system minimally functioning were discontinued. In 1922 the last of the British settlers moved away.

It would be two decades before the marquis was finally free of the place. In 1940, Canadian rancher Harry Ferguson leased the property for grazing land. Seven years later he bought all the bench land, except for the actual townsite and three other lots on which families in Britain had continued to pay taxes. Ferguson used the land for the same purpose that the rancher Charles Pennie had — winter grazing of cattle. He paid the marquis $40,000, almost $190,000 less than what the BCDA had paid two Canadian ranchers for half the land only forty years earlier.

In 1953 a B.C. Department of Agriculture study of the Walhachin benches determined that none of the land was suitable for fruit farming; only 160 acres could support vegetable production. A subsequent study concluded Walhachin was best used for nothing but casual winter grazing of cattle.

A few years after its abandonment little remained. Buildings quickly fell into disrepair, collapsed, were torn down, or simply weathered away. The irrigation flumes toppled and rotted. Scattered across the bench land the occasional fruit tree continued to struggle for life, to blossom and even bear fruit. Of the hopes and dreams of 150 British settlers, there remained few traces.

CHAPTER NINE

DUNCAN — CANADA'S MOST ENGLISH TOWN

If one part of Canada most replicated Britain's climate and lushly vege-tated landscapes brushed by sea breezes, it was the Cowichan Valley on Vancouver Island's east coast. Sheltered from the Pacific Ocean storm tracks that battered the island's west coast by a wide range of soaring, saw-toothed mountains stretching up the island's length, this narrow shelf of fertile ground bordering the Georgia Strait became home to the country's largest and most enduring colony of British upper-class emigrants. Climate was not the only draw. The promise of cheap land and bountiful opportunity to pursue blood sports proved equally com-pelling lures. So in the late 1890s, a steady flow of well-heeled, British emigrants started drifting northward from Victoria to settle around the rough-and-tumble town of Duncan.

Only thirty years earlier, the region had been a wilderness of tall old-growth Douglas firs, and western red cedar forest in the foothills, and hardwood forest in the valley bottom. Settlers from eastern Canada and Britain first started hacking small, mixed farms out of these forests with their axes in the 1860s. Among them was Ontario-born Scotsman William Duncan. On a rectangular pre-emption of rich bottomland overgrown by maples, alders, and cedars identified on survey maps as Section 17, Range 6, the twenty-eight-year-old carved out a small farm linked to civilization by only a foot trail that followed the Cowichan River to the steamer stop at Maple Bay.

Duncan and his neighbours were tough men who possessed little formal education. The British settlers in their ranks came from lower-class farming stock. Most were single and lived alone in rough cabins. From these cabins they emerged each morning to tackle the timber, cutting it back foot-by-foot. The process of transforming forest into open farmland was a task that took years. Every fallen tree had to be chopped into lengths that could be moved by hand. When enough timber was down, shortened into sections, and piled together, it was burned. The stumps also had to be dug out and burned. It took a serious, single-mindedly determined person to stick with this arduous, sometimes dangerous, task rather than be lured off to the adventure and chance at quick riches offered by the goldfields of the British Columbia interior. Duncan and most of the other men stuck, forming the core of the Cowichan Valley's community.

By August 13, 1886, when Sir John A. Macdonald banged the last spike into the E&N Railway line running seventy miles from Victoria to Nanaimo, Duncan was a married man with a prosperous farm and a surveyed townsite standing alongside the railroad right-of-way. He called this site, located near the midway point of the line, Alderlea. The hard-bitten locals referred to it as Duncan's Crossing. When a small railroad station went up, a hamlet-sized commercial centre rose around it. Webbing out from the town centre alongside a network of wagon roads were an ever-increasing number of farms. Good soil, a warm climate, and dependable rains produced abundant crops. Grass grew year round in a land seldom touched by snow or bitten by frost, yielding perfect conditions for dairy operations. In just a few years, Cowichan Valley was second only to the Fraser Valley in numbers of dairy cows in British Columbia. Farmers also raised pigs, cattle, and sheep, and grew vegetables, fruit, and tobacco.[1] Foodstuffs were loaded onto the trains, while supplies and new arrivals came off.

By 1890, the farmers and Duncan shopkeepers were facing a small-scale invasion of men they derisively called Longstockings. The term referred to the British gentlemen's preference for knickers and puttees over ankle-length pants. They came off the trains burdened with the usual bulging steamer trunks, fishing rods, hunting rifles, and shotguns. Word was out. Duncan was an angler's paradise, a shooter's heaven. Within a fifteen-mile radius of Duncan, Cowichan River provided fast-running fly-fishing, Cowichan and Quamichan lakes offered reputedly the finest freshwater angling in Canada, and the salt chuck of Georgia Strait held some of the richest salmon grounds in the world. From these waters, British gentlemen jerked cutthroat, brown, and rainbow trout, catfish, Dolly varden char, coho, and spring salmon.

Then there was the hunting; Roosevelt elk, deer, cougar, black bear, wolves, ducks, geese, and quail all close by.

Remittance men, farm students, India Army officer veterans, retired East India Company men, and well-financed, or poorly-financed, upper-class men straight from the Motherland stepped off the train, purchased a rural tract of land, and erected English manor-style houses situated down shady lanes and surrounded by flower gardens. Some of the first to arrive in Duncan were those who had grown tired of the increasingly commercial air of Victoria or who had found it too rich for their meagre pensions or remittances. Sir Edward Phillips-Wolley gave up Victoria for the Cowichan Valley in early 1900, putting up a massive wood and stucco manor he named The Grange. The sportsman-writer-adventurer by now was ardently concerned that the "British" character of British Columbia, and all of Canada, must be preserved against the threat of Americanism and republicanism. From The Grange he issued stories, poems, and letters-to-the-editor that extolled all things British, including driving the few cars beginning to appear in the area on the left side of the road rather than the right, as was the American custom.[2]

While the Canadian and lower-class British settlers might disdain them for their lack of work ethic and thrift, Duncan also thrived from an upper-class infusion of cash. Behind their backs, the Canadians generally described this burgeoning new group of settlers as incompetent, lazy, and general social misfits. In addition to Longstockings, they called them Brass Hats and Namby-Pambys. Even the hardest working of the British gentlemen was likely to be burdened with the remittance man tag. They mimicked their speech and unwittingly adopted many of the patterns themselves, so that a garbage can was known as a receptacle, and numbered the best among them as jolly good chaps.

Stories, mostly apocryphal, abounded of gentlemen suffering from a lack of business acumen. The most popular regarded a supposed English gentleman from a moneyed background who bought an over-priced dairy farm from a wily Canadian. After six months struggling with the fact that the "damned cows had to be milked every day," he purportedly sold at a loss.[3] The gentlemen retaliated in kind, nicknaming Canadians Short Stockings or Mossbacks, and ridiculing their lack of social graces, education, and, just generally, *class*.

Like it or not, however, the two communities had to co-exist and it was ultimately to the advantage of all to do so more or less peaceably. One Canadian baker went out of his way to maintain good relations with the British upper-class families. When Longstockings came into his shop he offered them free counsel on how to get by in Duncan. "I used to feel sorry for the ladies just in from China, India and Africa," he recounted. "They had been used to a houseful of native servants, and they were lost when they got to Canada. Why, they couldn't even make a rice pudding. They'd come in to the shop with all the mixings — rice, sugar, milk, and so on — in a basin and plead with me to make a pudding. I always did."[4]

When a gentleman decided to clear land for an estate and construct a fine manor house, Canadian contractors did the work, Canadian gardeners generally maintained the grounds, and Canadian housekeepers performed the domestic chores. Canadian storeowners happily stocked overpriced English pipe tobacco, Scottish single malt whiskey, Eccles cake, and beef kidneys. The drugstore was renamed a chemist's shop and the Tzouhalem Hotel offered a breakfast of toast upon which was ladled kippers and grilled kidneys. The tudor-style Tzouhalem Hotel became a favourite haunt of British gentlemen and

The Tzouhalem Hotel was a popular refuge for the British upper classes that settled in Duncan. Cowichan Historical Society N993.3.2.1.

their less numerous gentlewomen. The hotel was opulently furnished, mounted heads of hunting trophies adorned the walls, fur skins were draped over stairwell banisters, potted lush tropical plants stood in the corners, and whist, bridge, and billiards were played in the bar late into the night.

The remittance men of the Cowichan Valley gathered almost nightly at the Tzouhalem Hotel to participate in the fun and pour down notable quantities of whiskey or gin. One remittance man, who soon found he had drunk away his funds, fired off a desperate cable to his father for assistance. "John destitute," the cable read. A prompt reply arrived, "John destitute. John must work." According to the legend around this exchange of cables, John happily ran around Duncan showing the response to his friends, pondered its meaning for a short time, then rather serious-mindedly sought and found employment, transforming himself into a solid member of the community.[5]

For the most part the British gentleclass emigrants proved largely an amusing, economically stimulating, and only occasionally irritating segment of Duncan society. Most were more eccentric than outrageously behaved. There was, however, one immensely grand exception, and he came to symbolize both the worst and best of the influence of remittance men upon Duncan. Arthur Edward Cecil Lane arrived in the Cowichan Valley in 1904, taking up a twenty-acre property on the shore of Quamichan Lake with an access onto Maple Bay Road. Whereas most of the Longstockings attached lofty-sounding names to their estates, such as The Maples, The Bungalow, The Firs, The Grange, or names drawn from the old-world estates from which they originated, Lane stuck his tongue in his cheek and aptly named the estate Stoney Ground for boulders were common coin there, not that this mattered to Lane, who had more than enough money to make of the land whatever he wished.[6]

Born in 1871, Lane was the second son of Lieutenant Colonel J. Henry Bagot Lane, the Lord of King's Bromley Manor Estate near Lichfield in Staffordshire. His family claimed a lineage back to the first Normans who arrived in England brandishing swords alongside King William the Conqueror in 1066. A forebear of Lane's had fought as a knight during the twelfth century Crusade. In 1651, when Cromwell routed King Charles II's army at the Battle of Worchester, the king was hidden by a Lane and then, disguised as a servant of the young Mistress Jane Lane, spirited by her to safety from Bentley to Abbotsleigh where he took ship to France. As a result of the young woman's heroism, future female Lane family members were awarded royal pensions and the Arms of England in a canton was added to the Lane's paternal coat.

Bromley Manor, more a privately owned baronial village than large estate, sprawled over 2,314 acres or 3.6 square miles of farms, parkland, and woodlands. The manor itself was surrounded by 140 acres of park and flower gardens. Built of stone and brick in the Georgian Era, the manor had a main drawing room that measured thirty-four feet by twenty-two feet, and a dining room that was thirty-eight feet by twenty feet. There were two libraries, fourteen bedrooms, three dressing rooms, a nursery, and an additional nine servant bedrooms. Outside one found a private cricket pavilion, tennis courts, and a croquet lawn; nearby stood a gardener's cottage, three lodges, and various sheds. There were thirteen farms on the estate — operated by tenant farmers — the fully-licensed Royal Oak Inn, numerous cottages, a grist mill, a sawmill, a blacksmith shop, an electricity plant, and large stables.

As a child, Arthur rattled around the manor house alongside his two brothers. John Henry was the elder son, George the youngest. Like most upper-class youth, Arthur was sent to a public school, attending Charterhouse School at Godalming. When he was only fifteen years old his father died suddenly from a heart attack on March 22, 1886 at the age of fifty-seven; John Henry was cited as his heir in the obituary.

Upon finishing his public school education, Arthur entered Christ Church at Oxford University to study toward a Master of the Arts degree. Although he was awarded his degree shortly before sailing to Canada, pursuing his education was not Arthur's main priority in life. He was far more enthusiastic about pleasure and sport. He was a keen cricket player, an avid sportsman who loved to ride to the hounds, and a devoted socialite. Arthur filled one scrapbook after another with programs saved from the numerous balls he attended in whirlwind-like fashion over the span of two decades from 1884 to 1903. There were endless county balls, the Meynell Hunt Ball, cricket club balls, the Cheltenham Ladies' Fancy Dress Ball.

His public school mates and university chums nicknamed him Fats, although he was more large built than overweight. A powerful, slope-shouldered young man with a good-natured, gap-toothed grin, Arthur even saved character-reference letters written by friends that suggested he would perish from consumption and other maladies resulting from an ill-led life. Shortly before deciding to immigrate to Canada, he consulted with several experts in palmistry, learning that he would have a good future but marry late.

Five years before immigrating, his mother, Susan Ann, died at the age of sixty-seven. His elder brother having inherited King Bromley's Manor Estate, Arthur had little reason to remain in Britain and decided to try his luck in Canada. Once there, he travelled almost directly to the Cowichan Valley, and was soon developing Stoney Ground Estate and a smaller recreational property on Cowichan Lake that he called The Outlook.

Everything Arthur Lane could have possibly sought in a community, he found in Duncan and the surrounding Cowichan Valley. There was the Duncan Lawn Tennis Club, founded in 1888, and reputedly the second oldest lawn tennis club in the world after Wimbledon. The latter had been formed in 1875 as an offshoot of Wimbledon's All-English Croquet Club just a few months after the first official lawn tennis rulebook was published. When *The Field* magazine featured articles on the game and sponsored a Tennis Championship in 1877 at Wimbledon, the game's popularity was assured among the British upper-classes. Croquet was wildly popular among the gentlemen and gentlewomen of Cowichan Valley, too, and soon lawn tennis was equally in vogue. A year after Lane's arrival, the tennis club raised $300 to develop eight courts alongside the existing cricket pitches. Cricket was another of Lane's passions, as was duck hunting along the marshy shoreline of Quamichan Lake, and galloping about with more enthusiasm than skill on a polo field. Lane became a popular member of Duncan's British upper crust.

There was no denying, however, that Lane was vying, albeit unintentionally, to be the most eccentric person among many eccentrics. Even the German count Captain Charles E. Henry Lengnick, who took up residence on the banks of Cowichan Lake about the same time as Lane built Stoney Ground, seemed relatively staid by comparison. Lengnick lived with his maid-turned-wife in a Bavarian monstrosity surrounded by a high, wire fence. A big, burly man, Lengnick kept his head shaved and wore a peculiarly stitched together one-piece khaki outfit resembling a kilt and open-chested jerkin. He insisted that anyone approaching his estate by water ring a bell on the boat dock, and wait five minutes before approaching the manor house. This provided sufficient time for the count, who generally preferred to stride about his grounds and home naked, to don his kilt-like outfit.[7]

Lane, meanwhile, was establishing Stoney Ground as Cowichan Valley's most popular party venue. But these were not the usual upper-class British extravaganzas that ran late into the evening with the host

Arthur Lane, indulging his penchant for wearing costumes, sports a mixed riding and naval commander ensemble. Cowichan Historical Society N991.4.5.34.

lavishing his guests with endless amounts of food and liquor. Lane's parties fulfilled his deep abiding need to wear a wide assortment of costumes. Closets at Stoney Ground fairly burst with a vast assortment of regalia that allowed Lane and his guests to instantly adopt a variety of personas. Edwardian-era gentlemen and gentlewomen emerged from the changing rooms as Mississippi River steamboat gamblers, Chinese mandarins, Old West buffalo hunters, and American Civil War-era southern belles (Lane donning skirts and hoops with a wide sunhat brimming with flowers). It was all frightfully good fun with the endless theme parties generally running through the night — most of the guests only staggering home after the sun had risen and they had partaken of an early breakfast to cut the worst effects of an inevitable hang over.

Theatre also provided Lane with an opportunity to try his hand at being someone else. Lane became a keen member of the Cowichan Bay

Amateur Dramatic Society, which staged many plays as fundraisers for various worthwhile local causes. On April 21, 1909 the society performed a play entitled *Valentine* by upperclassman George Cheeke, Esquire of nearby Shawnigan Lake. Lane played the villainous Leroux, who the program noted, went by the alias of Monsieur Montijo and was a professional gambler. Three years later almost to the day, Lane moved deftly from one role to another as he played both Merriman the butler and Lane the manservant in *The Importance of Being Earnest: A Trivial Comedy for Serious People* by Oscar Wilde.

This same year, Lane became an active member of the Cowichan Yacht Club, assuming the job of secretary. The following year he was elected Commodore, a position he would hold for many years. Lane was a fervent boatsman, having bought a powerboat, the *Flutterby*, soon after coming to the Cowichan Valley. The *Flutterby* had no cabin, but Lane made up for this shortcoming by extending over its entire length a raised canvas canopy. In July, 1909, he sold the *Flutterby* and purchased the bigger *Sokum*, which had a cabin and more powerful engine that allowed him to easily venture afield throughout the Gulf Islands, up the east coast of Vancouver Island, and down to Victoria on a regular basis. When Lane slipped *Sokum* into a berth at the Royal Victoria Yacht club he evoked good natured laughs from those sitting on the clubhouse deck by playing the role of captain and ringing a bell to signal to the engineer to stop engines. Then, doffing his captain's cap to become the engineer, he would run to the stern of the boat and shut off the motor.

The money from Britain continued to flow Lane's way, giving him no reason to pursue business or anything other than his own pleasure. Deciding Stoney Ground was too small, he set about building a grand manor on Cowichan Bay in 1913 that he named Wilcuma. While work proceeded on the mansion, Lane lived in a small cabin nearby. In the summer, he strode about the grounds and into Duncan in knee-high English riding boots, thigh-length shorts, and cotton long johns so that the underwear covered the part of his legs that would otherwise have been bared. By November the mansion was complete and Lane held a grand banquet at which the main course was cougar meat, or what he termed "panther."

Commodore Lane undoubtedly would have gone on partying and living the good life without pause had it not been for the serious matter of a world war intervening. Lane, like most of his British fellows in the Cowichan Valley, quickly enlisted. He joined the 50th Gordon

Highlanders in Victoria as a lieutenant and, until being called to active service, gave himself over to tirelessly promoting the Canadian Patriotic Fund, raising money to assist dependents of servicemen in need. In July 1915, the 50th Gordon Highlanders became part of the 52nd Battalion, Canadian Expeditionary Force and started training in Vernon. On October 1, 1915 Lane's battalion sailed from Halifax for Britain on the *Scandanavian* and he was soon a soldier with the 3rd Canadian Pioneers in Belgium. Promoted to the rank of captain, he earned a Mention in Despatches for bravery under fire, but never spoke about what he had done to earn the honour.

In August 1917, Lane acquired a copy of a popular book *A General's Letters to his Son on Obtaining a Commission*. After reading it, he wrote on the cover: "Something worth reading." He underlined various passages, including one to the effect that an officer must make his men the "first consideration." He also underlined: "Men love an officer who enters into their sports with them," but scribbled "Rot" next to a

A group of English gentlemen indulge in some good sport during a party at Arthur Lane's estate. Cowichan Historical Society N991.4.5.59p50(3).

143

long treatise on how the greatest cause of drunkenness among the men stemmed from those who misguidedly attempted to display their patriotism by "rendering His Majesty's soldiers incapable" with drink. In red ink, he underlined: "The only reward really worth having is knowledge that you have done your duty."

Such musings might have indicated that Lane was becoming a more serious man due to his exposure to the horrors of war. He had served in the front lines from early 1916 through to November 11, 1918, when the Canadians reoccupied Mons and the war came to a sudden end. By April 1919, Lane was back in the Cowichan Valley and life was again a grand, unending party.

The good times, however, were slightly cramped by the specter of Prohibition. Lane threw himself into the campaign for a provincial referendum to either endorse the ban of liquor or to return the province to "wet" status. On April 29, 1920, he chaired a meeting in Duncan that the *Cowichan Leader* headlined as a "Gathering of Three-Hundred in Sympathy with Government Control — Good Speeches." Lane set the tone by draping a flag of St. George behind his chair and telling the audience that the "Moderation party [pro-wet party] represented St. George and Prohibition the dragon." Lane said "he hoped the moderation party would do the same to the prohibitionists as St. George did to the dragon."[8] The referendum swept Prohibition aside, allowing Lane and his friends, who had also argued that Prohibition was simply "unBritish", to once again easily access endless supplies of liquor for their parties.

Lane was, however, ready to give up the single life and somewhat settle down. In October 1922, he married Beatrice Margaret Booth, nicknamed Trixie, in Victoria. Driven back to Wilcuma by one of Lane's chums, the newlyweds arrived to find a large gathering of friends. "The happy pair," declared the *Cowichan Leader*, "were deeply impressed with the very great kindness evinced by everyone." Lane, the paper wrote, "is one of the best known figures in Cowichan. He is commodore of the Cowichan Bay Yacht Club, prominent in amateur dramatic circles, and a good all round sportsman. His friends are legion here and they join in wishing him and Mrs. Lane the best good fortune in the years that lie ahead."[9]

The era of good fortune was, however, drawing to an end as Britain sunk into a post-war recession; the wealth of the Lane family was seriously eroded, based almost entirely on old money and rather modest revenue versus the costs generated by King's Bromley Manor Estate. On January 21, 1927, the estate was sold by auction. The same year, Lane was forced to sell Wilcuma, and in September, he and Trixie held a farewell dance. The rooms of Wilcuma were, said the *Cowichan Leader*, "tastefully decorated with gladioli and delphiniums."[10] Lane moved his wife to a smaller home, Cheslyn Hay, on nearby Cherry Point, and thereafter the pace of the partying slowed dramatically. Although Lane continued to host social events at his new home, he gave himself over to more sedate activities. Chief among these was the building of a collection of toby jugs that soon was one of the largest and most valuable in Canada.

Duncan and the surrounding Cowichan Valley remained one of the last bastions of the remittance men. By the early 1940s, there were so many grey-haired gentlemen with an upper-class British background wandering the streets that Duncan became famous throughout the nation as "The Most English Town in Canada." One Victoria journalist described coming to Duncan with a friend from Winnipeg and "on the first street we found a man in khaki shorts and the invariable tweed coat ... Down the next street strode a lovely Colonel Blimp, with fly hooks all over his tweed hat ... And on my honour, with sworn evidence to support it, we found in the liquor store an old English gentleman in shorts, six inches of cotton drawers, and those long shiny boots that the Life Guards wear on sentry duty at Whitehall." The old gentleman was, of course, Lane in his casual summer outfit.[11]

Although Lane died suddenly on March 2, 1947, the era of the Longstockings in Duncan did not end with his demise. There were far too many of his fellows to uphold the tradition of the upper-class leisured lifestyle. They were, however, a dying breed as age and an oft-careless life took its inevitable toll. Drinking binges sometimes proved deadly, as was the case for R. A. Meade. A remittance man who maintained a broken down ninety-acre horse ranch, sporting only a few tired-looking nags, on the north arm of Cowichan Lake, Meade was a renowned hard drinker. When the man failed to retrieve a remittance cheque from the local post office for three weeks, some of his friends went over to the ranch. They found a line of whiskey bottles stuck into the dirty scum of snow bordering either side of the path leading to his front step. Meade's frozen body was discovered inside the house.[12]

By the early 1940s, it was estimated that the Longstockings in the community had shrunk from a population high of about two thousand souls to less than half that number. Most were like the faltering Major Laurence Chapman Rattray, who had retired from the British army to Duncan after World War I to grow roses and fish. Arrogant to a fault,

Rattray was often seen striding out in front of cars without so much as a glance their way. When behind the wheel himself, Rattray was a menace to all. He once drove in front of an oncoming train,and although his car was destroyed in the collision, he miraculously survived. "I don't know why it didn't stop," he complained of the train. "I honked at it."[13]

The Longstockings final moment of notoriety came in 1951 when the clutch of survivors learned that the newly-married Princess Elizabeth and Duke of Edinburgh planned to bypass Duncan without stopping during a tour of Vancouver Island. A delegation of Old Boys descended on Duncan mayor James Chesterfield Wragg and demanded that he pressure Buckingham Palace into ordering the Royal procession to stop in Duncan or they would block its passage with a human chain of their cohorts.

No doubt with images of aged Longstockings leaning on canes in their tweed caps and coats facing an honour-guard of Mounties, Wragg did his best to convince Buckingham Palace to include Duncan on the itinerary of stops to no avail. Wragg went public, endorsing the human chain idea on local radio talk shows. Newspapers from around the world showed up before the Royal tour to photograph a mock staging of the human chain roadblock.

On the day the royal procession was to pass through Duncan, some 10,000 residents from the Cowichan Valley area turned out to witness the impasse. Driving the lead car was the Duke of Edinburgh himself, who, upon approaching the town, slowed to a walking pace. The blockade was hastily abandoned as everyone — Longstockings and Canadians alike — was able to see the elegant couple, and in some cases, exchange pleasantries as the car slipped slowly past. When Wragg met the princess a few hours later at a formal reception in Nanaimo, she said, "That was quite an exciting reception you gave us in Duncan today."[14]

The following year *Maclean's* magazine reporter McKenzie Porter came to Duncan and wrote an article entitled "The Last Stronghold of the Longstockings." Much of the article was little more than, as Major Rattray described it, "pure invention, a lot of jolly nonsense." Porter summarized his findings as indicative that "Canada's most die-hard community of old-fashioned British aristocrats is finally petering out."[15] In this, he was correct, for the Old Boys were dying off rapidly and their era in the Cowichan Valley was consequently coming to a natural end. They did, however, leave an indelible stamp upon the community. Duncan and the rural area of Cowichan Valley would continue to resemble a small British county in terms of the kinds of farming operations, the many grand and less grand British-style homes dotting the landscape, and the nature of the small businesses that lined its commercial streets.

CHAPTER TEN

ADVENTURES ON THE PRAIRIE

Most remittance men didn't attach themselves to an exclusively British Edenic community, such as Walhachin or Cannington Manor or even heavily English-influenced Vancouver Island communities, like Duncan and Victoria. They either had insufficient financial backing to invest in farmland and housing or they lacked interest in so closely replicating upper-class British life. Although Walhachin and Cannington Manor offered the comfort and security of social and cultural familiarity to their residents, for many a remittance man these were the very things they sought to escape by coming to Canada. What they wanted was adventure, the chance of profit through a well-planned and -executed get-rich scheme, or simply the opportunity to live from day to day with no cares or responsibilities. It was men like these who provided the grist for the legends.

Jimmy Simpson was an archetypal remittance man. Practically from the day he first learned to walk, Simpson was a disgrace to his parents and a subject of scandal within the conservative community of Stamford in England's Lincolnshire County. "I was one of those kind that was born for the outdoors," he recalled many years later, "but everywhere you turned in England someone was telling you to keep off the grass."[1] Even before reaching his teens, Simpson was poaching on the large estates surrounding his village — shooting pheasants and rabbits for the sheer sport of it. His family, including an uncle who was Stamford's mayor, tried every conceivable strategy to force the young boy to conform. Hoping to teach him fiscal responsibility, they arranged a job for him as a newspaper delivery boy. After throwing the papers into the river Simpson slipped off into the estates to continue poaching. As a teenager they tried forcing him to become a carpenter. He rebuffed this last-ditch effort to inculcate responsibility into him (even at the risk of reducing one of the family's own to a lower-class occupation) by learning some carpentry skills but applying them to what he considered wildly amusing stunts. His grand finale involved cleverly sawing a coffin in half so it wouldn't fall to pieces until it was en route from mortuary to grave.

Simpson's last and final disgrace occurred inside the sanctified walls of Stamford's Anglican Church. The minister, having himself been brought down by scandalously spending far too much time with the pretty, but married church organist, delivered his last sermon before moving to a new diocese. As the minister led the processional out of the church, Simpson brayed with delight and pointed with both loud gesture and word toward the reverend's ample posterior — to which he had earlier attached a sprig of mistletoe.

After this antic the family gave young Simpson a choice: Canada, Australia, South Africa, anywhere but England. A few weeks later the teenager arrived in Halifax, travelled by train to Winnipeg, and then hitched a lift on a wagon to a farm outside the city where he was supposed to take up residence as a farm pupil. Simpson slopped pigs, shovelled manure out of barns, and hoed vegetables in a garden for merely one day before deciding this wasn't the life for him. Pocketing what was left of his remittance and carrying only a light bag he lit out for Winnipeg in the dark of night.

Six weeks of drinking and running wild on the streets left Simpson broke. He was also bored; Winnipeg seemed far too tame. Pawning his gold watch and chain, the young man raised enough cash to buy a train ticket to Calgary. He rolled into the ranching town in 1896. "Coming from an upper-class Victorian family in Stamford with all its Elizabethan, Jacobean, and Georgian homes to the west in the 1890s and seeing all this wild country around me, and meeting hardened railroaders, rum-soaked remittance men, horse thieves, and Indians would be too much for most teenagers, but this was just the crowd I liked," Simpson recalled. "The very first day I was in Calgary I was shot at by a drunk Belgian."[2]

Simpson fit right in. Within days he had assembled a cowboy outfit of his own, including a wide-brim North West Mounted Police — style hat — a personal affectation he would feature for the rest of his days. A

Jimmy Simpson (right). Taken in Banff, circa 1900. GAI NA-1438-2.

few weeks later he was up in the Rockies hunting with a high-powered rifle and succeeded only in blowing the rim off his hat. The resulting headache lasted longer than the fright he had given himself.

For the first few years Simpson drifted from job to job, adventure to adventure. He worked on the railroad near Lake Louise in the summers and spent the winters in California. Jailed in Fresno for riding a train without a ticket, he met Jack London in a cell. "He was a London tough, a wharf-bred rat, who didn't know his father, but still pulled himself out of the gutter to become California's greatest author."[3] These were the kind of men Simpson respected and admired, not British-bred aristocrats who fancied they deserved respect because of their social position.

Returning to Canada, Simpson hired on as a cook with the CPR outdoor guide Tom Wilson. He enjoyed working with Wilson and learned from him the business of running an outdoor guiding company. When Simpson turned twenty-one he was surprised to find that a relative he never knew had left him a sizeable legacy. There was enough money from the inheritance to buy a pack team and establish his own guiding outfit. Over the next sixty-one years Simpson established a reputation as one of the nation's most capable outdoor guides and became a Rocky Mountain legend in his own right.

He also continually surprised contemporaries by demonstrating a deep appreciation for culture that belied his rough and wild manner. He surrounded himself with a vast library of books that in the early 1900s was reputedly one of the largest private collections in Alberta. On the walls of his hunting lodge hung paintings and prints given to him by western artist friends, such as Charles Russell. While people didn't always like his opinions or theories, they were impressed by how Simpson seemed capable of opining on just about any subject with sufficient knowledge to persuasively argue his position against all comers.

Yet he retained both the irreverence and bizarre sense of humour that had got him into so much trouble back in Britain. Once, when he was still building his hunting lodge, a young, British, upper-class woman accompanying her husband on one of Simpson's trips came across Simpson breaking rocks with a sledgehammer for use as stone facing. Not recognizing this sweat-lathered labourer as her famous guide Jimmy Simpson, she asked if he were a prisoner or something, for surely that was the only place a man would have to spend his time breaking rocks. Simpson, with a deadpan expression, told her he was indeed a prisoner working off his sentence at the lodge. She asked what he had done to become a convict. Narrowing his eyes slightly, and offering not the slightest trace of a smile, Simpson said, "I killed a woman who asked too many questions."[4] Years later, at the age of ninety-three, Simpson, recalling this tale, would still fall into paroxysms of laughter.

Long after he became a successful guide Simpson continued poaching for the hell of it. The police believed he was the best, and most dedicated, poacher in Banff National Park, which was created in 1885. Arrested on several occasions, he usually beat the charge by drawing on the legal chicanery of the notorious criminal lawyer Paddy Nolan. Only once was he convicted and then, he said, it was because the Crown prosecutor cleverly boxed him into a situation where the only way he could have escaped the charge was to commit perjury, a crime carrying a stiffer sentence than poaching. "They claimed that the pelt of a mountain sheep that was in my house perfectly fit the body of a sheep they found in the hills. I had burned part of the body that pelt was from so I knew this was a lie but there was no way I could get up in court and tell them how I knew the sheep's pelt wasn't from the carcass they said it was. There was never a law, though, that you couldn't get around. I learned that in England and I never forgot it."[5]

Simpson's nature was such that it seems likely he would have been a rogue no matter what his circumstances; being shipped to the Canadian west only gave him a freedom to live the life he wanted. Simpson's lifestyle was well-suited to the country; in a land with wilderness as rugged and spectacularly pretty as the Rocky Mountains a man who could hunt, shoot, and guide others to satisfying outdoor adventures was destined to make a good living. Most remittance men, however, were more likely to be only fair to middling shots and lacked the dedication to the sporting life essential to making a career from hunting. But the average remittance man was anything if not inventive, and many were the ways in which they managed to cajole family into continuing to send remittances, or lure those around them to contribute funds to sustain their carefree lifestyles.

Out on the banks of Sheep Creek Charles Sturrock and Eric Buckler had, after two years of living in a tent, finally completed construction of their two small houses in 1905. Despite the time they had lived on the land little farming or ranching had been done. With regular polo, cricket and dance events at nearby Millarville, coyote hunts, and unending opportunity to hunt grouse and game in the surrounding hills there was no time, or necessity, for the diversion of agricultural labour.

Both young men received regular remittances. Eric Buckler particularly seemed to always have a good-sized roll of cash. Buckler, thinking ahead to how to earn even more money, proposed they set up a small dairy. They put up a barn, invested in some cattle and milking equipment, and suddenly found themselves dairymen — a hard, endlessly repetitive life, full of early mornings and late evenings spent keeping up with the pace of bovine lactation. This was not the lifestyle either Sturrock or Buckler had envisioned.

What was needed was some cheap labour to do the chores. With this in mind Sturrock fastened onto the idea of cashing in on the farm pupil system that was proving quite successful for other Millarville farmers. He placed an advertisement in a British newspaper that read: "Farming tuition by expert in Canadian farming. Premium reasonable."[6]

And so to Buck Ranch came an assortment of young gentlemen farmers. First names tended to get lost as the young men mimicked public school tradition and referred to each other only by surnames.

There was Feggis, a tall, lanky man; Swartz, a soft-spoken lad whose culinary skills earned him the duty of being the establishment's cook; Buckler's cousin Eddy, who liked to sport riding boots and a top hat; two Scottish brothers named Harry and Charlie Lusk; and about ten other young men of good family. They arrived with the usual kit of new saddles, rifles in beautiful leather cases, tailored riding breeches, and leather boots. Between them all they also brought to Buck Ranch a small menagerie of hunting dogs, including Irish wolfhounds, Scottish deerhounds, a bull mastiff, and more than a dozen foxhounds. About the same time as the Buck ranch pupils were arriving, Eric Buckler imported a piano and some furniture from England. Soon the possibility of music and comfortable seating transformed the two small houses into a popular gathering spot for other Millarville gentlemen farmers.

Buck Ranch operated with surprising success considering the chaotic way in which work was undertaken. Neither Sturrock nor Buckler knew enough about farming to pass on anything of much value to their pupils, but this seemed to matter little as long as the young men continued to receive their remittances and were able to enjoy sport and partake of the small Millarville British community's social life.

The pace of agricultural practices at Buck Ranch is well illustrated by the events surrounding the day of a pig slaughter. The finnicky chef

Charles Sturrock (with parasol) with pupils Feggis, Swartz, Wilson Jones, Eddy Buckler, and Ted Lewis. GAI NA-2520-30.

153

Swartz, who professed to be a Baron, precipitated events by complaining about the seemingly endless diet of mutton the men had been living on for months. Sturrock, aware of his responsibility as teacher and guardian of the younger men, mulled over the problem and then announced they would butcher a pig. Swartz had named the fattest of the pigs Jeremy and Sturrock logically singled this plump specimen out for slaughter. "I couldn't eat a bit of him," Swartz protested, "he's as tame as a dog."

Sturrock chastised Swartz for having made a pet of the pig and ordered a fire built in the corral so that a large pot of water could be set to boil while Jeremy was dispensed and prepared for cooking. "I'll have nothing to do with killing pigs," Swartz declared and fled inside the house to knead some bread he had earlier set to rise.

One of the other pupils asked Sturrock if the pig should be bathed before it was slaughtered. Sturrock, after careful consideration, informed him that the pig would be soaked to get its hide off after he had shot it. By this time all the pupils had gathered to witness the event and Charles Lusk offered Sturrock a swig of Scotch from a bottle he kept inside his jacket. Sturrock declined as this matter of slaughtering pigs required a steady hand.

Inside the house Swartz heard the pigs being rounded up and the men running this way and that to try and cut Jeremy out of the herd. He decided then and there that farming, or ranching as they all preferred to call it, was a nasty business. At the end of the year when his premium was paid out, Swartz thought, he would return to England. Suddenly the sounds outside the house stilled. Swartz risked a furtive glance out a window. All he could see was Sturrock, Lusk, and the others crouched behind some logs near the corral. They appeared to be hiding from something. "They're turning killing a pig into a game," he thought. Disgusted, Swartz decided to distract himself by playing the piano so loudly that he was certain the sound of Jeremy's grisly demise wouldn't reach him.

Midway through a tune he was interrupted by Lusk walking into the room. "Finished already?" Swartz asked grudgingly.

"No, not even started yet," Lusk replied. "They saw a coyote and they're off to chase it." Swartz went to the window just in time to see Sturrock and the other gentlemen farmers swinging into their saddles and setting off after the baying hounds that were already in hot pursuit. The hunters returned at noon after chasing the coyote almost to Millarville before a hound named Lynx managed to run it to ground and make the kill. Unfortunately, just before they had ridden off,

Bradfield Ranchhouse 1910. GAI NA-639-7.

Sturrock had dispensed Jeremy with one shot drowned out by Swartz's piano playing. Sturrock had then dumped the pig into the boiling water with the assumption that Lusk and Swartz would see to turning the body regularly and ensuring it didn't boil too long. The pig, boiled beyond salvation, ended up being cut up and fed to the hounds. For some reason Sturrock could never explain, however, the dogs all stank afterward and became badly bloated. With a shrug Sturrock and the others wrote the whole experience off as a bad job and continued to gain notoriety throughout the Millarville area for the unpredictable method by which they operated their ranch.[7]

The farm-pupil program Sturrock and Buckler operated at Buck ranch was a modest affair compared to the nearby Bradfield College Ranch owned and operated by the Reverend Dr. Herbert Branston Gray. Unlike the owners of Buck Ranch, Gray's motives for establishing an agricultural school to educate young upper classmen in farming and ranching methods derived from a matter of principle. Gray was warden and headmaster of Bradfield College in Berkshire, a renowned social reformer in Britain, an Anglican divine, and a liberal theologian. As an educator in the British public-school system he was dismayed to see so many young graduates, unable to find useful positions in society, being shipped off by their families to lives in the colonies for which their education left them totally unprepared. After penning many missives on this dreadful situation he decided to take an active role in bringing about reform: Bradfield College Ranch was to demonstrate that young remittance men could be successfully trained in agricultural arts. The reputation of young public school graduates in Canada would thus be redeemed.

In 1909 Gray delved into his own funds to purchase the twenty-five-hundred-acre Melrose Ranch, near Millarville. Gray chose the ranch for two reasons. First, Millarville was within twenty miles of Calgary and he knew that southern Alberta was more popular with the public schoolboys than most of the prairies. They associated the region with the romantic life of a rancher rather than the drudgery they ascribed to Canadian farming practiced throughout Manitoba and

Bradfield Ranch pupils, circa 1909. GAI NA-639-8.

Saskatchewan. The second reason Gray chose Melrose Ranch was its house, which was elegant and large enough to accommodate a farm manager, housekeeper, and about twenty students.

For students Gray carefully selected young men who had graduated from classes in agriculture and engineering he offered at Berkshire's Bradfield College. With great care he chose those judged to be of "solid character." They were charged two hundred dollars per annum and signed on for two years' training before they would graduate and be ready to set up an agricultural operation of their own. Much of their per annum fee could be recovered if the students assisted with household chores and other duties. In the first year those students who worked on the ranch would earn ten dollars a month; in the second year wages doubled.

Buck Ranch and Bradfield College were as different as night and day. At Bradfield, mornings began with a prayer and ended with all gathering to sing *God Save the King*. The pupils laboured in the ranch's creamery, carpentry shop, vegetable garden, or helped tend the ranch's livestock: three hundred head of cattle and more than two hundred Angora goats.

For the most part the college was deemed a success by Gray and his students, but there are few records of any of the graduates going on to establish agricultural operations of their own. In 1914, with the outbreak of war, the college was closed and most of the students immediately volunteered for service. At war's end the college ranch was not reopened.

One remittance man who often visited with the students at Bradfield College was Edward A. Melladew. The son of a Liverpool cotton manufacturing family, Melladew drifted into the Millarville area in 1905. He became a member of the Millarville Race Club and was one of the founding members of the community's polo team. In 1907 another young man, Arthur Barrett, reputedly a nephew of Admiral Cunningham, came to Millarville and became one of Melladew's closest friends. The two soon established a local reputation as scoundrels for their extravagant and scandalous ways.

Melladew and Barrett both drew upon money from their families in Britain to establish small homesteads, but they put scant effort into their operation. They preferred to concentrate their efforts on racehorses and improving their polo swings. Both were notorious drinkers and many of the Canadian ranchers in the area were amazed at the quantity of liquor the two of them could put away and still remain steady on their feet. But at the Millarville Race Days in 1909 they finally met their match.

The Millarville Polo Team, 1907. Arthur Barrett is third rider from the left.
GAI NA-3627-40.

As events turned from rowdy to riotous at one of the bars set up for the celebration, the police moved in to shut things down and confiscate the liquor supply. The bartender, having anticipated such an occurrence, had stashed a large supply of bottles in some nearby bushes; when the police departed he planned to reopen and business could continue as usual. Unfortunately for the bartender Barrett discovered his stash. Without hesitation he bundled up most of the cached liquor and he and Melladew lit out in a Democrat buggy for Melladew's home.

Millarville resident Sid Bannerman saw the two men make off with their ill-gotten liquor stock but kept his mouth shut about it. The next morning he rode out to the homestead to see how they were doing — he suspected that as long as the liquor lasted the two men would keep putting it back and was consequently concerned for their health. Finding two horses saddled up and tied to the hitching post outside the shack he wasn't surprised to discover Barrett and his friend inside dressed for some serious cowboying. "They were all dressed up in their cowboy outfits, including boots, chaps, and spurs, and were making a bet as to who could swim Sheep Creek with all their cowboy outfit on."[8] Both were also so drunk, he recalled, they could barely remember their names. It was a relatively simple thing for Bannerman to talk them out of the idea, as they quickly forgot what it was they had been planning. While they shucked off their cowboy regalia, Bannerman unsaddled the horses and set them loose. Going back inside to say goodbye he found both men passed out on bunks amid the scattered bottles of what must have been one of their best drunks ever.

In 1910 Melladew came into a modest inheritance that allowed him to buy a small ranch. The amount of ranching that went on was minimal, but the parties he hosted were renowned throughout the region.

Barrett meanwhile was falling on harder times; his remittances were becoming increasingly irregular and the family was talking of cutting him off entirely. Barrett devised a scheme to realize one last big score and it was to the tolerant Bannerman that he turned for an accomplice. "Arthur came to me one day and wanted me to write to his people in England and tell them he had died and that I had taken care of all funeral expenses which amounted to $650. Of course I was to explain to them that he was a personal friend of mine and I wanted him to have a respectable funeral."[9] Bannerman refused to get involved and a little while later Barrett returned to Britain to try and make amends with his family; he never returned to Canada.

About the time Barrett moved away, Melladew's drinking worsened and his behaviour became more eccentric. He took to carrying a revolver which he would brandish about in the region's bars. In 1911, while performing pistol tricks in the Grand Central Hotel in Okotoks, Melladew was fatally wounded in the head when the gun accidentally discharged.

Barrett's plan to get money out of his family by faking his own death was by no means the most ambitious of attempts to dupe family back in Britain into continuing to finance the lifestyles of remittance men. Perhaps the most audacious plan was hatched by R.C. "Dicky" Bright on the Bow River at Cochrane, just northwest of Calgary. Bright came to Canada in the early 1890s and established a small homestead. Prior to leaving Britain he had been, adhering to family tradition, studying medicine to become a physician. Bright's grandfather was Richard Bright, who in 1827 was the first to describe the clinical manifestations of the kidney disorder that in his honour was called Bright's disease.

Grandson Bright was little interested in following in his grandfather's, or his father's, foot-steps. What he much preferred was riding (something his contemporaries on the prairies said he did badly) and having a good time partying in nearby Calgary (which he did very well). To ensure a steady flow of remittances Bright wrote regular letters to his father describing how well his ranch was doing with a band of horses and countless cattle all soon to reach marketable age. In the meantime, however, he would ask his father for the loan of a few quid "of short money to tide me over until the long money from the cattle comes in."[10]

Bright's ranch existed only in his imaginings; in reality he had one horse and no other livestock besides that run on the homestead by C. Dawson, who had gone into partnership with Bright in 1893. The partnership consisted of Bright providing Dawson with range for his stock in exchange for a limited share in the price his horses fetched when sold. Bright liked this arrangement as he need do nothing but provide grazing land.

For several years Bright's mythical cattle continued to grow but never to reach marketable age; and Bright's father provided ever increasing sums of short money to his struggling rancher son. Eventually Dr. Bright grew suspicious and decided to come to Canada and see his son's ranch. It was not until he was almost in Calgary, however, that he telegrammed Bright to advise him of his imminent arrival.

A panicked Bright intercepted Dawson on the range and relayed the news of the impending disaster. Panic quickly gave way to cunning and Bright went to work displaying what to Dawson seemed amazing resourcefulness and quickness of action. Galloping from one Cochrane ranch to another he arranged to rent or borrow enough cattle to assemble a large herd. He also convinced a small group of neighbouring cowpunchers to bring the cattle to a pasture about two miles out of Cochrane and pretend to be his ranch crew.

He then rented the town's best driving team and fanciest buggy. Suitably attired in his Sunday best Bright took the buggy into town and met his father at the train station. Together son and father returned to Bright's rundown ranch. He explained away the condition of the buildings by saying that all his capital was concentrated in the livestock, which was where the future profit would be found. After his father had rested for a few hours, during which time Bright raced to the pasture to ensure all was ready, Bright took him over to the corral to see a demonstration of cattle branding.

As part of his grand deception Bright had bought one calf from a neighbour so he could brand it with his own mark as further proof that he was on the road to becoming a cattle baron. His physician father, more at home in cities and hospitals than on the open prairie, failed to notice that the brand didn't match the various other brands on the cattle purportedly constituting Bright's herd.

Well-satisfied with the extent of his son's achievements to date, Bright's father returned to Britain and continued to send large remittances. But a pall hung over Bright's head that robbed life of some of its pleasure, for he knew that the following summer his sisters were to come for a visit. This was to be no short stay, so there was no way he could pull together another deceptive herd and keep it assembled through several weeks. Over drinks in the local bar Bright would tell his friends that he was a doomed man, that he would be disgraced, and more importantly that he would lose his remittance.

But everyone who knew Bright realized the young man was one of those born with both silver spoon and extraordinary luck, so they expected something by way of good fortune to turn up for him, which it did. The winter before his sisters arrived was brutally harsh and many old and weak cows throughout the Cochrane area perished before the coming of spring. By summer, when the women arrived, the carcasses and skeletons of cattle still lay thick upon the prairie.

His herd had perished, Bright lamented to his sisters at the train station. From the modest ranch house he rode out each day with his sisters to tour the countryside. Sometimes Dawson rode along to break in a new horse. He had a hard time keeping a straight face whenever they came across another carcass. Looking down upon the unfortunate corpse, Bright would shake his head sadly and say to his sisters, "There's another one of my poor beasts which perished that terrible winter."[11] Suitably dismayed by their brother's misfortune the young women returned to Britain and relayed the news to their father of how Dicky had been wiped out by an act of nature. To rebuild, of course, more money would be necessary.

But by summer's end Bright seemingly tired of the deceptions. He talked his father into sending him funds so that he could return home and do some travelling abroad. Bright left Canada sometime in late 1896 or early 1897. On June 17, 1897, he wrote Dawson a letter from Geneva on Grand Hotel National stationary saying he was planning to return soon to Canada, but Dawson never heard from him again, nor did Bright ever return to his homestead.

The tendency of remittance men, such as Dicky Bright, to come into a region, idle there for a time, and then out of boredom, or continued decline in their fortunes, set off to try their luck somewhere else was common. E.F. Waldy, a tall, cheerful Englishman, came to the High River region sometime in 1894. He built a cabin on a homestead in some nearby woods and soon became a fixture in the community. Waldy spent most of his time hunting or riding about the countryside on a large white appaloosa. No one recalls him doing much in the way of work, but as he received generous monthly remittances this wasn't much of a surprise to anyone.

In 1898, Waldy, who was a crack shot, headed north to the forests near Edmonton for an extended hunting trip. He was gone for several months. During this time the remittances rolled in on a monthly basis, piling up at the High River post office. Waldy did not return from his expedition until spring of 1899. He returned then only to volunteer for service in the Boer War.

But Waldy was concerned to find that he now had a large sum of cash waiting for him. As he had been living rough on the land for many months, he hadn't needed much money and had quite forgotten his remittances. The young man didn't fancy travelling across Canada by train with so much cash in his pockets. To do so was to risk being robbed and possibly even murdered. While quite prepared to die hero-ically on an African battlefield, Waldy was horrified at the prospect of being knifed to death in some place like a railroad station lavatory because of his money roll. He could put the money into a bank, of course, but he was on the way to war; who knew if he would die in bat-tle and what need would he have of money then?

Waldy mused about this problem all the way to Calgary, where his troop was to embark by train to meet a ship in eastern Canada. By the time he reached Calgary the solution to his problem seemed obvious. Waldy told everyone he knew that he was staging a going-away party for himself and that all were invited. It's said that almost the whole town participated and that the liquor flowed, and the music and danc-ing continued until Waldy's last dollar was spent. Waldy found little glory in South Africa and, except for an injury received when he fell overboard while getting off the ship at Cape Town, came through the war unscathed. Rather than returning to High River at war's end he went to Britain, where he received a hero's welcome from his family.

While many remittance men aspired to return to Britain and reunite with their families, there were probably an equal number who cared little if they ever saw the Old Country's shores or the faces of family again. Undoubtedly Lionel Brooke fit into this group. Lord Brooke, as he was to be known throughout southern Alberta, the youngest son of

Sir Reginald and Lady Brooke of Runcorn in England's Cheshire County, was born in 1858. He was also related to Queen Victoria and was an older cousin of Alexander Augustus Frederick William Alfred George Cambridge, who as the Earl of Athlone would serve as Canada's governor general from 1940 to 1946. Brooke was a lean man who stood about six-foot-four. He was described as being the spitting image of the earl, who was to have been appointed governor general of Canada in 1914 but asked his name be removed because he wished to serve in the military.

Brooke followed the normal route for the scion of such a family of good blood by attending public school, graduating, and then enduring parental attempts to determine a suitable career path for a son who was establishing a reputation for ungentlemanly behaviour. For his part, Brooke appeared disinterested in any career that would distract him from his two life passions — hunting and travelling. Just before his twenty-fifth birthday, Brooke somehow disgraced himself in the eyes of his parents. Neither he nor his family ever disclosed the cause of this disgrace, but in 1883 he was summarily exiled by his family from Britain. As long as he stayed away, Brooke received a quarterly remittance. The value of the annual remittance probably rose over the years, but toward the end of his life in the 1930s the quarterly cheques that arrived at Pincher Creek's Royal Bank were said to equal about five thousand dollars in Canadian funds.

For the first two years of his exile Brooke travelled extensively. He saw most of South America, toured India, visited the West Indies, Japan, Iceland, and Bermuda, and rambled through California before finally arriving in Canada to visit friends who owned the Jug Handle Ranch near Pincher Creek. Brooke immediately fell in love with the foothills. Within weeks of his arrival he purchased the Butte Ranch in partnership with another Englishman. The partnership soon failed. Brooke sold his interest, and bought another ranch in Pincher Creek's Beauvais Lake district, which he named Chinook Ranch.

Brooke established the ranch as a horse-breeding operation and lavished money on the venture. He hired Englishman John Brown to manage the ranch and arranged for Brown's wife to do the housekeeping and cooking. The Chinook Ranch quickly became one of the most popular party locations in the Pincher Creek area, especially with the many other young remittance men living there.

There was no life like the ranching life in Brooke's mind. He loved riding, was a crack shot and a hard drinker, and gloried in the regalia and lifestyle of a cowboy. Brooke's common garb was a curious blend

Lionel "Lord" Brooke at his home in Pincher Creek, circa 1890. GAI NA-1403-1.

of British Old Country gentleman and rugged western Indian scout. This usually took the form of knickers and longstockings topped by a western shirt, a beaded buckskin jacket that the local Indians gave him, and a cowboy hat with an overly wide brim. After serving in the Boer War, where he was captured and imprisoned by the Boers until the armistice, he often tied the brim of the hat up at the sides in an Australian bushman's style. For most of his life, Brooke sported a large handlebar moustache. He also wore a monocle, which caused the local Indians to give him the name Whaw-pa-moon-hess-ki-sic, which was said to translate into "White man with the big glass eye."[12]

While Brooke's parties and good food ensured his popularity with everyone in Pincher Creek, his generosity also helped. With a remittance that far surpassed his personal needs, Brooke often gave money away to friends who had burned through their more meagre allowances. Once a young man known as Hassett offered Brooke his horses as security against a two-hundred-dollar loan. Brooke dismissed the security. "Horses, hell," he said, "you know you'll never pay me back."[13] At the same time Brooke was busily scribbling out a cheque for two hundred dollars, which he gave Hassett without further comment.

Although the horse stock Brooke raised on his ranch was excellent, there was, due to the fact few locals could afford their value, no market. Brooke once tried to overcome this problem by holding an auction where he could dispose of surplus horse stock by selling it to the highest bidder regardless of the cost. To ensure a good turnout he advertised free drinks and a complimentary lunch. All of Pincher Creek — and some say southern Alberta — attended.

Before the sale began the crowd lined up at the bar. An hour or so later the auction began and the bids poured in. Horses sold for two hundred dollars; teams went for three hundred dollars or more. Brooke snorted in mock disgust. Everyone knew none of the bidders had the money to back up such extravagant bids.

Climbing up on the auctioneer's stand, Brooke glared down at the crowd. "Now you beggars I fed you freely," he said, "you drank my liquor and now I have to take back all you bought, so come to the corral for I'll make you all ride a bucking horse."[14] In chastised silence everyone followed Brooke to the corral and looked about for the wild horse. To their amazement Brooke, who had been partaking of the free liquor in quantities surpassing that of his visitors, climbed into the corral and got down on all fours. For the next hour he bucked one after another of the bidders off, while the crowd sitting along the corral rail laughed so hard tears ran down their faces. Brooke's life was to be typified by these kind of anecdotes until his death in Pincher Creek at the age of eighty-one on January 12, 1939.

Not all were so free of cares or woes as Brooke appeared to be. Some, such as William Henry Sumerton, were slowly pulled down into despair by their seemingly footloose lives. Sumerton came to High River in 1887 to learn the ranching business. He was an affable fellow, well liked by all the other settlers in the area. While he was learning the ranching trade as a pupil on the McPherson spread, Sumerton spent many hours visiting Tom Lynch's ranch and watching Lynch and his cowboys break horses. Early on he illustrated a good way with horses. When he finished his period as a pupil, Sumerton purchased the ranch from Lynch with money provided by his parents.

He travelled to Britain to assemble breeding stock for the ranch, returning with two Cleveland Bay stallions and a thoroughbred mare called Silver Cross. In Ontario he bought some more mares to complete his stock.

Sumerton operated his breeding ranch until 1898, at one time owning as many as two hundred horses. Despite the excellent quality of his stock, however, the ranch never prospered and Sumerton's own temperament grew more melancholy with each passing year. Shortly before the ranch failed in 1898 Sumerton was taking a carload of horses east by train. After becoming quite drunk in the coach bar Sumerton stepped out into the breezeway, drew a knife, and slit his throat. A conductor found Sumerton lying in a pool of blood, managed to staunch its flow, and found medical aid in time to prevent his death.

After this incident Sumerton sold the failing ranch and left for the Klondike. He found no gold and eked out a living hauling mail by dog team for a year. In 1900 Sumerton received news that he had inherited a large sum of money. He returned to Britain to claim his legacy, but not long after his arrival in Britain news reached High River that Sumerton had drowned himself. There was much speculation as to why the young man would wish to take his own life, but some said it was nothing more than that he had become bored with the monotony of a life lived without meaningful purpose.

CHAPTER ELEVEN

ROUGHING IT WITH STYLE

Many Canadians thought the remittance life futile, empty, even corrupt. The drinking, partying, hunting, chasing around after one failed dream or another, lack of family ties, and the refusal by most to ever truly settle down to serious work rendered the lives of these well-educated, usually pleasant, and well-mannered young men pointless. But for remittance men, the very things that seemed dissolute to their Canadian counterparts and more seriously inclined British compatriots were what made life sparkle. On the prairies the majority of remittance men maintained a pretence of respectability and responsibility through their ranching efforts. In British Columbia's interior, however, hundreds of remittance men lived on the boundaries of British enclaves and offered no apologies for their actions. The largest concentration of these young men was in the Okanagan Valley, where a significant British community developed between 1880 and 1914.

"An Englishman always seems to do things thoroughly," recalled Okanagan pioneer J. R. Dennison. "If he came out here and decided he was going to go to the dogs no one could do it more thoroughly than he could. You very seldom heard anybody say about an Englishman, 'Well, he's a fairly decent chap.' It was always, 'Well, he's a damn good chap, or he's a bloody scalliwag.'"[1]

The Okanagan had many a "scalliwag" in the late 1800s and early 1900s, for it was a region well suited to the enjoyment of a carefree and wild lifestyle. In the hills overlooking the fruit farms on the bench lands and valley bottom, they found excellent sites next to creeks or rivers where they could erect a rough shack. From their shacks they forayed into the woods of the surrounding mountains to hunt or lazed away the days fishing in the valley's string of lakes. With meat free for the taking by anyone who could competently wield a rifle or a fishing rod, basic survival was relatively assured. All the remittance cheque need cover, then, was supplementary food and provisions, clothing, and, it seemed most importantly of all, liquor.

Charles Holliday joined other young British gentlemen living rough in the north Okanagan at Vernon. In 1889 the community was in transition from a cowtown to a fruit-farming centre. The town sported several hotels, each with a bar, and a growing number of services and businesses. Scattered along the dirt streets were a few unpainted cottages. There were no sidewalks and water was drawn from an irrigation ditch running through the middle of the flat upon which the town was built. As the town grew this water system was enclosed in a boxed culvert so the townspeople could no longer pollute the supply by dumping grey water into the ditch or putting clothes into the ditch to soak. Every three hundred feet a wooden tank with a pump provided a water outlet. These pumps were also the only source of water for fighting fire.

Fronting the buildings was a system of wooden plank sidewalks raised two feet off the ground to slow rotting. Holliday found the elevated sidewalk a bit perilous after having had a bit too much to drink. The sidewalks were, however, the perfect height for sitting on, so it was a common sight to see rows of men and even well-dressed ladies clustered in groups on the sidewalk's edge.

A few years later Holliday realized Vernon's informal lifestyle was endangered when he overheard the daughter of the town's lawyer saying, "I do wish Pa wouldn't sit on the sidewalk." This was, he reflected with regret, "about the time we began to burden ourselves with all the other restrictions of civilization, many of which are after all no more sensible than some of the taboos of so-called savage tribes."[2]

One thing that Vernon's town fathers had neglected to establish was a cemetery. When people died they were buried somewhere in their backyard or, if they didn't have family, were buried by friends up in the hills. The lack of foresight in this manner of burial became evident when a Chinese man no one knew came to town and promptly expired. Not surprisingly, given the anti-Oriental feeling that was prevalent throughout British Columbia at the time, no one wanted the man buried on their property. The town's government agent wrote to

Vernon as it was when Charles Holliday arrived. Provincial Archives of Alberta B.2340.

Victoria for instructions, but direction from the provincial government was slower than the body's decomposition rate. As Vernon's casual approach to disposing of its dead had not made it an attractive venue for anyone in the mortuary business, nobody knew how to embalm the corpse. Finally the government agent grew desperate and impressed several men into helping him bury the body in his own backyard. Shortly after this event the townspeople purchased a small plot of land for use as a community cemetery.

Within a few years the railroad was extended to Vernon from the CPR mainline and the town grew rapidly, along with the orchard land around it. But Vernon would retain much of its rustic nature until well after World War I. This was the community in which Holliday and an ever-increasing number of remittance men chose to base their activities.

Holliday, with his experience on a windjammer and consequent ease with a lifestyle devoid of many creature comforts, was initially surprised at how well the other British public schoolmen did at fitting into a western community, such as Vernon. He later wrote, "There was no

169

snobbishness about these public school boys....They were invariably what we nowadays call 'good mixers.' A few may have been wasters, but I cannot recall one who truthfully could be called a rotter."[3]

When a remittance cheque came in, the lucky recipient usually gathered up his friends from their shacks and everyone headed to Vernon to celebrate. "Some of the more careful ones," Holliday later wrote, "would hand over part of their roll to the bartender, with strict orders not to let them have any of it back until they had sobered up."[4] The liquor available was almost inevitably Canadian rye, Scotch and Irish whiskey, and little else. When Holliday first came to Vernon he once made the mistake of ordering a beer. The bartender

gave me a curious and rather pitying look, as if he might say to himself, "What's wrong with these English fellers, anyway?" After a search behind the bar he disinterred a couple of bottles of very flat and lukewarm beer. There was no such thing as soda water or other such like sissy stuff — there would be a jug of water on one end of the bar; you drank your whisky straight and diluted it in your insides with a follow-up drink of water from the jug if you felt that it needed diluting — this was known as a 'chaser' and was usually taken apologetically. There was also no measuring of one's tot as in England, the bottle was put on the bar and you helped yourself....However, there must have been a large profit, as the smallest sum taken over the bar was fifty cents; this was good for either two or three drinks — such a thing as ordering a lone drink was one of those things that simply wasn't done — if you needed one very badly and no one else was available, the correct thing was to treat the bartender.[5]

When remittance men started drinking they usually stayed at it until the allotted sum of money was gone or the liquor ran out. Sometimes this could go on for days and they would bunk out between drinking sessions with friends who were inevitably drawn into the ongoing party. A frequent participant in these parties was Coutts Marjoribanks, who was supposed to be managing Lord and Lady Aberdeen's Coldstream Ranch but was more often in town raising hell in one of the hotels.

Marjoribanks loved a grand entrance and so would always come into town on a big black horse called Cap at a clattering gallop, pull up short in front of the Kalamalka Hotel, and dismount with a cavalier

Tennis match in front of the Kalamalka Hotel, Vernon, B.C. in 1895.
BCARS 32334 F-2469.

flourish. Holliday was on the hotel verandah one day when
Marjoribanks galloped up and saw one of the local doctors, a small,
meek man, sitting near Holliday. Marjoribanks "being in an extra festive mood, rode up the porch steps and seizing the little doctor with
one hand swung him up on the front of the horse and charged up and
down Bernard Avenue with joyful whoops — he said it was time for
the doctor to learn to ride."[6]

Occasionally Marjoribanks did turn his hand to ranching, especially if the activity meant he could do so by dispatching orders to the
hired hands. Holliday was once idling away time watching
Marjoribanks and his crew loading cattle onto a train for shipping to
market. Marjoribanks peppered his commands with a string of obscen-
ities, all issued at a bellow that carried far on the early morning air. The
Presbyterian minister, a Mr. Langill, happened along, and, mortified by
Marjoribanks's language, strode over to the big man. "Really, Mr.
Marjoribanks," he said, "don't you think that a man in your position
should be showing a better example to the men in your employment?"

171

"Hell, man!" exploded Marjoribanks. "I'm not teaching a Sunday school, I'm loading cattle, and I'm giving the boys the best example I can. And I'll bet that Noah swore when he was loading his animals into the ark."

Later he turned to Holliday, who he considered a chum, and said by way of explanation for his rough manners "You know my sister has so much godliness that there wasn't enough left to go around the rest of the family."[7]

At least once Marjoribanks's behaviour went too far even for the lenient nature of Vernon's citizenry. On August 2, 1894, Marjoribanks appeared before the local court and pleaded guilty to "being disorderly and throwing stones." He was fined ten dollars, and charged costs of $3.25 and damages of $2.50. There is no indication of either the reason for, or the target of, his stone throwing.[8]

Marjoribanks gave the impression to his contemporaries that he feared no man; but he was desperately afraid of offending his sister. Once, upon learning that Lady Ishbel Aberdeen was coming to visit Coldstream Ranch, he sought Holliday out. By this time Holliday was supporting himself as an itinerant photographer and had also taken up water-colour painting. His paintings, mostly Okanagan Valley land-scapes, would eventually be included in showings at the Vancouver Art Gallery between 1932 and 1934. Marjoribanks, stating he knew nothing of art, asked Holliday out to his house to examine the various pictures decorating the walls so as to evaluate their moral propriety.

"You know my sister has such infernally straight-laced ideas about modesty," he told Holliday, "that she thinks all the figures in life sub-jects should be dressed from the ankles right up to the neck." Holliday toured the house and found the paintings — mostly reproductions — of which a few were of slightly draped figures all in good taste and clearly not candidates for any form of public censure. But Marjoribanks was not reassured. "You don't know what my sister is," he said, so they weeded out anything displaying skin other than that of a face. Holliday, puzzled as to why Marjoribanks bothered to seek his counsel, given his subsequent decision to remove anything that showed the slightest flesh, decided his initial plan had been, should his sister object to any of the paintings, to "say that that artist fellow had said they were all right."[9]

Not surprisingly, considering the large population of young bachelors in Vernon, and the absence of many single women, the town soon enjoyed the presence of a number of small brothels. The most famous of these was situated on the opposite side of a small creek from the main community, so became known as Across the Creek. In the local vernacular the women were referred to as "sporting ladies." The community was quite tolerant of the presence of prostitutes in their midst, but some of the staunch Presbyterian Scots were not so equanimous. One such man was Jock McNab, brought from Scotland by the Aberdeens to work on the Coldstream Ranch, and probably to temper Marjoribanks's behaviour. Among McNab's duties was operation of the ranch's small milk-delivery route. ·

McNab, directed by Marjoribanks to include Across the Creek on his milk route, balked. "I dinna think it right that I should be delivering the milk to they pented ladies," he told Marjoribanks. No amount of bluster could get the dour Scot to change his mind, so Marjoribanks finally went to McNab's wife and convinced her that business was business and the sporting ladies' money was as good as any other. Mrs. McNab quite agreed and ordered her husband to deliver the milk. "Ye'll be taking they puir bodies their bit milk, just the same as ither folk; but ye ken, Jock, ye'll no be gaen in," she told McNab that evening. The sporting ladies henceforth got their daily milk delivered by McNab, who was careful never to put a foot over the threshold of Across The Creek's doorway.[10]

The town prostitutes were on the leading edge of fashion trends and often adopted styles of dress before they became popularized in Vernon. Such was the case in 1891 with their appearance on the streets in white shoes. Quickly the other women of the community determined that any woman wearing white shoes outside the home was obviously "fast" and would attract the wrong kind of attention from men taking their ease on the town's sidewalks and hotel verandahs.

So the arrival of a new schoolmarm from Vancouver in the early summer of 1891 caused quite a stir when the young woman got off the train wearing white shoes. "My dear," one lady meeting the woman at the station exclaimed, "for heaven's sake take off those shoes!" She hastily explained about the profession of the only women in Vernon who went about so attired. By summer's end Holliday noticed that some of the town's more daring young women were also sporting white shoes and soon all the others followed suit.[11]

This development prompted Holliday to observe:

It is rather a curious fact that women's fashions are, generally speaking, introduced to the feminine world by the ladies of the demimonde. The costumers design them; any new fashion in ladies' clothing is, to say the least, a bit startling at first, and the courtesans with a desire to be conspicuous or perhaps hoping their astonishing garments will have an aphrodisiac effect, will be the first to wear them. Then the stage...adopts them, and the more daring of the female public, and so by easy stages these at first so bold and garments become respectable.[12]

Such may be the case, but for the most part Vernon's social gatherings, especially the regular and very popular dances, required that specific customs of dress be rigorously followed — customs that reflected British values and traditions. Everyone, except the sporting ladies, was welcome to attend the dances, which were, remembered Vernon resident Charlie Shaw, fashionable affairs where the men "had to have a tuxedo and dancing slippers and silk handkerchief, as women would be in silk gowns, and so you'd drape your handkerchief over your hand and it'd keep from staining her gown."[13]

When Holliday first arrived in Vernon the dances were less formal and he found the variety of costumes people wore amazing. "Cotton dresses buttoned up to the neck; stiff silk dresses in the fashion of fifty years before, chic ball gowns fresh from London or Paris, or perhaps a peasant woman from Europe in her gala costume. And the men? Anything from a crumpled dress suit smelling of mothballs to cowhide boots and overalls."[14]

Initially there was some difficulty coming up with musicians for the dances. Several dances had to rely on the fiddle music of Billy Buker, whose single waltz tune was *Oh Where, Oh Where Has My Little Dog Gone?* There were also the Knapps. Mrs. Knapp played the piano, while her husband comprised the rest of the band by simultaneously playing fiddle, mouth organ, a pair of cymbals between his knees, and a drum he occasionally walloped with his foot.

The shortage of musicians was only somewhat less irksome than the lack of women. This problem plagued the community for some years and many a remittance man was heard to lament the absence of females while the bottles were passed about the town's bars. One night Holliday and a group of young men were sitting in the lounge of the Kalamalka Hotel complaining of this state of affairs when the Vancouver superintendent of the CPR, a Mr. Marpole, happened to walk into the establishment.

Seeing this morose group of men, he suggested they should hold a dance at the hotel, but they pointed out the lack of dancing partners. "Suppose you haul us in a carload," joked a man named Hankey.

"By Jove!" said Marpole, slapping his thigh, "you fellows will have the dance, that's just what I will do."[15] A short time later Marpole invited

> a bevy of Vancouver girls and brought them, complete with chaperon, in his private car all the way up to Vernon; the only fly in the ointment being that they all had to go back again....This Kalamalka dance, the first of the "bachelor balls," was quite different to our usual ones; rather a "high-toned" affair at which dress suits, in deference to the Vancouver ladies, were in evidence; afterwards the bachelor's balls became large annual events in all the towns.[16]

Eventually Vernon grew to a size where it could raise its own orchestra, capable of playing many waltzes, and the formality of dress that Holliday tended to spurn became the required outfit that Shaw remembered. Vernon and the rest of the Okanagan were becoming more sophisticated and settled, but throughout this period the area continued to attract ever-growing numbers of remittance men. Despite bemoaning the absence of women from their lives, the way they lived was such that not many women of the time would have comfortably fit in with them.

Bob Gamman drifted into the valley in 1908, coming from Chicago after immigrating to America from Britain. His father had arranged for him to learn farming from a man he knew in Summerland, a community in the south end of the valley, but Gamman ended up first in Vernon. There the twenty-six-year-old fell in with the town's group of "ne'er do wells, rolling stones, remittance men. We had a wonderful time....They were men of my type. We did just about anything — broke horses, trapped, prospected."

Gamman didn't have a remittance but he was adopted as one of their own by those that did. "The country was full of those people," he recalled years later. "They had all had experience. They had hunted in Africa, been to India. They were real men, wonderful people. They were people you could depend on. And money, that was nothing, the least of their troubles. We got along splendidly. We never had any money, but we always lived well enough."

His first winter in the valley Gamman settled in a beachfront cabin on the west shore of Okanagan Lake across from Okanagan Landing, where there was a small dock backed by a few houses and a store. On

Gamman's side of the lake, heavily forested mountains fell sharply down to the lakeshore and population was sparse. Gamman rented the cabin from a remittance man named Brixton.

Gamman moved into his cabin with little more than the clothes on his back and a rifle. Stacked outside the cabin he found some wood and there was a small boat down at the water's edge. No sooner had he settled in than the temperature plunged to fifteen below zero. Gamman worried he might freeze to death. The morning after the cold spell set in Gamman opened his cabin door and saw a deer standing nearby. Grabbing his rifle he snapped off a shot and killed the deer. "I didn't know what to do with it, however. Like a lot of English lads, I knew how to shoot but didn't know the first thing about skinning an animal or anything." Luckily for Gamman, a Norwegian logger happened by later in the day. The man, recognizing that Gamman was "as green as grass," volunteered to stay a few days and lend him a hand. Gamman gratefully accepted.

The Norwegian taught Gamman how to dress meat and how to fall a tree for firewood; he also made the young man a pair of snowshoes. When the logger left, Gamman was a little better prepared to cope with living alone in the bush. This form of informal education helped many of the young Britons survive in their harsh new surroundings.

Gamman soon discovered that the woods around him were dotted with other cabins and that he was actually in the middle of a small, scattered remittance community. One of them was an Englishman named Starkey, who until recently had been employed as a cook on the Athabasca Rail Line survey in northern Alberta's Slave Lake country. Starkey offered to cook Christmas Eve dinner for everyone at the largest of the cabins, a place near where Gamman lived. The men gathered together some money and one of them set off by boat to buy some liquor from the store across the lake. Starkey, meanwhile turned to preparing an elegant dinner.

"We picked the wrong man to go for the hooch, however," Gamman recalled, for he came back tight and without anything for the rest of them. "Starkey was greatly annoyed at this, so he packed up and went away." By the time Starkey left, a heavy snowfall had started which continued all through the night. Gamman wandered off to his cabin for the night, but he returned the next morning to make sure Starkey had come back. Gamman learned Starkey was still missing. Worried, Gamman went looking for him and discovered some nearly snow-filled tracks running off down a hill toward the lake. He followed the tracks and soon came upon Starkey sitting under a tree. "He was frozen solid, sitting under the tree, with his pipe stuck in his mouth. Here was a man who had spent winters in the Athabasca country and he comes down here and freezes to death."

Lacking any lumber to build a coffin, the men tried to figure out what to with the body. It was so cold they couldn't dig a grave for him and no one much cared for the idea of keeping Starkey at their place until the ground thawed. One of them, however, had an old wicker wash bucket. They tried stuffing Starkey in the bucket but his legs stuck out. Finally they broke his legs and folded them up over his back and then wired the bucket's lid on. With Starkey so packaged they put the bucket into a boat and rowed out onto the lake to intercept a passing tugboat hauling logs. Telling the tug crew what was in the basket, they handed it over, and asked them to deliver Starkey to the police. Then Gamman and his companions in the boat went fishing.

With spring Gamman left the cabin and went back to Vernon where he discovered the local Okanagan squadron of the 30th British Columbia Horse was scheduled to participate in a three-week training exercise at an encampment near town. Gamman quickly joined up as he rather fancied the idea of riding around on drills and going on parades. He soon discovered that many of his friends were already members of this unit. They quickly smoothed the way for him to be enlisted. The squadron's dress uniform was quite striking. A scarlet serge tunic with yellow facing contrasted sharply with blue breeches trimmed with yellow stripes on the side seams. Puttee leggings and a cavalry helmet completed the uniform. For ordinary occasions and field drills the uniform comprised a cavalry field service cap, khaki shirt, tunic, breeches, and a leather belt and bandolier.

Gamman loved the squadron's flashy dress uniform but was unable to find either style of uniform large enough to fit his tall frame. After some scrounging about, his chums came up with the uniform of a British Indian policeman. In this uniform Gamman joined the rest of the squadron on three weeks of drills and living in tents.

During his time in the military camp Gamman went to the Kalamalka Hotel one day and happened across a tall fellow dressed in full cowboy regalia. It turned out to be Guy Ford, a British friend just in from the prairies. Gamman hardly recognized Ford, who had been a willowy, delicate boy in Britain, but who was now nearly as tall as Gamman and seemed as raunchy as they come. Ford stuck around Vernon until Gamman's soldiering stint was completed, then the two of them set out on some serious celebrating.

The 31st British Columbia Horse in training at Vernon, 1912. BCARS 24570 G-1232.

They spent the next few days drunk before deciding they should travel around a bit. That night they stole a buggy and team. Armed with two cases of whiskey and two barrels of rum, they escaped with the buggy to Okanagan Landing. They then stole a boat and took to the water. Rowing across the lake to the small settlement of Fintry, they abandoned the boat and followed the beach on foot — dragging their liquor supply with them. Although it was August and a hot night, they decided they should have a fire. The roaring bonfire they built got out of control and ignited the surrounding grass. Gamman and Ford narrowly averted starting a wildfire by desperately stamping the spreading flames out. But the danger the fire had posed drew the attention of Fintry's residents, who came after the two men with a small posse. As the posse members were all armed with shotguns and appeared to be in a foul mood, Gamman and Ford fled, abandoning much of their liquor supply.

For the next few weeks they lived on fish and whiskey, but Gamman soon found himself getting sick. "I'm going south and you go north. I can't stand this," Gamman told Ford. The two men parted ways; Gamman walked to the nearest boat dock and hopped on one of

178

the CPR stern-wheelers. He was broke and told the ship's captain he didn't care where they were going just so long as he could come along. To pay his passage, he helped the crew load and unload freight at the various Okanagan Lake landings. He finally got off at Summerland, took a room in the community's small Chinatown for two dollars a night, but remembered the next morning that he had no money. The owners spotted him trying to slip away and gave chase. Gamman scrambled down to the wharf and saw the ferry that ran between Naramata, which was on the opposite shore, and Summerland just starting to pull away. Throwing himself off the wharf, Gamman managed to grab hold of the ferry's rail and pull himself aboard. The ferry owner wasn't going to delay his schedule by taking the fugitive back to shore. Once in Naramata, Gamman was relieved to discover, no one could be bothered coming over from Summerland to arrest him. Tired by now of living rough, Gamman settled down in Naramata and got a job. He remained there until 1914.[17]

Gamman and his friends were wilder than most. Other remittance men, such as John Wilson who came to the valley in April 1910, lived pretty quietly. "In those days," Wilson later remembered, "there was an Englishman every mile between Kelowna and the head of the lake because the fishing and hunting were so wonderful. If word got around that one of us had shot a deer then every Englishman was down to have a change from fish by sharing the man's venison."

They lived a vagabond life. "Mostly we just went whichever way the wind blew and traded fish for groceries. There was no money around, but some of us usually had remittances. We lived on fish three meals a day: fish balls for breakfast, fried fish for dinner, and cold fish for supper."

Wilson came to the Okanagan from Britain as an advance scout for his family who were planning to eventually come and grow fruit in the valley. Passing through Winnipeg, he had been surprised to see so many Europeans filling the streets who couldn't speak English and wore scarves around their necks. Minister of the Interior Clifford Sifton's "stalwart peasants" immigration program was in full swing and many Britons, Wilson included, were discomfited by the effect this was having on western Canada's ethnic mix. But he found the Okanagan to be comfortably British in its composition and becoming more so with each passing day as the land developers opened up one fruit-farming community after another to British immigrants drawn mostly from the upper classes.

Wilson was about as well equipped for the farming life as most of his peers. "I'd never done a day's work in my life. I was absolutely useless. Yet you had to be a real pioneer to survive in those days. Had to be able to wield an axe or a pick, to drive a team. I didn't know how to cook." Like all the other young men who were similarly unskilled, Wilson got along by muddling through; moving from one job to another or just living off the land.

Settling in Peachland, where J.M. Robinson had started an orchard community on the basis of his seeing two peach trees growing wild on a hillside, Wilson lived the typical young British bachelor's life. "Most of us Englishmen went to the Anglican Church on Sunday in hopes of being asked over to someone's home for dinner. This usually worked. The married folk always looked after the bachelors if they were half respectable."

Peachland was a temperance town, but the young men still managed to get some drinking in by racing aboard the CPR ship each time it came to port and furtively downing shot after shot in the ship's lounge during its ten-minute stopover. "Everyone always met the boat anyway as it was all the excitement there was in the town."[18]

While life in Peachland was pretty quiet, the size of the British community in Kelowna ensured that everyone could fervently participate in the same recreational activities they had enjoyed in Britain. Cricket, tennis, and private dances, to which primarily only British residents were invited, were regular events. Dorothea Walker, who had married and some said consequently rehabilitated the reputation of remittance man William Walker, remembered: "There were plenty of private dances and riding parties. I always had two beautiful saddle horses. My two hobbies were riding or gardening. I never missed a paper chase, or a hunt, or a gymkhana."

Lacking foxes, she said, the hunts were, as elsewhere in western Canada, for coyotes. "It was just as good as hunting in England had been, just as difficult."

The hunts were also carried out with just as much attention to correct dress and protocol as had been the case in Britain. Participants were required to be properly groomed; no overalls or slouchy cowboy hats were allowed. "We rode in well-tailored riding habits. The men wore proper bowler hats and proper riding boots. We all had tailored riding clothes. Sometimes we wore peaked riding caps and chamois pants. We women always rode sidesaddle. After sixteen it would have been indecent for a girl to have ridden astride. The hunting was very

Paper chase party forms in front of Guisachan ranchhouse in 1905.
The Kelowna Museum 43.

good." The hunts were a weekly affair during hunting season, from early autumn to whenever winter temperatures froze the ground too hard for safe galloping of horses.

"Usually we would ride across Mission Creek and up into the benches beyond. The fences were those great high log fences that were about the height of four high, enormous logs. For the hunt we'd just lay down two logs and leave two up so the good horses could take the fences on the jump," Walker remembered. Her own favourite horse was a sixteen-hand-high hunter that could manage even the most difficult jumps. The dogs used were Canadian deerhounds. If they failed to flush a coyote, the riders had a circuit that took them from one side of the highlands surrounding Kelowna to the other. "We always stopped to have afternoon tea on the Brent Estate where a man named Davis and his wife had a home. 'Dinky' Hardner had an English horn which he'd blow to announce we were coming for tea. Sometimes he'd blow it during the hunt and the riders would shout tally-ho and all such phrases. No one minded people galloping over the land, there were no wire fences."

After the hunt, everyone would gather at someone's home for supper. "Then we'd turn back the rug and dance until 4:00 a.m. Then after the dance we'd get back on our horses and ride all day again. A great deal of sport went on. You could get up a cricket match any day of the week." Many of the young Britons came to the events decked out in their public-school uniforms. Because the men behaved as gentlemen and were seldom seen drunk, Walker never considered them to be remitters. They were just nice young men who made living in Kelowna even more enjoyable than it would otherwise have been. "We had an awfully good time here you know," she later said. "People didn't work as hard then as they do now."[19]

About two hundred miles east of the Okanagan Valley, Jack and Daisy Phillips would also have claimed to be having an awfully good time but certainly not that their life was free of hard work. Daisy's letters home to her mother and sister in Britain were full of cheery descriptions of how the two of them were thriving from their labour on the land. When her mother thought of her, Daisy counselled, she should "think of a slightly rounder face, very brown and freckled for me even. My hands have got harder and do not get so rough or dirty as they used to, and I suppose the same with my face, as my lips and skin used to peel. It is the dry air, and the alkali in the air whatever that may be."[20]

As for Jack, Daisy described him one day as "sitting resting in the shade as he has just come up from the potato field, reading the *Overseas Mail* which he dearly loves. He is covered in dust with a very dirty face, in an old flannel shirt, khaki breeches and puttees, and nearly black arms and neck he is so sunburnt. All the same, I really believe he is happy as a king, and very proud of his 28 acres."[21]

Two months after their arrival in Windermere the couple managed to get a rough little house finished enough for them to move into it. Their days were spent breaking land in preparation for planting an orchard. In some of her less bubbly moments Daisy told her sister that mosquito bites on her eyes had caused them to nearly swell shut and that Jack's hands were covered in cuts and bruises she treated with oil of lavender. She also expressed the first hints of what would become an ongoing loneliness for the regular companionship of other women.

By July, four months after their arrival, they were making plans for the agricultural development of their property. "We have decided to plant two acres of apple trees next year to make a start," Daisy wrote.

> Our kinds will be 'Johnathons' and a 'Mackintosh' for permanents, and 'Wealthy' for fillers. These grow quicker and bear sooner, but are pulled up when the other trees grow and spread. We are also going to plant about 100 raspberries, gooseberries, and red and black currants. The ground is ploughed in the fall. I believe they dig the holes then and plant in the spring, but nous verrons. The ground all round the

house will have to be ploughed too and the garden mapped out ready for the irrigation. Such lots to do for Jack.[22]

For the next year-and-a-half there would be lots for both Phillipses to do. Daisy's weeks took on a routine of household chores that transformed her from a woman who had only recently been at a loss to know how to wash handkerchiefs to someone capable of maintaining a farming home that met Jack's rigorous and orderly requirements. Despite the hardships, Daisy was careful not to complain to Jack. She never questioned that her role was to be the supporting, uncomplaining wife; Jack's role was to determine the course of their lives and, with some fairly copious assistance from the family in Britain, support them both. In several letters Daisy dismisses the suffragettes with the same contempt Jack affords them. But beneath the surface it was evident that at times Daisy found Jack's ways, so common among public schoolmen of the time, a trial. "Don't think I am complaining of him," she wrote in March, 1913, "but he is so unused to 'women-folk.' I sometimes find he does not realize they are different flesh and blood, and that hardships, if one may call them that, are more difficult for them to bear. I find it better to say nothing as after a bit he sees for himself, or a chance word from Mrs. Poett (a neighbour) or some other female does it!"[23]

In the summer of 1913, Daisy gave birth to a daughter, Elizabeth. About that time, too, Daisy began to tell her family that she doubted that Jack would ever decide to return to England, even could they afford to do so. For her own part she professed to be happy about this prospect. Still her letters were full of nostalgia for Britain. On the rare occasions when she and other Englishwomen of the small community got together for tea the conversation often revolved around their lives in England. "I admire the mountains," she wrote of the Rockies that towered over her Windermere home, "but I shall never love them. My heart, or really my true love, is and will be England!"[24]

After the lofty promises of the Columbia Valley Irrigated Fruit Lands Company, Jack Phillips and the other gentlemen farmers grew increasingly dismayed by the slowness with which the planted fruit trees grew and the snail's pace with which irrigation canals and other company-guaranteed improvements proceeded. They struck a Settlers' Association which tried to negotiate with the company and finally to exact financial redress from them for the deceptions and lack of performance on promises. The group had little success.

"Our small fruits, apples, and clover are all fair," Daisy wrote with her usual optimism on June 3rd, 1914, "but we shall not make a fortune just yet!"[25] After that one cautionary note she quickly changed the subject back to general gossip.

But in the end the failure of the orchard to blossom quickly and yield salable fruit was of little import, for events on the world stage were to change their lives forever. On June 28, 1914, Archduke Francis Ferdinand was assassinated in Sarajevo, Bosnia, by a Serbian nationalist. One month later, on July 28, Austria declared war on Serbia and World War I began. In three days Germany invaded Luxembourg and Belgium. After waiting four days for Germany to respond to a withdrawal ultimatum, Britain declared war on August 4, 1914. Canada and, more importantly for the British remittance men who remained fiercely loyal to the Old Country, Britain were at war.

Still unaware of the maelstrom into which she and the world were being swept, Daisy, joyous to see some harvest at last, scribbled a postscript on the top edge of the first page of a July 13 letter to her sister: "We have had six raspberries!!!!!!!!!!!!"[26]

CHAPTER TWELVE

THE HAZARDOUS UNDERTAKING

Four days after Britain's declaration of war, Jack Phillips wrote to Freda:

> This war will I'm afraid modify our plans very much. At any moment I may be called up, either back to England or to any part of the globe and during the uncertainity it is useless to go on developing so we have cut down all our expenditures. Unless we are extremely lucky we shall, in the event of my being called on, lose most of the money we have put in here. Still, we both realize we have duties to perform, and if that is the only sacrifice we have to make for our share in a successful war we cannot complain.[1]

By August 26 Daisy was writing to Freda that when Jack was inevitably called up she would return to England. Daisy proposed that she and her sister pool financial resources and live together. "The Mother Country is just magnificent, I think, in the way she is facing things and an example to the world at a time of crisis. I am sure the Colonies can supply her with food and men to fight as well. All the corps at Calgary are full up I heard yesterday....All the youth of the Valley (Windermere) has enlisted, Mr. Pope's son, Mr. Lunn, Acheson — all nice English boys — and various reservists called up."[2]

Jack, a reserve officer, would, she advised, be called up only as required. Never, however, did either of them hesitate in answering to

Jack and Daisy Phillips on the porch of their Windermere home shortly before the outbreak of World War I. BCARS 56114 F-1926.

what they saw as Jack's duty to serve. Nor did they hope the call might come later rather than sooner. On September 28 Daisy advised her sister that Jack had written to the War Office to confirm a report that all retired officers were being called immediately to the Colours. "Jack wants to go badly, very badly, and chafes and frets. At the same time he feels he is not justified to volunteer, having sunk his capital here and worked so hard....of course if we leave here it means giving up all and unfortunately in this country it is almost impossible to find an honest man to look after things. Honour is a thing that is little known or practised in any business dealings."[3]

Daisy continued: "If we do return, I expect Jack would go straight to his Regiment in Belgium, so do not picture him on home service in Kitchener's Army. For my own part, I am ready and willing to come if Jack has orders but I do not let myself think too much about it."[4] Daisy was torn by two conflicting emotions. On one hand the war would return her to England and suddenly she found herself wishing to be with her friends and family again. At the same time the war would place Jack in peril and the young wife of only two years found herself confronted with the dreadful possibility of what the ultimate outcome of Jack's racing off to war could be. Uncertain of their future, the couple continued to work hard maintaining a farm they were resigned to inevitably abandoning. In the evenings they rolled bandages to send to the Red Cross and later, exhausted from their chores and volunteerism, fell into bed. "I would far rather be with Jack dead licked than as fresh as paint without him!"[5] Daisy confided to her sister.

Just before Christmas the telegram Jack had anxiously awaited arrived. Daisy and Jack hastily gathered up all the belongings they had unpacked only two years earlier and left for England within a few days. "I shall be really glad when the wrench of leaving is over and I have really been able to put all I want in boxes and packing cases," Daisy wrote in a final letter to Freda and her mother on December 22, 1914.[6] A few weeks later the two, with their daughter, were back in England. Jack reported immediately to his regiment, the Lincolnshires, and received orders posting him to France. At the Waterloo Station in London Daisy slipped past the military police providing security and joined Jack on the troop train. She travelled with Jack and his unit to Southampton, where the soldiers boarded a ship and sailed off across the English Channel to war.

Jack Phillips was but one of the many recent British immigrants to Canada who, having seen prior military service in the British Army, returned to their former regiments. The majority of these men were retired officers, who, like Phillips, had fought in South Africa or served with regiments posted to colonial service throughout the empire. Added to this number was a wave of young British immigrants who sailed immediately back to Britain to enlist in home country units. Many of them naively feared that the Canadian Expeditionary Force (CEF) being hastily cobbled together in Quebec wouldn't be deployed in Europe until after the fighting was over. The Boche, they were sure, would soon be thoroughly licked by the courageous British troops and their plucky French and Belgian allies. For some remittance men the coming of war was a godsend: a chance to return to Britain, do noble service in a worthy cause, and possibly as a result of this service be reconciled with a family that could hardly cast them out again after they had risked their life for king and country.

From Walhachin, Windermere, the Okanagan Valley, Vancouver Island's Comox Valley, Victoria, southern Alberta, anywhere they had established an enclave, the remittance men left for war. Forty-three men from Walhachin's small British population of 150 were gone within a month of the declaration. About 20 of these left to join the 31st British Columbia Horse, which had been ordered to Quebec to become part of the Canadian Expeditionary Force. The others returned to Britain to rejoin their regiments. By 1916 all British males of military age were gone from the community. Walhachin had the dubious honour of having the highest per capita rate of enlistment in Canada — an achievement that would prove the final nail in the coffin for a settlement already fighting a losing battle for economic survival against the environmental handicaps of water shortages, poor soil, and the residents' lack of agricultural skill.

In Millarville, Charles Sturrock and Eric Buckler turned Buck Ranch over to the care of Buckler's cousin, Eddy Buckler, and hurried to war; both returned to Britain to serve initially in the British Lovat Scouts. By early 1915 the editor of one Calgary newspaper commented on how the city streets were virtually barren of the remittance men who for so many years had given them a dash of colour and through their wild antics had provided so much local entertainment.

Initially the problem facing Britons trying to enlist in the Canadian forces was that there were more volunteers than ranks to be filled. Minister of Militia Sam Hughes called for twenty-five thousand volunteers to report to a training camp at Valcartier, Quebec — thirty-three

August 27, 1914, the 31st British Columbia Horse boards trains at Kamloops for deployment overseas. BCARS 24576 G-1238.

thousand men appeared. Most of these men were noted to be recent British immigrants. On October 3 the first contingent drawn from the volunteers sailed for Britain.

"The world regards you as a marvel," Hughes declared as men, horses, and equipment muddled about the Quebec docks. Finally, as harried officers abandoned hope of retaining unit integrity, the whole works was just jammed pell mell aboard ships.[7] Speed was deemed of utmost importance, getting to Britain the essential goal, and units could be sorted out in the CEF's overseas encampment on the Salisbury Plains.

Given that it had been whipped together with few transportation services other than the nation's long rail lines, this small Canadian army — assembled, equipped, and ready to deploy overseas a mere sixty-one days after the declaration of war — was indeed a "marvel." The CEF was, however, anything but ready for war. Ill-trained, badly equipped, and overconfident, Canada's troops were as ignorant of what was to come as all the other armies across Europe.

Prewar Canada had only 3,000 men in its regular army, but this was reinforced by a militia numbering about 60,000. These forces now became the backbone of the CEF. By July 1915 the Canadian army would be expanded to 150,000 as it became evident that the war was going to be anything but a quickly resolved affair. In October, after returning from a grimly revealing trip to Britain, Prime Minister Robert Borden announced Canada would increase its manpower commitment to 250,000. In his New Year's message for 1916 he doubled that number. At the time Canada's total population numbered 8 million. Only about 1.5 million were believed to be men of military age, and Borden was promising that one-third of these men would go to war. Before conscription was invoked 330,000 men volunteered. Of these, 232,968 men went into the infantry. This total amounted to one of every six Canadian men aged between fifteen and fifty-four. Conscription, enacted in the spring of 1917, would add another 99,561 to Canada's manpower commitment.

Long before the nation's conscription crisis erupted, most British immigrants who were fit to serve had gone into the army. In early 1916, in answer to Prime Minister Borden's plea for new recruits, the Okanagan residents of Kelowna responded with a last patriotic outpouring of volunteers that took most remaining men of military age to war. The residents staying behind turned out en masse at the Kelowna wharf to wave goodbye to the one thousand men who sailed up Okanagan Lake to catch the train at Vernon and start the long journey to the trenches. Banners aboard the stern-wheeler SS *Sicamous* declared the soldiers to be "Kelowna's Gift of 1,000 Men." Although it was 1916 and the casualties from the first battles were beginning to make their impression on Canada's civilians, a general spirit of optimism and patriotism prevailed throughout the land, and nowhere was this more true than in the western Canadian British enclaves. Everyone seemed willing and eager to do their bit. The heavy casualties Canadians suffered in their first major engagement during the second battle of Ypres fought in spring of 1915 served only to motivate more men, such as those in the Okanagan, to enlist.

Not even veterans of the South African war, such as Jack Phillips, had any concept of the kind of war they were entering. The nature of battle fought in the European trenches was unlike anything that had preceded it. Between the opposing lines of fortified trenches lay "no-man's land," a shell-cratered, barbwire-strewn wasteland liberally scattered with abandoned equipment, unexploded shells, and the decomposing corpses of men and animals who had fallen in conflict. The rattle of the machine-guns, whose overlapping and devastating rate of fire was largely responsible for the creation of the trench war, provided a near-constant din, interrupted regularly by

Kelowna's Gift of 1,000, 1916. The Kelowna Museum 357-A.

190

the deeper crumping rumble of artillery barrages or the crack of a sniper's rifle.

The trenches struck many of the soldiers as being a portent of what hell must be like, but it was a hell of mud, cold, unceasing noise, and the putrid stench of death and decay. Engorged rats fed on unburied corpses. The mud was often so deep that walking became almost impossible; during assaults men sometimes drowned when they fell into shell holes filled to the brim with rainwater and mud. Their eternally filthy uniforms were infested with lice. The food was poor and there was never enough. They lived on a monotonous and nutrient-deficient diet of corned beef, biscuits, or bread called hardtack, tea, and watery jam. The water was often polluted. Men dropped all their excess body weight. In their ragged uniforms they looked more like scarecrows than soldiers.

New diseases thrived in this macabre environment. Trench fever, identified by doctors in 1915 as a disease transmitted by body lice, perpetually plagued the troops. It left afflicted soldiers exhausted by fever, chronic headaches, and sore muscles, bones, and joints; the condition was further compounded by outbreaks of skin lesions on the chest and back. Recovery usually took two months, but for many there was scant chance to recover as the sick were seldom evacuated to rear area hospitals. Trench foot was also common — a literal rotting away of feet that could never be properly cleaned or dried. The constant stress, the perpetual racket of shelling and gunfire, the witnessing of thousands of horrors as friends were killed or maimed led to battle fatigue, which resulted in many soldiers becoming inordinately irritable and insomniac. Men so afflicted were easily identified by their overreaction to the slightest of noises with body jerks and other startled gestures. The germ-ridden mud caused even minor wounds to become infected and gangrene was a constant danger. Men went mad; some committed suicide, others, seemingly surrendering all hope, threw their lives away needlessly during combat.

The casualties were appalling. Thousands were routinely killed or wounded in a day's battle in which gains and losses in captured terrain were measured in less than one hundred yards. Just as no statistics exist to show how many remittance men came to Canada before the war, there are no statistics on how many died or were badly wounded. But public schoolmen in the British Army suffered inordinately heavy casualties (due to their often serving as line officers who were a preferred target for enemy fire), so it is probable that remittance men died in equal numbers.

Jack Phillips was among the first to fall. He was serving as a platoon commander with his regiment, the British Lincolnshires, in the trenches of Ypres, where the previous fall the initial British Expeditionary Force (BEF) to Europe had been virtually eliminated when it sustained casualties of fifty-eight thousand during a month of brutal fighting in what was to become known as the first battle of Ypres. The Lincolnshires were among the dozens of British regiments thrown into the line to replace the shredded BEF. In early April Phillips was wounded at Hill 60, during a buildup in German offensive activity along the Ypres line. He was evacuated to an army hospital in Boulogne where a leg was amputated. Somehow Daisy managed to obtain permission to travel from Britain to Europe to visit her wounded husband. She was by his side on April 18 when he died as a result of complications caused by the stump of his leg becoming infected with gangrene.

Four days later the newly deployed Canadian Expeditionary Force would find itself caught in the centre of the maelstrom of the second battle of Ypres. On April 22 German forces launched an attack against the Canadian, British, and French divisions with the first use of poison gas. They released 5,730 cylinders of chlorine gas onto a spring evening breeze. The rolling green cloud decimated a French-Algerian division. During the night Canadian troops rushed to fill the gap opened in the lines by the destruction of this unit. On April 24 the Germans launched a second gas attack; this time the Canadians were the target. Waves of grey-uniformed German troops, looking like faceless ghosts behind their gas masks, fell upon the Canadian lines. Lacking gas masks, the Canadian troops urinated into handkerchiefs and tied these over their faces to reduce the effect of the gas enough for them to breathe and keep fighting. Two leading battalions were butchered, but somehow the Canadians hung onto their positions. The battle seesawed back and forth for thirty-three days until the Germans finally abandoned their offensive and faded back into their trenches. At battle's end, 6,035 Canadians had fallen. Many of the veterans would be plagued for the rest of their lives by a condition called gas lung.

After Ypres came little-known battles such as Fesubert where the Germans pretended to fall back in order to lure the Canadians into a cauldron of overlapping machine guns and tangles of barbed wire that left 2,468 dead for no worthwhile gain. In a later battle that was unremarked with even a name, Eric Buckler died. Charles Sturrock had to go on soldiering without the companionship of the friend who had been at his side since they set up ranching together in 1903. Sturrock developed a heart condition in early 1917 and was demobilized from the army in August 1917. He returned to Canada to find that Buckler's cousin Eddy had drowned while trying to ford Sheep Creek during a spring flood. The ranch was being cared for by a neighbour who had lost his own home to a fire and so had moved into the house at Buck Ranch. The happy, carefree days when Buck Ranch served as a base for Millarville's remittance men were forever gone. Sturrock and the other survivors were never again to be as frivolous and unrepentently irresponsible as they had been in those prewar years.

On the battlefield Edward B. Seymour, a renowned Calgary remittance man, showed the same dash and spirit he had brought to the bars and streets of the western city. Seymour was the third son of the marquis of Hertford. One of his ancestors, Jane Seymour, had been the third wife of Henry VIII and the mother of the king's only legitimate son, Edward VI.

Edward Seymour came to Calgary in the early 1900s. Soon after his arrival he volunteered for service in the Boer War with the Lord Strathcona Horse regiment, and was known afterward around the city as a good fighting man who unfortunately couldn't leave liquor alone. If asked what he did for a living, Seymour said he was involved in real estate and livestock export. This might or might not have been true, as in 1906 the Calgary City Directory did list a company called Seymour, Woodhouse, and Robinson, Real Estate and Livestock Exporters. Whether he was the Seymour mentioned has never been confirmed. When World War I broke out, Seymour was with the first troops to rejoin his old company in the Canadian Lord Strathcona Horse regiment. He enlisted as a common trooper.

Seymour established a reputation for disregarding the rules of soldiering and being incapable of staying out of trouble when the regiment was not involved in battle. His first major gaffe is said to have happened within days of the Strathcona's arrival at the Canadian depot on the Salisbury Plains. The unit's commanding officer, Lieutenant-Colonel Archibald Cameron Macdonnell, was invited to a meeting of the neighbouring hunt club. While attending the affair Macdonnell was surprised to come face to face with Seymour elegantly attired in a hunt uniform and helping his uncle, who was acting as Master of the Foxhounds, receive the guests. Just that morning a report had crossed Macdonnell's desk advising that Seymour had been absent without leave for several days and was being sought by the military police. Not wanting to spark a scandal in the middle of the hunt, Macdonnell made no comment at the time other than to suggest to the cheeky young man that he report for duty the next day.

When Seymour showed up at the command post he was ordered to remove his headdress, sword belt, and spurs and was marched before the lieutenant-colonel. His meeting with the commanding officer lasted only a few minutes, after which he was taken to the guard room to serve a sentence for being AWOL. Stories proliferated afterward that the soldiers on guard duty had game pies and other delicacies delivered to them by servants of Seymour's uncle who was anxious to ensure that his nephew was well taken care of during his stay in jail.

Seymour's military service was to be punctuated by periods spent under guard. As the war progressed and many of the young men with whom he had first come to Europe were killed or wounded, Seymour took pains to avoid being identified with his noble heritage. Whether this was because he was afraid of being treated with scorn by the rugged western Canadians now filling the ranks or because he didn't want his dubious military record to reflect badly on his family is unknown. Whatever the reason, he told newcomers his first name was Bob and was vague about where in Alberta he had come from.

The truth, however, kept creeping out. A young Calgary trooper named A. Turner found himself on guard duty on February 26, 1916. Seymour was typically in the lock-up. The young prisoner entertained guards and prisoners alike by singing bawdy songs through the evening. Turner was passing the tedious hours of duty by reading a recent edition of the Calgary *Eye-Opener* when he came across a piece in which the editor, Bob Edwards, asked the rhetorical question: "Where are all the remittance men that used to be around Calgary?" He went on to make special reference to Lord Edward Seymour, as Seymour had been nicknamed. "Where is he now?" Edwards wrote. "We don't know, but I'll bet he's over there doing his bit."

The next morning Seymour was released from the guardhouse and Turner confronted him. "Bob, are you really Lord Seymour?" he asked. Seymour snarled back, "No." Turner mentioned the item from the Calgary paper. Later in the day Seymour came up to Turner and asked if he could see the news item. Turner gave it to him. Later he said, "Well, was that you?" Seymour hung his head sheepishly and said, "I guess so."

After that he no longer pretended to be Bob Seymour. As the war drew on and the fighting grew worse Seymour went to his commanding officer and requested to serve in "any hazardous undertaking that might arise." On November 20, 1917, Seymour's request was answered when the Canadians joined with British forces in supporting the war's first use of tanks in a major assault at Cambrai. Seymour was in the guardhouse awaiting sentencing on a minor misdemeanour charge when the Canadian's cavalry brigade, including the Strathconas, were ordered to move out to a forward assembly area in preparation to go forward with the tanks. Seymour was left behind in jail but pleaded with guard commander Sergeant Tommy Price to let him go so he could join his unit. Price vacillated, Seymour cajoled. Finally Price opened the jail door. Seymour hastily gathered his kit together, stole a horse, and set off bareback toward the front line. Minutes later Price rode up beside him on another stolen horse. The sergeant had torn off his stripes, demoting himself for permitting a prisoner to escape. The two men reached the front lines just as the Canadians were preparing to go over the top into no-man's-land. They reported to the Strathcona's commanding officer, Lieutenant-Colonel MacDonald, who had replaced Macdonnell years earlier when Macdonnell was promoted to major-general, and were ordered to join their units.

Within minutes the Canadians went into the attack. Seymour, who rode bareback through the entire engagement, fought hard and well until the bloody battle ended, as was usually the case in this war, in a stalemate in which little was achieved. After this battle Seymour's stays in the guard room were infrequent and he seemed to take on a more serious countenance. This was not surprising; Seymour was now one of the "Old Originals," a nickname given to the few who had been among the first volunteers who had survived and were still serving as combat troopers.

In early August 1918 the static war that had held for almost four years finally began to move as the German defensive line started to crack open before relentless Allied assaults on the vital railway town of Amiens. From August 8 to 11 a coordinated offensive, spearheaded by nine divisions of the Australian and Canadian Corps, pushed the Germans back. The Allies used new, devastating tactics that involved the coordination of air, artillery, armoured, cavalry, and infantry forces. Two thousand heavy guns supported the assault. Four hundred and seventy tanks went forward with the troops. Scores of aircraft dived in against German strongpoints and blasted them with bombs. Platoons and companies advanced as teams, rather than in the long lines that had for years marched to slaughter before the enemy machine guns. When a German strongpoint put up tough resistance the Canadians broke before the enemy guns and then slithered around its flanks, leaving the bypassed Germans to be mopped up by follow-on forces.

On the first day the Canadians advanced an unheard-of eight miles. The distance cost them 1,306 dead and 2,803 wounded. But the German frontline divisions they met were shredded. General Erich Ludendorff, German Chief of Staff, called this day, "the black day of the German army in the history of this war." Among the 1,306 who died that day was Edward Seymour, reportedly struck down by a bullet wound to the head when the Strathconas mounted a charge on horseback against a machine-gun nest. The battle of Amiens would be one of the last times in military history that cavalry would be used in combat.[8]

Amiens marked the beginning of the war's end but it would take another three months of slaughter before the German surrender at 11:00 A.M. on November 11. The war had cost the lives of 60,611 Canadian men and women. After four years of a war many truly believed must, because of its horror and devastating cost, be the war to end all wars, the world was at peace. Peace came, however, to a world forever changed by war's experience. Throughout the nations that had fought and sacrificed so many of their young, there was a feeling that mankind had somehow lost its innocence on the battlefields. The period between World War I and the outbreak of World War II would be punctuated by political upheaval, failed attempts at economic recovery that would culminate in the Great Depression, the decline of European empires, and the birth of philosophies of despair, such as existentialism and nihilism. In the midst of this more serious, darker world there was little room or tolerance for the remittance lifestyle. Weighed against the other historical periods that ended with the final shots on the battlefield, the passing of the age of remittance men in the Canadian west was little noticed, but it ended all the same.

CHAPTER THIRTEEN

A WASTED YOUTH?

Within four years of the war's end the last of the British settlers at Walhachin drifted away from the settlement. Many returned to Britain, leaving behind the homes they had established twelve years earlier in the high hopes that they could create in the middle of the B.C. interior dry belt a small Eden for British gentlefolk.

Daisy Phillips never returned to Windermere. The Phillipses' plot of land was sold for less than Jack Phillips had paid. In time the house they had built was torn down, the fruit trees withered and died, and the land was never again farmed. For Daisy the two years in Windermere would come to be remembered as the most idyllic time of her life and she would romanticize those days. In her mind, and in the stories she told her daughter, family, and friends, the experiences she shared with Jack in the Kootenay wilderness came to resemble the false images presented by the development company that had originally lured the young couple into investing everything they had in an impossible dream. She never remarried and died in 1960.

Many remittance men never returned to Canada after the war. Of those who went to war seeking glory, honour, and redemption in the eyes of their families the survivors often got their wish. It was a wish all too likely earned out of the death of siblings, especially older brothers who fell in battle and cleared the lines of inheritance for a younger brother. Many a remittance man found himself suddenly transformed from ne'er-do-well to lord, marquis, or duke.

Britain had fielded an army of 6 million — 750,000 of those died, 1.7 million were wounded. The United Kingdom had lost the better part of a generation to the war. Britain, of course, wasn't alone in this — Canada, Australia, France, Germany, and other nations had all paid similar costs. In addition to its 60,000 dead, 153,422 Canadians had been wounded or were still deemed to be missing in action as of 1919.[1]

For the survivors, postwar British society offered an opportunity to fit into the economic and cultural life of their community. Rather than the surplus that had existed prior to the war, men with a public-school education were suddenly in short supply. They became teachers, took up professions, joined banking firms, and entered family businesses that due to the nation's loss of young men would make use of any youthful talent they could find.

Part of this transformation of remittance men into upstanding members of society came about as a result of changes in the men themselves. In western Canada, remittance men had been renowned for their naiveté and lack of even the simplest skills. After four years in the trenches those who had been inept at the skills of war were likely to either be dead or maimed. Remittance men who had gone to war and survived had learned competence in a brutally tough training school.

They had also shed much of their innocence and optimistic good cheer. The contrived, world-weary cynicism that young public school-men had often affected before the war now gave way to a world-weariness that was quite genuine. Gertrude Stein, the avante garde Parisian writer, would eventually label the survivors of the young generation that went to war "The Lost Generation." Long before she came up with this sobriquet it was evident that the war had left an indelible impression on many of the veterans. After witnessing the futile butchery of years of trench warfare, the veterans, especially those who were better educated, saw life as just a meaningless passage that ended in death. In the world of the trenches there had been no glory, no death with honour.

After the horrors of war it was hard for veteran remittance men to return to western Canadian British enclaves, take up playing cricket and riding to the hounds with the married ladies of the community, and still evince that same festive good cheer that had so permeated and defined these settlements. With war's end there was a marked decline in polo competitions, coyote hunts, cricket matches, and race weeks.

Some of this was due in part to a lack of young remittance men. Okanagan resident John Wilson remembered that after the war there were hardly any left in the valley. "There were tons of them here

After World War I, Coutts Marjoribanks emerged as one of Vernon's leading citizens.
Vernon Museum & Archives.

before the war," he recalled, "but most of them got killed off in the First War."[2]

And those who died were not likely to be replaced. From 1918 through to the next war British emigration slowed from the frenetic pace it had sustained from 1890 to 1914. The number of immigrants to Canada from Britain in 1919 totalled only 9,914, the highest level claimed in 1924 was 72,919 — a far cry from the four postwar years when the totals had annually ranged from a low in 1911 of 123,013 to a 1913 high of 150,542.[3] The flow of British immigrants into western Canada dropped off significantly, especially the influx of British public schoolmen.

Some of them returned to western Canada and picked up their lives where they had left off, but even this group largely set aside the wildness of their youthful behaviour. While in Britain convalescing from his heart condition prior to being demobilized, Charles Sturrock had met a young Englishwoman. The two kept in touch after he returned to Millarville in 1917. In December 1918, with the war over and the seas again safe and open to civilian passage, the woman joined thirty other brides-to-be and sailed to Canada. Sturrock and she were married several days before Christmas. They had two children and Sturrock ran Buck Ranch as a viable operation until his death in 1938 at the age of fifty-three.

His life after the war was typical of those who went to battle and returned to western Canada. Their turn to serious pursuits perhaps made it doubly hard for those remittance men who had not served in the forces and sought to carry on the traditions that had given them a sense of community in the prewar years.

Crippled when he was thrown from a horse, Lord Lionel Brooke, a veteran of the Boer War, was unable to serve in World War I. After the war he carried on with the same wild behaviour, fuelled by heavy drinking, for which he was famous throughout the Pincher Creek region. He continued to wear incongruous outfits of knickers, plus-fours, a buckskin jacket, a cowboy hat, and a monocle.

Tom Kirkham remembered Brooke coming each year during the early 1930s to a resort near Waterton Lake where Kirkham worked first as a clerk and later as the manager. "Brooke at his best made a

Some remittance men, such as Mr. Craufurd on the left, continued to live off allowances from Britain long after the age of remittance men had ended. For most, however, the era came to a close with the war. GAI NA-4942-3.

hell of a lot of noise," Kirkham said. "He'd let out cowboy yells, Indian yells and drink an astounding amount of beer...He could drink beer all day long and other than getting noisier he didn't get any drunker." About once a week during the several months he would remain at one of the Waterton Lake resort chalets he would hire someone to drive him to Pincher Creek so he could cash a cheque at the Royal Bank to which his regular remittances still came from Britain. "He paid cash for everything," Kirkham said. "Sometimes he would chat with me. He'd show me gambling games he had learned when he was in India at the Punjab Light Horse mess. He would insist on gambling for drinks in the bar, which was illegal but we didn't worry about that. He deliberately lost so that he would have a following of people around to hear his stories." When he died, on January 12, 1939, at the age of eighty-one, Kirkham claims, he was buried at Pincher Creek in a solid oak casket lined on the inside with lead.[4]

Brooke never lost his zest for life, but it was, Kirkham reflected, a seemingly empty life. Perhaps he thought it quite lonely, as in these later years Brooke seemed to have few friends.

Lord Brooke was lucky in that his remittances kept coming in throughout his life, even during the Great Depression. Others were less fortunate; some found that eventually family in Britain were unable, or unwilling, to continue sending the cheques that were vital to sustaining them. Edward Ellis Edwards from North Wales found himself in this circumstance. Born in 1885, Edwards had come to Canada in 1905. His was a large family consisting of five brothers and two sisters. One of the brothers was killed in the war; a second immigrated to Canada and lived in Edmonton, but shunned Edwards because of his way of life. The rest of the family remained in Britain.

Up until the end of the war, and possibly for some years after, it appears that Edwards lived in Calgary and was supported by a small remittance from Britain. By the time he was fifty-seven, however, life had taken a severe downturn for the former remittance man. He wrote to his family's solicitors Allington, Hughes & Bate at Wrexham, North Wales to advise that he was "in very poor circumstances." He was hoping that some funds from an inheritance he anticipated might be released to him as quickly as possible.

Less than two years later Calgary Lawyer Thomas Underwood, who had known Edwards for years, tried to act on Edwards's behalf and straighten out the middle-aged man before his lifestyle took him to an early grave. Underwood advised the Welsh solicitors that Edwards was in jail because he had received a bank draft in error for $160 "belonging to another man of the same name....He cashed the draft and of course disposed of the money. He was arrested by the authorities and now he is working for the Government to right the amount." Three years earlier, Underwood wrote, Edwards had turned his business affairs over to the lawyer. Edwards was now broke Underwood reported, and he asked the Welsh solicitors: "Would it be possible to secure any more from the estate?"[5]

A few months later Underwood wrote to Edwards care of the Lethbridge Jail in Lethbridge, Alberta.

> Once again you are in jail. Will you never have sense enough to conduct yourself properly so that you would not be taken up every once in a while? Do you ever think of your father and mother? What would they think of their son, brought up as you were brought up in a good Christian home? I have talked to you and tried to bring you to understand these things, but it evidently has no affect, you just keep on in the same old way....I am sorry at this Christmas season that you are in jail....Why not take a firm stand now and cut out all this drinking and be a real man?[6]

On Jan. 8, 1945, Edwards wrote back to Underwood advising that he expected to be released shortly and asking for five dollars "because I am broke because coming out of here broke is not very comfortably. That is all at present. Trusting you are in good health." On April 17, 1945, he wrote Underwood to advise him he was again back in jail and asked for a further loan of ten dollars. He had been, Edwards said, very sick but was feeling better now. The letter ended with him saying "I think I will let you handle the next money that comes."

One year later, on May 28, 1946, Edwards died in an Old Men's Home. He was sixty-one.[7]

Not all of those that missed service in the war tried to sustain their wild way of living after the war was over. Many joined the veterans, like Sturrock, in settling down and undertaking a traditional life by marrying, finding an occupation, and having children. In the Okanagan Valley, Charles Holliday had started settling down prior to the war when he married Vernon school teacher Elizabeth Harding in 1906.

Holliday had enlisted in the army during World War I but was never sent overseas. As a consequence, perhaps, he retained much of his youthful optimism and irreverence for authority right up until his death.

In his memoirs, *The Valley Of Youth*, Holliday probably summa-
rizes the feelings of most of the young men who came to Canada from
Britain between 1880 and 1914. When it was all over many critics, and
many of the people with whom they had mixed and who now sought
to distance themselves from the legacy of the remittance men, would
declare their lives to have been wasted, frittered away needlessly without any goal, purpose, or achievement.

Holliday had no time for this assessment of the lives he and so
many British public schoolmen had enjoyed in their youth. "We...boys
certainly did wander about, jumping from one thing to another in a
casual way when probably most of our friends at home thought we
would have been better in some steady business or profession...but I do
not think it was a waste of time...anyway I have no regrets about my
'wasted youth;' if I could only get it back wouldn't I just waste it in the
same old way, again!"[8]

NOTES

Chapter One

1. C.E. Vulliamy, *Crimea: The Campaign of 1854-56* (London: Jonathon Cape, 1939), p. 341.
2. Pauline Gregg, *A Social and Economic History of Britain: 1760-1960*, rev. 3rd ed. (Toronto: George C. Harrap and Co. Ltd., 1962), p. 350.
3. Johnathon Gathorne-Hardy, *The Old School Tie: The Phenomenon of the English Public School* (New York: The Viking Press, 1977), p. 126.
4. Ibid., p. 141.
5. Ibid., p. 145.
6. Ibid., p. 147.
7. Frederick M. DelaFosse [Roger Vardon, pseud.], *English Bloods* (Ottawa: Graphic Publishers, 1930), p. 10.
8. James McCook, "Peers on the Prairie," *The Beaver* (June 1953), pp. 10-13.
9. Clive Phillipps-Wolley, *One of the Broken Brigade* (London: Smith, Elder and Co., 1897), p. 16.
10. Harvey J. Philpot, *Guide Book to the Canadian Dominion Containing Full Information for the Emigrant, the Tourist, the Sportsman, and the Small Capitalist* (London: Edward Standford, 1871), pp. 96-97.
11. Ibid., p. 98.

12. Charles Holliday, *The Valley of Youth* (Caldwell, Idaho: The Caxton Printers Ltd., 1948), p. 101.
13. Ibid., p. 102.
14. Ibid., p. 103.
15. Ibid., p. 103.
16. Ibid., p. 104.

Chapter Two

1. Lewis. G. Thomas, ed., *Our Foothills* (Calgary: Millarville, Kew, Priddis, and Bragg Creek Historical Society, 1975), pp. 104-105.
2. Frederick M. DelaFosse [Roger Vardon, pseud.], *English Bloods* (Ottawa: Graphic Publisher, 1930), pp. 10-12.
3. J. Ewing Ritchie, *To Canada with Emigrants* (London: T. Fisher Unwin, 1885), pp. 24-25.
4. Ibid., p. 26.
5. Ibid., pp. 29-30.
6. Ibid., p. 31.
7. Oxley Family Correspondence, 1912-1914, Apr. 6, 1912, British Columbia Archives and Records Service.
8. Ibid.
9. Ibid.
10. Ibid.
11. Ibid., Governor General's Car, Apr. 1912.
12. Ritchie, pp. 33-34.
13. Ibid., p. 35.
14. Ibid., pp. 42-43.
15. Charles Holliday, *The Valley of Youth* (Caldwell, Idaho: The Caxton Printers Ltd., 1948), pp. 110-111.
16. Ibid., p. 113.
17. Ibid., p. 113.
18. Ibid., p. 114.

Chapter Three

1. Oxley Family Corresponence, 1912-1914, Sunday near Ottawa, 1912, British Columbia Archives and Records Service.
2. Ibid.
3. Ibid.

4. Arthur E. Copping, *Canada, The Golden Land: The Story of the Present Day Occupation of the Great West* (New York: Hodder and Stoughton, 1911), pp. 18-20.
5. Ibid., p. 20.
6. Ibid., p. 23.
7. Oxley, Sunday near Ottawa, 1912.
8. J. Ewing Ritchie, *To Canada with Emigrants* (London: T. Fisher Unwin, 1885), pp. 129-130.
9. Oxley, Sunday near Ottawa, 1912.
10. Ibid.
11. Ibid.
12. Charles Holliday, *The Valley of Youth* (Caldwell, Idaho: The Caxton Printers Ltd., 1948), pp. 114-115.
13. Ibid., p. 115.
14. Ibid., p. 115.
15. Ibid., p. 116.
16. Clive Phillipps-Wolley, *The Trottings of a Tenderfoot* (London: Richard Bentley and Son, 1884), p. 49.
17. Holliday, p. 115.
18. *The British Colonist in North America: A Guide for Intending Immigrants* (London: Swan Sonnescheim and Co., 1890), p. 55.
19. Holliday, p. 130.
20. Ibid., p. 130.
21. Ritchie, p. 142.
22. Ibid., p. 143.
23. Oxley, Governor General's Car, April 1912.
24. Ritchie, pp. 168-169.
25. Doris French, *Ishbel and the Empire: A Biography of Lady Aberdeen* (Toronto: Dundurn Press, 1988), p. 100.
26. Ibid., p. 100.
27. Ibid., pp. 100-101.

Chapter Four

1. Dick Templeton, "The Greenhorn," *Westward Ho Magazine* (December 1907), pp. 90-91.
2. Ibid., p. 91.
3. Ibid., p. 91.
4. Harvey J. Philpot, *Guide Book to the Canadian Dominion Containing Full Information for the Emigrant, the Tourist, the Sportsman, and the Small Capitalist* (London: Edward Standford, 1871), pp. 97-98.

5. Bernard Darwin, *The English Public School* (New York: Longman, Green, 1929), p. 21.
6. J Ewing Ritchie, *To Canada with Emigrants* (London: T. Fisher Unwin, 1885), pp. 149-150.
7. Ibid., pp. 156-158.
8. Ibid., p. 175.
9. Ibid., p. 176.
10. Ibid., pp. 168-169.
11. Ibid., p. 177.
12. Ibid., p. 178.
13. H.R. Whates, *Canada: The New Nation. A Book for the Settler, the Emigrant and the Politician* (London: J.M. Dent, 1906), p. 159.
14. Ritchie, pp. 192-193.
15. Lewis G. Thomas, ed., *Our Foothills* (Calgary: Millarville, Kew, Priddis, and Bragg Creek Historical Society, 1975), p. 213.
16. Ibid., p. 213.
17. Ibid., p. 213.

Chapter Five

1. Buck's story related by Frank Gilbert Roe, "Remittance Men." *Alberta Historical Review 2* (January 1954), pp. 3-12.
2. L.V. Kelly, *The Range Men: The Story of the Ranchers and Indians of Alberta* (Toronto: William Briggs, 1913), p. 240.
3. Ibid., p. 240.
4. Dorothea Walker in interview with Imbert Orchard, Kelowna, B.C., 1965, British Columbia Archives and Records Service.
5. Ibid.
6. A.G. Adshead, "The British Emigrant in Canada: The Bright Side." *Travel & Exploration: A Monthly Illustrated Magazine* (June, 1909).
7. Kelly, p. 242.
8. Roe, pp. 3-12.
9. Kelly, p. 242.
10. *Leaves From the Medicine Tree: A history of the area influenced by the tree, and biographies of pioneers and old timers who came under its spell prior to 1900* (Lethbridge: The High River Pioneers' and Old Timers' Association, 1960), pp. 207-208.
11. P.W. Luce, "These Animals All Lived." *Canadian Cattlemen* (February, 1954), p8, pp. 24-25.
12. Dorothy J. Shea, "The Remittance Man." *Folklore* (Spring, 1983), pp. 7-8.

13. *Tribune*, 2 July 1895.
14. John Sandilands, *Western Canadian Dictionary and Phrase Book* (Winnipeg: Telegram Job Printers, 1912), p. 8.
15. Harry Aldred in interview with Imbert Orchard, Kelowna, B.C., 1965, British Columbia Archives and Records Service.
16. William Ward Spinks, *Tales of the British Columbia Frontier* (Toronto: Ryerson Press, 1933), p.5.
17. Rudyard Kipling, *Letters To The Family* (Toronto: Macmillan Company of Canada, 1907), pp. 36-37.

Chapter Six

1. Charles Holliday, *The Valley of Youth* (Caldwell, Idaho: The Caxton Printers Ltd., 1948), p. 180.
2. Doris French, *Ishbel and the Empire: A Biography of Lady Aberdeen* (Toronto: Dundurn Press, 1988), p. 119.
3. Ibid., p. 121.
4. Ibid., p. 121.
5. Ibid., p. 126.
6. F. Fairford, *British Columbia* (London: Sir Isaac Pitman and Sons Ltd., 1914), p. 64.
7. Holliday, pp. 181-183.
8. *Handbook of British Columbia, Canada: Its Position, Advantages, Resources, Climate, Mining, Lumbering, Fishing, Farming, Ranching and Fruit Growing — Official Bulletin No. 23* (Victoria: Bureau of Provincial Information, 1911), pp. 41-43.
9. Robert Randolph Bruce, "The Story of the Happy Valley," Windermere Promotion Brochure, British Columbia Archives and Records Service.
10. Ibid.
11. Mortimer Chambers et. al., *The Western Experience: The Modern Era* vol. 3. (New York: Alfred A. Knopf, 1974), p. 897.
12. W.A. Carrothers, *Emigration From The British Isles* (London: Frank Cass and Co. Ltd., 1965), p. 315.
13. Oxley Family Correspondence, 1912-1914, Apr. 20, 1912, Invermere, B.C., British Columbia Archives and Records Service.
14. *The British Colonist in North America: A Guide for Intending Immigrants*, pp. 5-6.
15. Oxley, Apr. 20, 1912, Invermere, B.C.
16. Ibid.
17. Holliday, p. 182.

18. Ibid., p. 182.

Chapter Seven

1. Ruth Humphrys, "Edward Michell Pierce: The Founder of Cannington Manor." *The Beaver* (Autumn, 1982), pp. 15-16.
2. A.E.N. Hewlett, *Cannington Manor Historic Park*, 3rd ed. by Brenda J. Stead. (Regina: Saskatchewan Tourist and Renewable Resources, Museums Branch, 1976), p. 2.
3. Humphrys, p. 17.
4. Ibid, p. 18.
5. Ibid., p. 17.
6. Hewlett, p. 5.
7. Ibid., p. 18.
8. Ibid., p. 20.
9. Ibid., p. 19.
10. Ruth Humphrys, "The Becktons of Cannington Manor," *The Beaver* (Winter, 1982), p. 43.
11. Ibid., p. 47.
12. Ibid., pp. 47-48.
13. Ibid., p. 43.
14. Ibid., p. 50.

Chapter Eight

1. Nelson A. Riis, "Settlement Abandonment — A Case Study of Walhachin." Unpublished Master's Thesis, Department of Geography, University of British Columbia, 1970, pp. 41-42.
2. Ibid., p. 37.
3. British Columbia Development Association Walhachin Promotional Brochure, British Columbia Archives and Records Service, Victoria, 1909.
4. Riis, p. 115.
5. Ibid., p. 115.
6. *Walhachin Times*, March 21, 1912.

Chapter Nine

1. Tom Henry, *Small City in a Big Valley: The Story of Duncan* (Madeira Park, B.C.: Harbour Publishing), 1999), pp. 9-35.
2. Ibid., 51.

3. Ibid., 49.
4. Ibid., 143.
5. E. Blanche Norcross, *The Warm Land: A History of Cowichan*(Duncan, B.C.: Island Books, 1975), p. 49.
6. All material on Arthur Lane drawn, unless otherwise noted, from "The Arthur Lane Collection," Cowichan Historical Society Archives, Duncan, B.C.
7. Lynne Bowen, *Those Lake People: Stories of Cowichan Lake* (Vancouver: Douglas & McIntyre, 1995), 19-20.
8. *Cowichan Leader*, April 29, 1920, np.
9. Ibid., Oct. 5, 1922, 7.
10. Ibid., Sept. 8, 1927, np.
11. Henry, 51.
12. Bowen, 5.
13. Henry, 142-143.
14. Ibid., 143-151.
15. Ibid., 155.

Chapter Ten

1. Jimmy Simpson taped interview on file at Glenbow-Alberta Institute Archives, Calgary, Alberta. Tape # RCT-58-1.
2. Ibid.
3. Ibid.
4. Ibid.
5. Ibid.
6. Lewis G. Thomas, ed., *Our Foothills* (Calgary: Millarville, Kew, Priddis, and Bragg Creek Historical Society, 1975), p. 213.
7. Ibid., pp. 213-214.
8. Ibid., pp. 213-214.
9. Ibid., pp. 213-214.
10. Campion Dawson to Dr. Dempsey, 12 March 1983. Campion Dawson papers, Glenbow-Alberta Institute Archives, Calgary, Alberta.
10. Ibid.
11. Marie Rose Smith, "Eighty Years on the Plains: Installment VI," *Canadian Cattlemen*, (September, 1949), p. 36.
12. Ibid., p. 19.
13. Ibid. p. 36.
14. Ibid. pp. 19, 36.

Chapter Eleven

1. J. R. Dennison in interview with Imbert Orchard, Kelowna, B.C., 1965, British Columbia Archives and Records Service.
2. Charles Holliday, *The Valley of Youth* (Caldwell, Idaho: The Caxton Printers Ltd., 1948), p. 178.
3. Ibid., pp. 126-127.
4. Ibid., p. 127.
5. Ibid., p. 128.
6. Ibid., p. 184.
7. Ibid., p. 184.
8. Police Records 1909-1916, City of Vernon Collection, MS 107 979.130, Greater Vernon Museum and Archives.
9. Holliday, pp. 184-185.
10. Ibid., p. 185.
11. Ibid., p. 186.
12. Ibid., p. 186.
13. Charlie Shaw in interview with Imbert Orchard, Kelowna, B.C., 1965, British Columbia Archives and Records Service.
14. Holliday, p. 329.
15. Ibid., p. 328.
16. Ibid., p. 328.
17. Bob Gamman in interview with Imbert Orchard, Kelowna, B.C., 1965, British Columbia Archives and Records Service.
18. John Wilson in interview with Imbert Orchard, Peachland, B.C., 1965, British Columbia Archives and Records Service.
19. Dorothea Walker in interview with Imbert Orchard, Kelowna, B.C., 1965, British Columbia Archives and Records Service.
20. Oxley Family Correspondence, 1912-1914, July 5, 1912, British Columbia Archives and Records Service.
21. Ibid., June 24, 1912.
22. Ibid., July 25, 1912.
23. Ibid., Mar (?), 1912.
24. Ibid., Jan. 20, 1913.
25. Ibid., June 3, 1914.
26. Ibid., July 13, 1914.

Chapter Twelve

1. Oxley Family Correspondence, 1912-1914, Aug. 8, 1914, British Columbia Archives and Records Service.

2. Ibid., Aug. 26, 1914.
3. Ibid., Sept. 28, 1914.
4. Ibid.
5. Ibid.
6. Ibid., Dec. 22, 1914.
7. Desmond Morton, *A Military History of Canada: From Champlain to the Gulf War*, 3rd ed. (Toronto: McClelland and Stewart Inc., 1992), p.131.
8. Material on Edward Seymour drawn from the R. Cunnife collection regarding Edward Seymour and Strathcona's Horse in World War I., Glenbow-Alberta Institute Archives, Calgary, Alberta.

Chapter Thirteen

1. J.F.B. Livesay, *Canada's Hundred Days: With the Canadian Corps from Amiens to Mons*, Aug. 8 — Nov. 11, 1918 (Toronto: Thomas Allen, 1919), p. 403.
2. John Wilson in interview with Imbert Orchard, Kelowna, B.C., 1965, British Columbia Archives and Records Service.
3. W.A. Carrothers, *Emigration From The British Isles* (London: Frank Cass and Co. Ltd., 1965), p. 316.
4. Tom Kirkham taped interview, Glenbow-Alberta Institute Archives, Calgary, Alberta, RCT-329-1.
5. Thomas Underwood papers, Box 3, Letters to E.E. Edwards, 1944, Glenbow-Alberta Institute Archives.
6. Ibid.
7. Ibid.
8. Charles Holliday, *The Valley of Youth* (Caldwell, Idaho: The Caxton Printers Ltd., 1948), pp. 346-347.

BIBLIOGRAPHY

Books

Bennett, Geoffrey. *Nelson The Commander*. London: C. Tinling and Co. Ltd., 1972.

Bowen, Lynne Bowen. *Those Lake People: Stories of Cowichan Lake*. Vancouver: Douglas & McIntyre, 1995.

——. *The British Colonist in North America: A Guide for Intending Immigrants*. London: Swan Sonnescheim and Co., 1890.

Carrothers, W. A. *Emigration From The British Isles*. London: Frank Cass and Co. Ltd., 1965.

Chambers, Mortimer et. al. *The Western Experience: The Modern Era*, vol. 3. New York: Alfred A. Knopf, 1974.

Church, H. E. *Notes From An Emigrant in the Canadian Northwest*. London: Methuen and Co. Ltd., 1929.

Copping, Arthur Edward. Canada, *The Golden Land: The Story of the Present Day Occupation of the Great West*. New York: Hodder and Stoughton, 1911.

Darwin, Bernard. *The English Public School*. New York: Longman, Green, 1929.

DelaFosse, Frederick M. *English Bloods*. Ottawa: Graphic Publishers, 1930.

Dunae, Patrick A. *Gentlemen Emigrants: From the British Public Schools to the Canadian Frontier*. Vancouver: Douglas and McIntyre, 1981.

French, Doris. *Ishbel and the Empire: A Biography of Lady Aberdeen.* Toronto: Dundurn Press, 1988.

Gathorne-Hardy, Johnathon. *The Old School Tie: The Phenomenon of the English Public School.* New York: The Viking Press, 1977.

Gregg, Pauline. *A Social and Economic History of Britain: 1760-1960.* rev. 3rd ed. Toronto: George Harrap and Co. Ltd.,1962.

——. *Handbook of British Columbia, Canada: Its Position, Advantages, Resources, Climate, Mining, Lumbering, Fishing, Farming, Ranching and Fruit Growing.* Official Bulletin No. 23. Victoria: Bureau of Provincial Information, 1911.

Harris, Cole R. and Elizabeth Phillips. *Letters From Windermere,1912-1914.* Vancouver: University of British Columbia Press, 1984.

Henry, Tom. *Small City in a Big Valley: The Story of Duncan.* Madeira Park, B.C.: Harbour Publishing, 1999.

Holliday, Charles. *The Valley of Youth.* Caldwell, Idaho: The Caxton Printers, 1948.

Kelly, L. V. *The Range Men: The Story of the Ranchers and Indians of Alberta.* Toronto: William Briggs, 1913.

Kipling, Rudyard. *Letters To The Family.* Toronto: Macmillan Company of Canada Ltd., 1907.

——. *Leaves From the Medicine Tree: A history of the area influenced by the tree, and biographies of pioneers and old timers who came under its spell prior to 1900.* Lethbridge, Alberta: The High River Pioneers' and Old Timers' Association, 1960.

Livesay, J. F. B. *Canada's Hundred Days: With the Canadian Corps from Amiens to Mons, Aug. 8 — Nov. 11, 1918.* Toronto:Thomas Allen, 1919.

Mitchell, David, and Duffy, Dennis, eds. *Bright Sunshine and a Brand New Country: Recollections of the Okanagan Valley, 1890-1914.* Sound Heritage Series, no. 8. Victoria: Provincial Archives of British Columbia, 1979.

Morton, Desmond. *A Military History of Canada: From Champlain to the Gulf War.* 3rd ed Toronto: McClelland and Stewart Inc., 1992.

Norcross, E. Blanche. *The Warm Land: A History of Cowichan.* Duncan, B.C.: Island Books, 1975.

Phillipps-Wolley, Clive. *One of the Broken Brigade.* London: Smith, Elder and Co., 1897.

Phillipps-Wolley, Clive. *The Trottings of a Tenderfoot.* London: Richard Bentley and Sons, 1884.

Philpot, Harvey J. *Guide Book to the Canadian Dominion Containing Full Information for the Emigrant, the Tourist, the Sportsman, and the Small Capitalist.* London: Edward Standford, 1871.

Ritchie, J. Ewing. *To Canada With Emigrants.* London: Fisher Unwin, 1885.

Sandilands, John. *Western Canadian Dictionary and Phrase Book.* Winnipeg: Telegram Job Printers, 1912.

Scott, David and Hanic, Edna H. *East Kootenay Saga.* New Westminster: Nanaga Publishing Co. Ltd., 1974.

Spinks, William Ward. *Tales of the British Columbia Frontier.* Toronto: Ryerson Press, 1933.

Surtees, Ursula. Kelowna: *The Orchard City.* Burlington, Ontario: Windsor Publications, 1989.

Thomas, Lewis G., ed. *Our Foothills.* Calgary: Millarville, Kew, Priddis, and Bragg Creek Historical Society, 1975.

Vulliamy, C. E. *Crimea: The Campaign of 1854-56.* London: Jonathon Cape, 1939.

Weir, Joan. *Walhachin: Catastrophe or Camelot?* Surrey, B.C.: Hancock House Publishers Ltd., 1984.

Whates, H. R. *Canada: The New Nation: A book for the Settler, the Emigrant and the Politician.* London: J. M. Dent, 1906.

Magazines, Newspapers, Interviews, Correspondence

Adshead, A. G. "The British Emigrant in Canada: The Bright Side." *Travel & Exploration: A Monthly Illustrated Magazine.* June, 1909.

British Columbia Archives and Records Service, Victoria, B.C. Imbert Orchard interview collection.

British Columbia Archives and Records Service, Victoria, B.C. Walhachin Promotion Brochure.

Chalmers, A. D. "The British Emigrant In Canada: The Dark Side." *Travel & Exploration: A Monthly Illustrated Magazine.* April, 1909.

Colvin, George. S. "Runners of the Wind." *Canadian Cattlemen.* September, 1949, pp. 14-16.

Cowichan Historical Society Archives, Duncan, B.C. "The Arthur Lane Collection."

Cowichan Leader, Duncan, B.C. April 29, 1920 and Oct. 5, 1922.

Glenbow-Alberta Institute, Calgary. R. Cunnife collection regarding Edward Seymour and Strathcona's Horse in World War I.

Glenbow-Alberta Institute, Calgary. Campion Dawson to Dr. Dempsey letters. 12 March 1983.

Glenbow-Alberta Institute, Calgary. Basil G. Hamilton. Diary, Saskatchewan area, 1896.

Glenbow-Alberta Institute, Calgary. Tom Kirkham interview. Summer 1978. Tape # RCT-329-1.

Glenbow-Alberta Institute, Calgary. Angus McKinnon. "Bob Newbolt, Pioneer 1884."

Glenbow-Alberta Institute, Calgary. Jimmy Simpson taped interview. Tape # RCT-58-1.

Glenbow-Alberta Institute, Calgary. Thomas Underwood Papers. Box 3, Letters to E.E. Edwards, 1944.

Greater Vernon Museum and Archives, Vernon. Police Records 1909-1916, City of Vernon Collection.

Hewlett, A. E. M. *Cannington Manor Historic Park*. 3rd ed. by Brenda J. Stead. Regina: Saskatchewan Tourist and Renewable Resources, Museums Branch, 1976.

Hewlett, A. E. M. "England on the Prairies." *The Beaver*. December, 1952, pp. 20-25.

Hughes, Ellen M. "Remittance Men." Glenbow-Alberta Institute, Calgary. 12 December 1978.

Humphrys, Ruth. "Edward Michell Pierce: The Founder of Cannington Manor." *The Beaver*. Autumn 1982, pp. 12-18.

Humphrys, Ruth. "The Becktons of Cannington Manor." *The Beaver*. Winter 1982, pp. 42-50.

Luce, P. W. "These Animals All Lived." *Canadian Cattlemen*. February 1954, pp. 8, 24-25.

McCook, James. "Peers on the Prairies." *The Beaver*. June 1953. pp. 10-13.

McFarlane, Larry A. "British Remittance Men As Ranchers: The Case of Coutts Marjoribanks and Edmund Thursby, 1884-95." *Great Plains Quarterly*. Winter 1991. pp. 53-69.

——. "The Remittance Man." *Scarlet and Gold*. 48th ed. 1966. pp. 117-119.

Riis, Nelson A. "Settlement Abandonment: A Case Study of Walhachin, B.C." Master's thesis, University of British Columbia, 1970.

Roe, Frank Gilbert. "Remittance Men." *Alberta Historical Review 2*. January 1954, pp. 3-12.

Shea, Dorothy, J. "The Remittance Men." *Folklore*. Spring 1983, pp. 7-8.

Smith, Marie Rose. "Eighty Years on the Plains: Installment VI." *Canadian Cattlemen*. September 1949, pp. 18-19, 36-37.

Templeton, Dick. "The Greenhorn." Westward Ho Magazine. December
    1907, pp. 90-92.
Tribune. Calgary, Alberta. 2 July 1895.
Walhachin Times. Walhachin, B.C. 21 March 1912.

INDEX

Photos in bold

A

Aberdeen, Ishbel, 27–28, 50–51, 55, 80–83, 170, 172
Aberdeen, Lord John Hamilton Gordon, 27, 50, 80, 117, 170
Administration of Estates Act, 16
Administrative Reform Association, 14
Adshead, A. G., 70
Alaska and North West Trading Company, 116
Aldred, Harry, 74–75
Allan Line, 29, 33
Amiens, battle of, 195-196
Anglesey, 129
Anson, Bishop of Diocese of Fort Qu'Appelle, 100
Ashcroft (engineer), 117
Ashcroft (Manor), 115, 126
Ashcroft Journal, The, 117

Asquith, Lord Herbert Henry, prime minister, 121
Athabasca Rail Line, 176

B

B.C. Department of Agriculture, 133
Badminton Library, 21
Baillie-Grohman, William Adolph, 22, 46, 76–80, *77*, 84, 93
Balaclava, 13
Banff National Park, 151
Bannerman, Sid, 158–9
Barnes, Charles E., 115–7, 121, 122, 132
Barren Ground of Northern Canada, The, 22
Barrett, Arthur, 157–59, **158**
Barrie, Ontario, 48
Bass, Sir William, 116
Battle of Spion Kop, 36
Beckton, Ernest and William, 102, 106, 107

Beckton, Ernest, Herbert, William, **105**, 107–13
Benvoulin, 81
Berkshire, 155, 157
Billinghurst, E. E., 117
Bird, Harry and Robert, 100, **105**
Boer War, 36, 112, 162, 164, 190, 193, 200
Booth, Beatrice Margaret, 144–45
Borden. Robert, prime minister, 189
Bow River, 56, 59, 61, 159
Bowden, Mr., 92
Bradfield College Ranch, 155–7, **155, 156**
Bradfield College, 155, 157
Briggs, Peter, 66
Bright, Dr. Richard, 159
Bright, R. C. "Dicky", 159–61
British Colonist in North America, The, 48, 92
British Columbia Development Association (BCDA), 116–22, 128, 129, 132
British Columbia Horticultural Estates Limited, 118
British Columbia House, Waterloo Place, 119
British Columbia Information Bureau and Agency, 119
British Expeditionary Force (BEF), 192
British Lovat Scouts, 188
Brooke, Lionel "Lord", 162–5, **164**, 200–201
Brooke, Sir Reginald and Lady, 163
Brown, John, 163
Brown, Osborne, homestead of, **66**
Brown, Shipley & Company, 32
Bruce, Robert Randolph, 87–88, 93
Bryce, Scotty, 103–4

Buck Ranch, 63, 152–3, 155, 193, 200
Buck, (Story of), 64–66
Buckler, Eddy, 153, **153**, 188, 192
Buckler, Eric, 61–63, 152–3, 188, 192
Buker, Billy, 174
Burns, Pat, 61
Burton, Richard, 20

C
Caledon, Lord, 21
Calgary, 48, 55, 56–59, 61, 64–66, 71, 121, 149, 156, 159, 162, 185, 188, 193, 194, 201
Cambrai, battle of, 195
Cambridge, Alexander Augustus Frederick William Alfred George, earl of Athlone, 163
Camps in the Rockies, 22
Canadian Expeditionary Force (CEF), 187, 188, 192
Canadian National Railroad, 115
Canadian Pacific Railway Land Department, 87
Canadian Pacific Railway Line, 29
Canadian Pacific Railway, 41, 45, 81, 97, 113, 169
Canadian Patriotic Fund, 143
Cannington Manor Race Track, **110**
Cannington Manor, 23, **33**, 80, 93, 94, 97–113, 118, 127, 148
Cape Horn, 25, 29, 39
Cape Town, 162
Cariboo country 72, 114
Cariboo Road 116
Cecil, Lord Robert, 17
Charge of the Light Brigade, 13
Charles I, king 95
Charles II, king, 138

Charterhouse School, 139
Cheeke, George, 142
Chetwynd, Sir Talbot, 118, 131
Chicago, 175
Chinook Ranch, 163
Church, Herbert Edward and
    Richard A., 30, 48
Church, Rev. Alfred John, 30
Churchill, Winston, 17, 20
Circassian, 107
Cochrane, 159, 160, 161
Coldstream Ranch, 28, 82–83,
    117, 172, 173
Columbia Lake, 78
Columbia River, 78, 79
Columbia Valley Irrigated Fruit
    Lands, **84**, 87, 93, 119, 183
Comox Valley, 80, 187
Copping, Arthur E., 34-35
Cowichan Bay, 141–42
Cowichan Lake, 135, 140, 145
Cowichan Leader, 144
Cowichan River, 134, 135
Cowichan Valley, 134–36, 138,
    140–42, 144–46
Cowichan Valley, 80
Craufurd, Mr, **200**
Crimea Peninsula, 13
Crimean War, 13
Cromwell, Oliver, 138
Cunningham, Admiral 157
Curtis, Sir John, 102, 106

D
Dakota Territory, 28, 50–51, 80
Dawson, Campion, 160, 161
De Winton, 61
Deer Lodge, Montana, 59
Dela Fosse, Frederick Montague,
    20, 21, 33, 38
Dennison, J. R., 167

Devonshire Commission, 18
Devonshire Regiment, 27
Dewdney, Edgar, 73
Didsbury Stock Farm, 108–9, **108**,
    112
Dominion Line, 29, 35
Dry Belt Settlement Utilities
    Limited, 118
Dublin, 53
Duke of Edinburgh, 146
Duncan of Camperdown, vis-
    count, 95
Duncan, **19**, 134–38, 140, 142–46,
    148
Duncan, William, 134–35
Duncan's Crossing, 135
Dunn, George, 10

E
E&N Railway, 135
East India Company, 136
Edmonton, 162, 201
Edward VI, king, 193
Edwards, Bob, 194
Edwards, Edward Ellis, 201–2
Eleanor Margaret, 25
Elizabeth I, queen, 95
Empress of Ireland, 36, 38
Englishman in Canada, The, 73
*Englishman's Guide-Book to the
    United States and Canada*, 30,
    32, 33
Eye-Opener, 194

F
Fairview, 68
Farwell, A. S., 78
Feggis, 153, **153**
Ferdinand, Archduke Francis, 184
Ferguson, Harry 132
Fesubert, battle of, 192

Field, 21, 46, 140

Fifteen Years' Sport and Life in the Hunting Grounds of Western America and British Columbia, 22

50th Gordon Highlanders, 142–43

52nd Battalion, CEF, 143

Fintry, 178

Flutterby, 142

Footner, B. C., 121

Ford, Guy, 177–8

Fort Garry, 21

Fraser Valley, 135

Fresno, California, 150

Fruit Farming on the "Dry Belt" of British Columbia, 119

G

Gamman, Bob, 175–179

Garry Club, Winnipeg, 49–50

General's Letters to his Son on Obtaining a Commission, 143

Geneva, 161

George V, king, 121

George, Henry Albert, Fourth Earl Grey, 83

George, Ross, 72

Georgia Strait, 134, 135

Gibson, Captain, 35

Godalming, 139

Golden, 44

Grasmere, 25, 39

Great Depression, 196, 201

Greaves, J. B., 117

Grey, Dr. Herbert Branston, 155–7

Guide Book to the Canadian Dominion Containing Full Information for the Emigrant, the Tourist, the Sportsman, and the Small Capitalist, 23

Guisachan Ranch, 28, 81, 83, **181**

Guisachan, Scotland, 27

Gulf Islands, 46

H

Halifax, 149

Handbook of British Columbia, 86

Harding, Elizabeth, 202

Hardner, "Dinky", 181

Harrison (Beckton servant), 108, 111

Harrow, 16

Hassett, 164

Hawaii, 39

Hayman, Henry, 17

Hazelton, 86

Henry VIII, king, 193

Hertfordshire, 95

High River, 21, 72, 162, 166

Hill 60, 192

Hippolytus, 21

Hobson, W. D., 68

Holliday, Charles William, 25–26, 29, 39–40, 44–46, 47, 49, 80, 85, 86, 93, 168–74, 202–3

Hughes, Sam, minister of militia, 188

Humphreys, James, 112

I

Industrial Revolution, 15

J

James I, king, 95

James II, king, 95

Jedburgh, Scotland, 59

Jug Handle Ranch, 163

K

Kaledan, 85

Kamloops, 114, 126, **188**

Kelly, L. V., 67
Kelowna, 81, 179, 180–2, 189–90, **190**
Kilcoursie, Viscount, 21
Kingston, Ontario, 59
Kipling, Rudyard, 75
Kirkham, Tom, 200–201
Klondike Gold Rush, 68, 112, 166
Knapp, Mr. and Mrs., 174
Knightsbridge, 27
Kootenay Lake, 76, 78
Kootenay Land Syndicate Company, 78–79, **79**
Kootenays 23, 36, 76–79, 83, 84, 93

L
Lachine, 21
Lake Louise, 150
Lane, Arthur Edward Cecil, 138–46, **141**
Lane, George, 139
Lane, Jane, 138–39
Lane, John Henry, 139
Lane, Lt. Col. J. Henry Bagot, 138
Lane, Susan Ann, 140
Langill, Mr. (Presbyterian minister), 171
Lengnick, Capt. Charles E., 140
Lethbridge, 202
Lichfield, Staffordshire, 138
Lincolnshire Regiment, 36, 192
Lincolnshire, 64, 148
Liverpool, 28, 29, 32, 120, 157
London Times, The, 69
London, 25, 26, 32, 46, 55, 56, 86, 95, 126
London, Jack, 150
Lord Strathcona Horse, 193
Ludendorff, General Eric, 196
Lusk, Charlie and Harry, 153–5
Lynch, Tom, 59, 165

M
Macdonald, Sir John A., prime minister, 96–97, 135
Macdonnell, Lieutenant-Colonel Archibald Cameron, 193
Maclean's, 146
Macpherson, David, minister of interior, 97
Making a Start in Canada, Letters from two young emigrants, 30
Maltby, Ernest, 100, 112
Manchester Guardian, 101
Manchester, 102, 108
Maple Bay, 134, 138
Marjoribanks, Coutts, 27–28, 50–52, 80–81, **82**, 170–3, **199**
Marlburian, 18
Marpole, Mr., 174–5
McKay, George Grant (G.G.), 80–82
McNab, Jock, 173
Meade, R. A., 145
Melladew, Edward A., 157–9
Melrose Ranch, 157
Michell, Brigadier-General Edward, 96
Michell, Elizabeth, 95
Military Colonization Company (M.C.C.), 59, 61
Millarville, 61, 152, 154, 155–58, 188, 193, 200
Miller, Captain John, 95
Mitre Hotel, 104–5, **105**
Mons, 144
Montreal, 38, 41, 64, 73, 120
Moose Jaw, 55
Moose Mountain Trading Company 100, 104, 112
Moose Mountains, 96, 100
Moosomin (Fourth Siding), 94, 98, 102

Mulgrave, Lord, 21
Murray, Bob, 53–54

N
Nanaimo, 135
Napier, Gerald, 102
Napoleonic Wars, 13
Naramata, 85, 179
Nelson, Lord Horatio, 95, 121
New Westminster Exhibition, 83
New York City 29, 32, 35
Newbolt, William Robert 59–61,
    60
Newfoundland Banks 38
Nicola Land Company Limited,
    116
Nightingale, Florence, 14
Nolan, Paddy, 151
North Pacific Wharves and
    Trading Company, 116

O
O'Connell, Geoffrey, 73–74
Okanagan Falls, 93
Okanagan Lake, 175, 179, 189
Okanagan Land Development
    Company 82
Okanagan Landing, 175, 178
Okanagan Valley, 9, 28, 47, 51, 67,
    68, **71**, 74, 80, 81–86, 90, 115,
    119, 120, 121, 167–8, 172,
    179, 182, 187, 202
Okotoks, 159
Oliver, John, B.C. premier, 132
111-Mile House Ranch and Hotel,
    116
One of the Broken Brigade, 21
Osoyoos, 78
Ottawa, 97
Ottoman Turkish Empire, 13
Overseas Mail, 182

Oxford, University, 21, 26, 139
Oxley, Frederick, 91

P
Paget, Charles Henry Alexander,
    sixth marquis of Anglesey,
    129–30, 132
Pall Mall clubs, 46
Palmer (agriculturalist), 117
Pandosy, Father Charles Felix
    Adolph, 81
Papillon, Rev. T. C., 55
Patience and God's Providence, 21
Peachland, 85, 89, 180
Pederewski, 129
Pennie, Charles, 114, 115, 116,
    117, 132
Penticton, 68
Perry, C. E., 48
Phillips, Daisy (Oxley), 35–37,
    41–44, 87, 89, 91–92, 118,
    120, 182–87, **186**, 192, 197
Phillips, Elizabeth, 183
Phillips, Jack, 27, 35–36, 41–44,
    87, 89, 91–92, 118, 120,
    182–87, **186**, 190, 192, 197
Phillips, Thomas Edward, 27
Phillips-Wolley, Edward Clive
    Oldnall Long, 21, 45, 136
Philpot, Harvey J., 23–24, 54–55
Pierce, Annie, 97
Pierce, Duncan, 94, 96
Pierce, Edward Michell, 94–103,
    99, 107, 108, 112–13
Pierce, Frances, 104
Pierce, Harvey, 112–13
Pierce, Jack, 112–13
Pierce, Jessie (Beckton), 108–9, 112
Pierce, Lily, 98
Pierce, Lydia, 95
Pierce, Richard, 95

Pike, Warburton, 22, 26–27, 46–47
Pincher Creek, 163–65, 200–01
Plains of Abraham, 38
Poett, Mrs., 183
Porter, McKenzie, 146
Price, Sergeant Tommy, 195
Primogeniture, 16
Princess Elizabeth, 146
Pryce, Charles, 100
Pullman, Washington, 131
Punjab Light Horse, 201

Q
Quamichan Lake, 135, 138, 140
Quebec City, 29, 38, 41
Queen Victoria's Rifles, 27
Queen's Plate, 110

R
Rangemen, The, 67
Rattray, Laurence Chapman, 145–46
Redmayne, John Fitzgerald Studert, 119
Regina, 110
Relief of Ladysmith, 36
Rhodes, Cecil, 121
Ridding, Dr., 18
Ritchie, J. Ewing, 34–35, 38–39, 43, 49–50, 55–57, 58–59, 64, 73
Robinson, J. M., 85, 180
Rocky Mountains and foothills, 21, 22, 56, 57, 61, 75, 150, 151, 152, 183
Roosevelt, Theodore, 76
Royal Agricultural Society, 83
Royal Horticultural Society, 86
Rugby school, 16
Runcorn, Cheshire County, 163
Russell, Charles, 151

Russell, William, 14
Russian Empire, 13

S
S. W. Silver & Company, 30
Salisbury Plains, 189, 193
San Francisco, 25, 39, 68
Sandhurst Military Academy, 15, 20, 27, 36, 118
Sandilands, John, 74
Sarajevo, Bosnia, 184
Sarnia, 34
Saskatchewan and the Rocky Mountains, 21
Savona, 126
Scandinavian, 33, 143
Scott, James, Duke of Monmouth, 95
Seattle, 40
Sebastopol, 13
Seymour, Edward B., 193–5
Seymour, Jane, 193
Shakespeare, William, 104
Shaw, Charlie, 174, 175
Shawnigan Lake, 142
Sheep Creek, 61–62, 152, 159, 193
Shuswap Indians, 114
Sicamous, 81
Sifton, Clifford, 90, 179
Similkameen Valley, 68
Simpson, Jimmy, 148–152, **150**
Sinclair, John, 51
Skaha Lake, 93
Skeena River, 86
Slave Lake, 176
Smith, Eustace, 81, **82**
Snodgrass, 93
Sokum, 142
Somersetshire, 95, 99
South Africa, 9, 90, 149, 162, 187
Southampton, 187

Southesk, Earl of, 21
Sportsman's Eden, A, 21
Spreckles, Adolph and family, 39
Sproat, Gilbert Malcolm, 78
SS *Sicamous*, 190, **190**
St. John, New Brunswick, 36, 38, 41
St. John's, Newfoundland, 73
St. Lawrence River, 38
Stamford, 148
Standard, 46
Starkey, 176–7
Steedman, Charlie, 102, **103**
Stein, Gertrude, 198
Strange, General Thomas Bland, 59
Sturrock, Charles, 61–62, 152–5, **153**, 188, 192–3, 200
Sullivan, Joe, 54
Sumerton, William Henry, 165–6
Summerland, 85, 179
Swartz, 153–5, *153*,

T
Templeton, Dick, 53–54
The Importance of Begin Earnest, 142
The Times, 14, 46
Theseus, 95
Thirtieth British Columbia Horse, 177
Thirty-First British Columbia Horse, 131, **178**, 188, **188**
Thompson River 114, 115, 125, 126, 130
Thompson River valley, 80, 114, 115, 121
3rd Canadian Pioneers, 143
Through the Sub-Arctic Forest, 22
Tidmarsh, Richard, 69
Titanic, 29, 35, 36, 37
To Canada With Emigrants, 34
Toronto, 73, 94, 96, 97

Travel & Exploration: A Monthly Illustrated Magazine, 70
Tribune, Calgary, 74
Turner, A., 194
Tzouhalem Hotel, 137–38, **137**

U,
Umatilla, 39
Underwood, Thomas, 201–2
Union Club (of Victoria), 46, 49, 90

V
Valcartier, Quebec, 188
Valley of Youth, The, 203
Vancouver, 80, 173, 174
Vernon, **47**, 81, 131, 168–70, **169**, **171**, 172–5, 177
Vernon, George Forbes, 82
Victoria, 39, 40 44–48, 51, 76, 77, 85, 90, 116, 117, 134, 135, 136, 142, 144, 145, 148, 187
Victoria, queen, 163

W
Waldy, E. F., 162
Walhachin Hotel, **124**, 125, 129, 130
Walhachin Times, 131
Walhachin, 23, 80, 93, 113, 114–33, **117**, **119**, **123**, **127**, 148, 187, 197
Walker, Dorothea (Thompson), 68–69, 180-2
Walker, William, 67–69, 180
Walla Walla, 40
Waterton Lake, 201
Wellington, school of, 20, 118
Western Canadian Dictionary and Phrase-Book, 74
Whates, H. R., 58
White Bear Indian Reserve, 96, 111

Whitlock, Sam, 98

Wilde, Oscar, 34, 142

Wilkinson, C. H., 117

Will, Andrew A., 51

William the Conqueror, 138

Williams, Jim, 105, **105**

Willow Bluff, 54

Wilson, John, 179–80, 198

Wilson, Tom, 150

Wimbledon, 140

Winchester, school of, 18

Windermere, 23, **24**, 36, 80,
87–88, 89, 91–92, 118, 119,
182, 183, 185, 187, 197

Windsor and Eton Express, 91

Winnipeg, 41, 44, 49–51, 53, 55,
56, 74, 80, 97, 110, 149, 179

World War I, 10, 69, 84, 89, 128,
131, 157, 184, 185–96, 197,
198, 202

Wragg, James Chesterfield, 146

Wrexham, North Wales, 201

Y

Yorkshire Gazette, 101

Ypres, first battle of, 192

Ypres, second battle of, 190, 192

AUTHOR INFORMATION

Mark Zuehlke grew up in the Okanagan Valley amid tales of British remittance men. The influence of those stories led to the writing of this book and its basis for the CTV documentary *The Remittance Men*, which he co-scripted and co-produced. He is the author of more than a dozen books, including the mystery novel *Hands Like Clouds*, whose main character is a modern-day British remittance man. Other books by Mark Zuehlke are: *Ortona: Canada's Breakthrough to Rome*. He lives in Victoria and has even lunched several times at that bastion of remittancedom, The Union Club.